Between Daylight and Hell

Between Daylight and Hell

and

Scots who left a stain on American history

Iain Lundy

Whittles Publishing

Published by
Whittles Publishing Ltd,
Dunbeath,
Caithness, KW6 6EG,
Scotland, UK

www.whittlespublishing.com

ISBN 978-184995-263-7

973·049163

Printed by
Charlesworth Press, Wakefield

To Be, who never lost faith that this project
would one day reach completion

Contents

Author's personal thanks

I have received nothing but endless and positive encouragement in my efforts to research and write this book, and for that I am grateful to many people. In particular, I would like to thank the following:

Susan Lunn, for her scrupulous sub-editing skills, and for displaying patience and attention to detail in reviewing the chapters of this book.

The Prints and Photographic Department of the Library of Congress in Washington DC.

Staff at the Mitchell Library, Glasgow.

Lorraine Forbes, of the local studies section of Aberdeenshire Libraries in Huntly.

Dougie Beck, for help in unearthing the whereabouts of old Scottish place names that have long since disappeared.

Colin Jose, American soccer historian, for help with background on Robert Millar.

Kathy Weiser-Alexander, editor of *Legends of America* website.

Lori Podolsky, archivist at McGill University, Montreal.

Jennifer Phillips, Communications Officer, University of Aberdeen.

Meghan Saar, editor of *True West Magazine*.

Katie and Rex Ginder, for use of their domestic office space.

John Ginder, for his graveyard navigational skills.

William Dolback, President of the Ticonderoga Historical Society for photographs of the fort and the sign for Abercrombie's landing.

Foreword

The United States became a regular holiday destination for me in the very early years of the 21st century. I sometimes crossed the Atlantic twice in a calendar year from my home in Scotland until I made the move permanent in 2015.

Compared to the land I left behind, America is massive. There is so much to see and of course, like all tourist types, I travel plenty and treasure my ever-growing 'collection' of cities and states. My wanderings have taken me to cities as diverse as New York; Los Angeles and San Francisco in California; Pittsburgh, Pennsylvania; Las Vegas, Nevada; Phoenix, Arizona; and smaller cities such as Peoria, Illinois; Williamsburg, Virginia; and Monterey, California.

In addition, there have been trips through the back roads of West Virginia, the Amish country of Ohio and Pennsylvania, the winding Highway One along the Pacific coast of California, the lakes of northern Wisconsin, and the shores of Lake Superior in northern Michigan.

Everywhere is different and fascinating in its own right. But there has been a constant something in every place I have visited – and that something was the inspiration and the genesis for this book. Throughout America, from the Atlantic to the Pacific, the Gulf of Mexico to the Canadian border, from big cities to tiny communities they call 'hoot an' holler' towns, there is evidence of Scottish pioneers having been there and having made an indelible mark.

I well remember standing in a remote part of central Arizona on a day trip to see a spectacular phenomenon known as Tonto Natural Bridge. It is a little-known geological wonder, an example of a travertine arch standing more than 180 feet above a creek and a 400-ft long tunnel. The wooded valley is surrounded by rugged but beautiful desert scenery.

At the entrance there is a car park and a shop where visitors pay an admission fee and buy souvenirs. I picked up the piece of paper that passed for an information guide to the place and started reading it. Gobsmacked is not a word I use too often, but it was appropriate for the moment of revelation I was undergoing in the little wooden shed as I read the document. It turned out that the natural wonder I was about to visit was 'discovered' by a man from Inverbervie, a fishing village on the east coast of Scotland.

Davy Gowan had been fleeing from Indians when he hid underneath the arch, stayed there for three days, and only emerged when he felt it was safe to do so. However, Davy was a canny gold prospector and miner who knew the ways of the old American Wild

West. Three days under the arch had been a long time and Davy went to the authorities and claimed squatter's rights. He won his claim and the land was his. In later years he invited some of his extended family over from Scotland. They came and lived in comparative luxury.

I remember standing there thinking what a ridiculous story this was – yet it was compelling and fascinating and when I got back to urban 'civilisation' I began a more extensive search for information on my fellow countryman. Old Davy turned out to be quite a character and the story set the wheels in motion for the labour of love that has resulted in the publication of *Between Daylight and Hell*.

When I visited Tonto Natural Bridge I had been working as a journalist in Scotland for almost 40 years. I had never heard of Davy Gowan and I figured there must have been many more like him – people who had been born in Scotland, left their homeland to start a new life in America, and done something that could be classed as remarkable.

So I started checking everywhere, on every internet site that provided information on Scottish settlers, the passenger lists of vessels that had carried immigrants to the so-called New World, genealogy sites and old documents in libraries that might just have recorded information about families or individuals leaving Scotland for America.

Almost two years later, I had collected more than 600 names, every one with an incredible story attached. Scots have done everything in the U.S. – one man helped build the Statue of Liberty, another saved the buffalo from extinction. There is not a corner of America untouched by the influence of Scots, not a branch of society they have not helped shape.

As I studied the list, my focus was constantly drawn to one category of people – the bad guys. Perhaps it was the memory of my first editor at the *Largs and Millport Weekly News* in Ayrshire telling me that everyone who buys a paper wants to read about 'other people's misfortune'. Of course John McCreadie was right and that sage piece of advice – delivered after a dram or two of whisky – has stuck with me throughout my career.

The slow, lingering death of newspapers is a cause of great sadness for me. I hope, however, that there are still enough people not only reading, but keen to read about the misfortunes of others. This book is filled with people whose behaviour was truly awful and impacted severely on the lives of many others.

One chapter in this book is devoted to a character from Perthshire called David Jack. He landed in California at the time of the gold rush, and when the area was transferring from Mexican to American control. Jack used his position in society to evict people from their homes, throw them off their farms and ranches, and generally grab their land and possessions. He was a thoroughly odious individual.

The Executive Committee of the local Squatters League wrote to him demanding restitution in the following terms:

If you don't make good that amount of money to each and every one of us…
you son of a bitch, we shall suspend your animation between daylight and
hell.

It was a quote I kept coming back to as I wrote and which has become the title for
this collection of stories. Very few people ever thanked David Jack but perhaps I should.

This book is not an academic study of the Scots diaspora in America, or an attempt
to explain the multitude of reasons for Scots leaving their native land for a fresh start
in the USA. As a long-time journalist, my great love is telling interesting and gripping
stories using the written word, and that is what *Between Daylight and Hell* is meant to
be – a good read. I sincerely hope you enjoy it.

1

Adam Stephen

...he is guilty of unofficerlike behavior...owing to inattention or want of judgement; and he has been frequently intoxicated since in the service, to the prejudice of good order and military discipline...

– COURT-MARTIAL VERDICT

The Scottish settlers who carved out lives for themselves in the new lands of America were among the most resourceful of the early pioneers. They were, for the most part, tough and determined individuals, formed in the harsh Caledonian climate and well-suited to the challenges that faced them in their new home.

Intrepid and innovative, the Scots brought many qualities to the colonial party. Yes, they worked hard and produced 'local heroes' by the score in towns and cities stretching from the Atlantic to the Pacific. But they also brought with them Scottishness in all its forms – they sang, they danced, they laughed at themselves as well as everyone else, they fought like demons, they were good neighbours, they mixed well with the hodge-podge of nationalities, they soldiered heroically, they preached fire and brimstone with the best.

And of course, like true Scots, they sustained their activities with alcohol. The hardy souls who sailed in wooden boats from ports like Glasgow, Greenock and Leith had stashes of beer and whisky, often by the crate and barrel load. Who could begrudge them a libation at this time? Many were émigrés, forced from their homes and destined never to see their native land again. They were embarking on voyages that some would not survive. America was filled with uncertainty and danger, not least from the hostile Native American Indian population. It was no wonder that the pioneer Scots, well used to the comforts of alcohol, felt they needed a drink or two to keep their spirits up.

However, if they had any notions that their love of whisky gave them some sort of monopoly on hardened drinking, they got the shock of their lives when they reached port on the other side of the Atlantic. In America they found a country that was simply awash with booze from top to bottom and in every sector of society. There were illegal stills producing moonshine and hooch by the gallon, the Irish had brought their whiskey – with an extra 'e' – and the continental Europeans from Germany, France, Italy, Poland, Lithuania and elsewhere had arrived with enough wine, beer, brandy and madeira to keep the new land drinking for years. Rum soon became a favorite tipple, and so did cider.

Every community, no matter how small, had a sprinkling of inns and taverns; many had their own breweries and distilleries. The innkeepers and tavern owners were important people, afforded esteem as high, if not higher, than the local clergymen. In Tombstone, Arizona, where the Gunfight at the O.K. Corral was fought, there were at one time 110 saloons serving a population of 14,000.

George Washington and Thomas Jefferson were among the many high society figures who loved a drink as much as the next man. Jefferson, the fledgling nation's third president, toured the vineyards of France and brought home thousands of bottles of fine wine and champagne. Drinking parties at his Virginia home, Monticello, were legendary and lasted long into the night. Everybody, even the Puritans and Presbyterians, found an excuse to drink morning, noon and night.

For those who made the journey from Scotland, this new land of opportunity was a bleary-eyed home from home. The 'Whisky Olympics' may not have been born in the Scottish Highlands after all; they seemed more a product of colonial America.

*George Washington
at Battle of Trenton*

Benjamin Franklin, the most celebrated of the founding fathers of the United States, enjoyed a tipple but in moderation. He once wrote that 'nothing is more like a fool than a drunken man'. Naturally, the one inevitable consequence of the American fondness for alcohol in all its forms was a seemingly endless list of casualties. These would not be confined to the bar-room brawlers; an alcoholic fall from grace has never been a respecter of status or society, privilege or position.

Just as naturally, this book would not be complete without a story of a Scotsman whose reputation was tarnished by his love of the hard stuff and who, despite his many achievements, will be forever remembered for the wrong reasons.

Enter Major General Adam Stephen. He was a son of the Aberdeenshire countryside; a man educated at two of the finest Scottish universities; a qualified surgeon who put his skills to use in the British Navy; a respected medical practitioner in Virginia; an early and trusted military colleague of George Washington who rose to become the great man's second-in-command; a skilled politician and a civic leader who founded the town of Martinsburg in what is now West Virginia.

During the American War of Independence, Stephen was in charge of troops at some of the conflict's most pivotal battles, often with great success. He should really be remembered as a great revolutionary leader, soldier and politician. Instead, his legacy is tainted by his booze-ridden downfall.

It speaks volumes of Stephen's abilities, both on the battlefield and in the debating chamber, that he was such a force to be reckoned with in colonial Virginia. Prior to achieving statehood in 1788, Virginia produced luminaries whose names live on in the annals of U.S. history. The roll-call of politicians and statesmen with whom Stephen rubbed shoulders included Washington and Jefferson along with two other future presidents, James Monroe and James Madison, as well as the great orator of the time, Patrick Henry.

Stephen distinguished himself during the French and Indian War of the mid-1700s. He was an extremely wealthy landowner and something of a bigwig in northern Virginia society, all of which made his capitulation that more spectacular and embarrassing. Nowadays just a footnote in American history, at the time his demise would undoubtedly have been a source of great gossip and tittle-tattle.

It was quite a fall for Stephen. After one major conflict he was hailed as a national hero, during the next he was written off by one of America's leading statesmen and intellectuals Benjamin Rush as 'a sordid boastful, cowardly sot'. The unfortunate truth is that Adam Stephen drank no more and certainly no less than the next man; it was the circumstances and the timing of his public aberration that proved to be his undoing.

Let's be honest, in Scotland we retain a certain affection for people who make it big while being able to enjoy a good 'bevvy session' now and again. But a liking for the hard stuff is one thing, leading troops into battle while 'incapably drunk' is quite another. And that was Adam Stephen's sin.

Stephen came to America in 1748, at a time when his native Scotland was still in a state of political and social upheaval following the failed 1745 Jacobite Rebellion. Many of those who crossed his path described him as a gruff and short-tempered character, something of a curmudgeon, but he was also a well-read, intelligent and eloquent man.

Details of his early life are sketchy. He was born between 1718 and 1721 and raised in the Aberdeenshire village of Rhynie, a small farming parish that formed part of the ancient lordship of Strathbogie granted to the Dukes of Gordon by King Robert the Bruce. Records show that in 1755 there were 172 houses in the village, with 836 people living there, all tenants of the Gordon family. It was a typical 18th century north-east Scotland rural community, where the local landowner held enormous influence, the church was responsible for law and order, and the regular cattle fairs were the high point of the social calendar.

The people among whom young Adam Stephen spent his formative years were hard-working sons of the soil. Rural Aberdeenshire can be a harsh and forbidding environment in all weathers. Even today, the 18-mile stretch of the A941 road between Rhynie and Dufftown is the first to close when winter snows hit. It would have been a tough and character-building upbringing for a boy who clearly saw his future elsewhere.

There are no Parish records giving details of his parents; in a 1696 'List of Pollable Persons within the Shire of Aberdeen', a miller by the name of Alexander Stevin and his wife are listed as living at Mill of Smistoun in Rhynie Parish. Adam had a brother called Alexander so it is possible that the couple were his paternal grandparents. In September 1746 a George Stephen and his wife Helen Crombie of Smithstown – possibly Adam's parents – had a son James baptised.

After his schooling in Rhynie, Stephen left home to study at King's College University in Aberdeen in the 1730s. It was a time of flux, and perhaps no little excitement for the student populations of both King's and Marischal Colleges in the city. The institutions, which later merged to become the University of Aberdeen, had come out in support of James Edward Stuart, the 'Old Pretender', in his bid to reclaim the thrones of Scotland, England and Ireland in the 1715 Jacobite Rebellion. Their punishment was to see many of their brightest academics unceremoniously kicked out, and swiftly replaced by more politically acceptable men.

Stephen graduated with a Master of Arts degree in March 1739. The university's alumni records list him as *Mr Adamus Stephen, Aberdonensis ex parochia de Rhinnie* (Adam Stephen of Aberdeen, formerly of the Parish of Rhynie). He went on to study medicine at the University of Edinburgh, where he graduated with a Bachelor of Science degree. In 1745 he passed an exam in London qualifying him to be a naval surgeon.

Life as a student in Edinburgh and London was a far cry from his days in the Scottish countryside; clearly, Stephen had an early taste for wanderlust. Student life may also have given him a taste for drink. Certainly, during his brief experience as a surgeon on board a Royal Navy ship, alcohol became part of his daily routine. Rum was not considered a luxury in the navy in the 1700s, it was a necessity, and a ration of a 'tot' of rum was given to every sailor on every vessel twice a day.

Stephen sailed on HMS *Neptune*, a 163ft fully rigged ship with 74 guns. The War of the Austrian Succession was raging in Europe and during Stephen's time on board the *Neptune*, the vessel took part in the 12 day siege of the French port of Lorient, a battle that ended in a British defeat. Stephen, however, won his combat spurs during a separate and potentially more frightening incident. While heading across the English Channel the ship was attacked by French pirates. The story goes that the young surgeon yelled to his captain that he was taking charge of the guns in the cabin and proceeded to blast the approaching freebooters until they retreated.

By all accounts Stephen was given a hero's welcome when he returned to London, although his life at sea was to be short. He suffered from chronic seasickness and called time on his naval career after a year. His discomfort, however, was not enough to stop him making the lengthy voyage across the Atlantic in 1748 for a new life in America. Stephen landed in the port of Annapolis, Maryland, then made the short journey into Virginia

So Adam Stephen was well set for his next great adventure, this time in the land of opportunity that was 18th century America. He possessed two university degrees, had a penchant for travel, could hold his own in an argument and, possibly most important given the almost constant state of war in the country he now called home, was already battle-hardened. At least two of his brothers, Alexander and Robert, joined him, and he wasted no time in settling into colonial life.

He moved to the town of Falmouth on the banks of the Rappahannock River and established a medical practice in nearby Fredericksburg. His brothers became rent collectors for Lord Fairfax, the only British peer who was a permanent resident in the colonies and whose land-holdings in Virginia amounted to more than five million acres. Fairfax was one of the most prominent men in America at that time and played a part in persuading Stephen that he should pursue a military career.

If Stephen ever had feelings of homesickness for the 'Old Country' then Fredericksburg was the perfect place for him to settle. The town was like a 'Little Scotland', tucked away in the Virginia valleys: there were familiar accents round every corner and many of the merchants and civic leaders were Scots. It was also home to a young George Washington, and the two men became firm friends, a relationship that was to sour over time.

For five years Stephen seemed content running a successful doctor's practice. At the same time, he accumulated land along the Opequon Creek in the Northern Shenandoah Valley in what is now West Virginia, carving out a reputation as a respected businessman, citizen and landowner. The years spent in Fredericksburg may have been the most peaceful in Adam Stephen's adult life.

However, in this new and developing land, the drumbeat of war could always be heard. The Seven Years' War, a conflict between Great Britain and France, had spread its tentacles to many corners of the globe. In North America, where the two European powers were seeking to increase their territorial influence, the conflict became a battle for supremacy known as the French and Indian War.

Stephen often claimed that his neighbour and friend Lord Fairfax had somehow 'forced' him into military life. Certainly, influential Virginians including Fairfax had recognised leadership qualities in the Scottish doctor. But Stephen was a single-minded individual. He marched off to war only because he was up for the fight – although he may also have been persuaded by Virginia's promise of free land for each soldier. In 1754 Stephen had 39 recruits under his command and was given the rank of captain in the 1st Virginia Regiment. The much younger Washington was his lieutenant colonel. By the time they reached the disputed lands of western Pennsylvania, Stephen had been promoted to Major and was Washington's second-in-command.

The two men were together at battles and skirmishes against the French at the Forks of the Ohio, a strategic spot at the confluence of the Ohio, Monongahela and Allegheny Rivers which the French had called Fort Duquesne. By the time the war was ended – and thanks in no small part to Stephen's efforts – the British were in control of the area and had renamed it Fort Pitt, later to become Pittsburgh.

Ironically, given what lay ahead, Stephen had to write to Washington on more than one occasion to tell him of drunkenness in the ranks. At the Battle of Fort Necessity in Pennsylvania, the Virginian troops broke into the liquor store and were too drunk to fight. Washington was ambitious and a hard taskmaster and warned that soldiers found guilty of drunkenness would be severely dealt with. Stephen should perhaps have taken note.

Nevertheless, by the end of the war, and with the French defeated, Stephen, by now a lieutenant colonel, had covered himself in glory and was feted as a hero.

In the 12 years between the end of the French and Indian War and the outbreak of the Revolutionary War, Stephen bought up land along the Tuscarora River in Virginia and lived the life of a gentleman farmer and part-time doctor. He also dabbled in politics, and it was this period that saw his big fall-out with his one-time friend and military comrade Washington.

The origin of the dispute was an attempt by Stephen to make sure he got the best of the land offered by the Virginia governor, Robert Dinwiddie, to troops who had fought in the war. Washington and his friends wanted the same land and the two men quarrelled openly and bitterly. Stephen then decided to oppose Washington in an election for the Virginia House of Burgesses, further deepening the divide. One of Washington's friends, Robert Stewart, wrote to him saying that Stephen was 'using his speculative wealth and an immensity of flummery…to attract the attention of the Plebeians, whose unstable minds are agitated by every breath of novelty, whims and nonsense'.

Washington won the election but did not forgive Stephen for what he believed was a dirty tricks campaign, and relations between the two men were never the same again.

Stephen's military career thrived between the two wars. He was successful in helping to broker a peace with the Cherokee tribe, helped to quell a rebellion led by the Ottawa Indian leader Pontiac and took part in Lord Dunmore's War against Shawnee and Mingo tribespeople.

In 1774, with revolution in the air, Stephen and a distinguished band of military and political brothers from Virginia published a hugely important yet long-forgotten declaration. Known as the Fort Gower Resolves, it was the first public statement that powerful men in high places, the movers and shakers of Virginia society, were prepared to go to war against the British King George III. After pledging allegiance to the King, the document states: '…But as the Love of Liberty, and Attachment to the real Interests and just Rights of America outweigh every other Consideration, we resolve that we will exert every Power within us for the Defence of American Liberty.'

Stephen's biographer, historian Harry M. Ward, wrote that, 'Stephen assumed the position that the American protest should not be compromised, and he was ahead of most Virginians in expecting a military solution'.

The veteran Scotsman got his wish. The document was political dynamite and fed the revolutionary fervour that spawned the American War of Independence. It also ushered in a series of events that were to end in Stephen's own drunken downfall.

Stephen was in his 50s when the war began. He was a much-lauded and decorated leader and was ready to fight for his adopted nation. But times had changed for the old warrior. His age did not help, nor did his increasingly cantankerous nature. George Washington – once again his commander – now distrusted and disliked him and was watching his every move. Rumours were rife that he was drinking heavily and, some felt, unfit to lead troops as a result.

There were also stories doing the rounds that Stephen, who never married but who fathered one child with a long-term 'mistress', had been regularly consorting with prostitutes. In his eventual court-martial it was alleged that he had 'taken snuff from the boxes of strumpets' while drunk and in full view of men under his command.

So when the war started in 1775, Stephen, now the sheriff of the newly-established Berkeley County, was far from the heroic figure he once was. Nevertheless, he was commissioned colonel of the Continental Army's 4th Virginia Regiment and rose through the ranks first to become brigadier general, then major general.

The Scotsman spent the early part of the war in action in Virginia and South Carolina. Some successful campaigns helped his reputation and secured his promotions. Unfortunately, it also encouraged his belligerent attitude, and his calls for the army to adopt a more aggressive stance towards the British further angered the master tactician Washington.

Adam Stephen House marker,
Martinsburg, West Virginia

Although Stephen was given command of one of five new divisions created when Washington reorganised his army, relations between the two men were becoming worse. On Christmas night 1776, in one of the most famous moments in American history, Washington's men crossed the icy Delaware River hoping to surprise the British troops and their German Hessian allies, who were guarding the city of Trenton, New Jersey.

All was going well until Washington, only two miles from the city, discovered that Stephen had independently sent troops of his own across a different stretch of the river and that six Hessians had been shot and wounded. Washington, glaring at his once trusted lieutenant, spluttered with exasperation: 'You, You Sir, may have ruined all my plans by having put them on their guard!'

In fact, Stephen's actions did no harm. The Hessians and the British had not anticipated any attack by the Americans and their Christmas revelry had continued long into the night. They were unprepared and many were in no fit state to resist the surprise attack.

However, it did reveal how low the Scot had sunk in Washington's estimation. Stephen frequently wrote to Washington and the future president often replied in brusque terms. After his troops took part in an engagement with the British near Piscataway, New Jersey, Stephen wrote to Washington that it had been a 'success' for the Continentals and that the Virginian troops had performed well.

Washington's reply was curt. It read: 'Your account of the attempt upon the Enemy at Piscataway is favourable, but I am sorry to add, widely different from those I have had from others (officers of distinction) who were of the party. I cannot by them learn that there is the least certainty of the Enemy's leaving half the slain upon the Field, you speak of in your letter of this date; that instead of an orderly retreat, it was (with the greatest part of the detachment) a disorderly route and, that the disadvantage was on our side, not the Enemy's who had notice of your coming and was prepared for it, as I expected.'

Despite Stephen's assertion, Piscataway had been a British victory. If he still thought of himself as one of Washington's favoured few, the letter must have left him in no doubt that he was in extremely bad odour with his commander.

On 11 September 1777, only a week after Stephen's alleged drunken encounter with strumpets, he commanded troops at the Battle of Brandywine in Pennsylvania. One of his fellow generals, Nathanael Greene, was reportedly told by a junior officer during the battle that Stephen had been drinking. Greene is said to have replied that such behaviour on Stephen's part was now 'common knowledge'.

Certainly in the army encampments there was no shortage of drink – or women for that matter. Liquor stores at the camps sold good quality alcohol, with rum, whiskey and beer in plentiful supply, although there is no indication as to what Stephen's favourite tipple was. It was proving a long, arduous war, and for a man of his rank, alcohol was virtually laid on a plate.

By now the war was at a crucial stage. Washington, who was trying to take the colonial capital Philadelphia from the British, had been defeated at Brandywine by British troops led by General William Howe. Though no blame for the loss could be attributed to Stephen, the knives were well and truly out for him.

Then, on 4 October, came the Battle of Germantown. It was the day when Stephen made one of the most calamitous – and embarrassing – blunders in American military

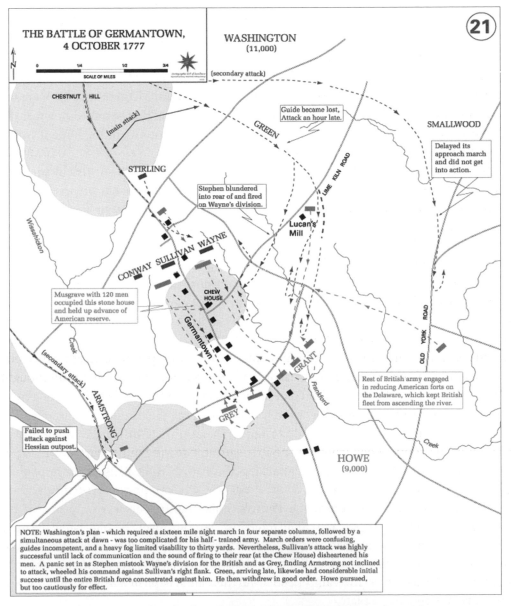

THE BATTLE OF GERMANTOWN,
4 OCTOBER 1777

SCALE OF MILES
0   1/4   1/2   3/4

WASHINGTON
(11,000)

(secondary attack)

CHESTNUT HILL

(main attack)

GREEN

Guide became lost,
Attack an hour late.

SMALLWOOD

Delayed its
approach march
and did not get
into action.

STIRLING

Stephen blundered
into rear of and fired
on Wayne's division.

LIME KILN ROAD

Lucan's
Mill

Wissahickon

CONWAY SULLIVAN WAYNE

Musgrave with 120 men
occupied this stone house
and held up advance of
American reserve.

CHEW
HOUSE

Germantown

Creek

(secondary attack)

ARMSTRONG

GRANT

GREY

OLD YORK ROAD

Frankford

Rest of British army engaged
in reducing American forts on
the Delaware, which kept British
fleet from ascending the river.

Failed to push
attack against
Hessian outpost.

HOWE
(9,000)

Creek

NOTE: Washington's plan - which required a sixteen mile night march in four separate columns, followed by a simultaneous attack at dawn - was too complicated for his half - trained army. March orders were confusing, guides incompetent, and a heavy fog limited visability to thirty yards. Nevertheless, Sullivan's attack was highly successful until lack of communication and the sound of firing to their rear (at the Chew House) disheartened his men. A panic set in as Stephen mistook Wayne's division for the British and as Grey, finding Armstrong not inclined to attack, wheeled his command against Sullivan's right flank. Green, arriving late, likewise had considerable initial success until the entire British force concentrated against him. He then withdrew in good order. Howe pursued, but too cautiously for effect.

Germantown battle plan showing Stephen's and Wayne's positions history. It was also the straw that broke the camel's back. The events that unfolded in the small Pennsylvania town persuaded Stephen's superiors that they had had enough of his undisciplined behavior, and initiated the surgeon-cum-soldier from Rhynie, Aberdeenshire, into the military 'Hall of Shame'.

Washington, Stephen and the rest of the troops had been re-grouping after the defeat at Brandywine. They were camped 30 miles north-west of Philadelphia, along the banks of Perkiomen Creek. An account of the events leading up to the battle, written by John Trussell, Jr., states: 'The ill-trained Americans were underfed and poorly-clothed; many were barefoot; and they had been defeated and out-manoeuvred. Nevertheless, their morale was good and they were still full of fight.'

The British commander, General Howe, had stationed 10,000 of his well-fed Redcoats at Germantown, located between the American forces and the city of Philadelphia. The little town had been established by a handful of Quakers and Mennonites who were the first German settlers in the United States and sailed on a ship that became known as the 'German Mayflower'. Ironically, they had set up their community in the hope it would be a place of peace.

Washington's plan, as at Trenton the previous year, was to take the British by surprise. He had 11,000 men at his disposal and he wanted them all in position 'precisely at 5 o'clock with charged bayonets and without firing'. He envisioned a four-pronged attack, with columns of men approaching Germantown from different directions. It was a complicated strategy – perhaps too complicated for his officers and men – and it very nearly paid off.

But for the Continentals to reach their positions, they faced a gruelling 16-mile march. A number of the divisions lost their way in the darkness and the early-morning fog. By 5am Washington, believing the majority of his troops to be in place, launched the surprise attack.

Stephen was nowhere near the battlefield. He and Brigadier General Alexander McDougall, a fellow Scot from the island of Islay, were in command of divisions as part of the 'fourth column' under General Nathanael Greene. Stephen had long been suspicious of Greene, whom he believed had been feeding the rumour-mill in regard to his behaviour. He thought of Greene as a 'spy in the camp' and distrusted him, perhaps with good reason. However, when the battle started Greene, Stephen and McDougall, whose troops were supposed to be attacking the British right flank, were hopelessly lost.

Wandering aimlessly around the Pennsylvania countryside was only one of the problems facing the veteran Scot that morning. True to form, he had been up most of the night drinking. Reports described him as 'still drunk by sunrise'. Whether he could command troops in such a state was highly doubtful; if Greene and the others he perceived as enemies in the camp needed further 'anti-Stephen' ammunition, he was handing it to them on a plate.

Meanwhile the battle was going well for Washington. The element of surprise had worked yet again and the British were in disarray. The thick fog on the battlefield was worsened by gunsmoke, but the Americans, despite being low on numbers, were in the ascendancy. Many of the British forces were holed up in the mansion house of Cliveden, owned by former provincial chief justice Benjamin Chew and the focus of much of the fighting.

The advancing Americans were being led by Generals John Sullivan, Thomas Conway and 'Mad' Anthony Wayne – the latter got his nickname because of his fiery temper. At one point things were looking so bleak for the British that their commander, General Howe, was preparing to order a retreat. Then Nathanael Greene, Alexander McDougall and the 'noticeably-intoxicated' Adam Stephen arrived on the scene – and the tide turned.

General 'Mad' Anthony Wayne
- Library of Congress

The three late arriving brigades were tired but they were gung-ho and keen to get involved in the action. It didn't matter that the battlefield was blanketed in such thick fog that they could barely see in front of them. Greene's men pushed forward towards the Cliveden mansion house but Stephen, who was on his right, had somehow managed to take a wrong turning.

By all accounts, Stephen had not sobered up. Perhaps he had a bottle of rum or whiskey stashed in his uniform? The battlefield fog was nothing compared with the alcoholic haze swirling round the general's head. He had led his men way off course but the wily veteran of many battles must have believed his instincts would keep him right. In fact he had gone so far off course that his men were now beyond Cliveden, where the fighting was at its fiercest.

Then, through the fog, he saw them. British troops lined up ahead of him. Stephen's men were approaching the deployed line from the rear and he knew that the attack he was about to launch would be a surprise. He ordered his men to form into battle line and fire.

The attack was a surprise all right. In fact it was one of the biggest surprises of 'Mad' Anthony Wayne's military career. It was also a huge shock for Adam Stephen when he realised what had happened. For these troops were no redcoat-clad British. They were the men of Wayne's Continentals. Stephen, in his drunken confusion, had ordered his men to fire at troops from his own side.

Wayne's men, who had been in the midst of attacking British forces, fired back, and for a short time, the two brigades carried on their own skirmish on the streets of Germantown. There were a small number of casualties, and Wayne, believing he had been flanked by enemy forces, ordered his men to retreat. The British then forced Stephen's troops off the battlefield and suddenly the initiative swung in their favour.

One by one the American units were forced to retreat. Wayne's departure left the forces of both Sullivan and Conway exposed and they had to withdraw. At one point Greene's men were left to take on the might of the entire British contingent until they too fled, and the British chased the Americans into the wilds of Pennsylvania. For Washington's men it was a classic case of snatching defeat from the jaws of victory.

Wayne was not so much mad, he was spitting blood, and beyond irate at what had happened. So was Washington. If he had prevailed at Germantown and won through to Philadelphia the war could have come to a premature end. A golden opportunity had been allowed to slip through his fingers, and while a number of factors had contributed to the defeat, there was one individual in Washington's sights – and he was about to be hung out to dry.

Stephen had disgraced himself at Germantown, of that there can be no doubt. After the battle he was reportedly found to be 'incapably drunk'. He wrote to Washington requesting that a military court of inquiry be set up to examine his conduct. Washington obliged and ordered that the court be headed by none other than General Nathanael Greene. Not surprisingly, the court members recommended that Stephen be court-martialled for 'unofficer-like behaviour'.

The court-martial was held under the presidency of Major General Sullivan on 7 November 1777 at Whitemarsh, Pennsylvania. It considered a range of charges against Stephen including the fraternising with strumpets claim. Six days later it handed down its verdict.

The outcome can have been of no surprise to Stephen. It read: 'The court having considered the charges against Major General Stephen, are of the opinion that he is guilty of unofficerlike behavior, in the retreat from Germantown, owing to inattention, or want of judgement; and that he has been frequently intoxicated while in the service, to the prejudice of good order and military discipline; contrary to the 5th Article of the 18th Section of the articles of war. Therefore sentence him to be dismissed the service. The court find him not guilty of any other crimes he was charged with, and therefore acquit him, as to all others, except the two before mentioned.'

It was an ignominious end to Stephen's career. Washington approved the court-martial decision and cashiered his former friend and long-term military colleague out of the army in disgrace. Stephen protested that 'a person of high rank' was out to get him and complained that two subordinate officers, Generals Charles Scott and William Woodford, had engineered his downfall. He appealed in writing to Sir Henry Laurens, President of the Second Continental Congress, to overturn the decision, but to no avail. Stephen, in truth, had no-one else to blame but himself.

Although Germantown had been a defeat for Washington, the spirit shown by his men persuaded France to enter the war on the side of the Americans. In a move that reeked of political expediency, Stephen's command was given to the 20-year old dashing French nobleman, the Marquis de Lafayette.

Stephen's military life may have ended in the days after Germantown, but he remained a formidable figure in Virginia. He put his oratory skills to good use as a delegate to the 1788 Virginia Ratifying Convention, in which he supported the successful ratification of the United States Constitution.

In a stirring speech he told fellow delegates: 'Where is the genius of America? That genius which formerly resisted British tyranny, and in the language of manly intrepidity and fortitude, said to that nation, Thus far and no farther shall you proceed! Yonder she is, in mournful attire, her hair dishevelled, distressed with grief and sorrow, supplicating our assistance against gorgons, fiends, and hydras which are ready to devour her and carry desolation throughout her country.'

Stephen spent most of his time in his 2000-acre plantation home, The Bower, where he grew wheat and kept cattle. He also sold off plots of land he had acquired from his old friend Lord Fairfax and established the town of Martinsburg in what is now West Virginia. It is said he wanted to name the town after himself but there was already a Stephensburg (now renamed Stephen City) in Virginia, so he instead named it after a nephew of Lord Fairfax, Thomas Bryan Martin.

He also built a beautiful limestone house in Martinsburg, nowadays known as the Adam Stephen House. It sits on the banks of the Tuscarora River in the old part of the town, and has been restored as a memorial to the town's founder by the General Adam Stephen Memorial Association.

Stephen, who died at The Bower on 16 July 1791, never reconciled with Washington, although curiously the two families remained connected after both men had passed away. In 1755 Stephen had a daughter, Ann, with his mistress Phoebe Seamann. Ann's first husband was Alexander Spotswood Dandridge, and his cousin Martha Dandridge became Washington's second wife. Ann and Alexander had one son whom they called Adam Stephen Dandridge.

Adam Stephen achieved a great deal after he departed Scotland for his U.S. adventure. His legacy should be as one of the great colonial pioneers who helped bring

Adam Stephen House plaque, Martinsburg, West Virginia

Adam Stephen House, Martinsburg

about the establishment of the United States. Instead, it is tainted by alcoholic excesses and his massive 'friendly-fire' misjudgment at the Battle of Germantown.

He is even demonised in the world of video gaming. A few years ago, the California-based company GMT Games brought out a series based on battles of the American Revolution. One was Germantown and a section of the game is simply called 'Stephen's Shame'.

2

Charles Forbes

You yellow rat! You double-crossing bastard.

– PRESIDENT WARREN HARDING TO CHARLES FORBES

It is doubtful whether any other country on earth – certainly in the Western world – attaches such reverence to its military men and women as the United States.

In a nation where patriotism and militarism go largely hand in hand, members of the U.S. armed forces are treated like heroes. On the streets, in bars and supermarkets, they are thanked 'for their service' on a daily basis. At baseball games and other sporting events, military veterans are routinely asked to stand and receive the applause of the crowd.

To the outside world it may seem a tad misty-eyed and overly patriotic, but it is very much the American way. The men and women who wear the uniform, who fight in theatres of war in distant lands, are seen as the defenders of that most cherished of American ideals – freedom. The U.S. Declaration of Independence lists liberty as an inalienable right, and from the civil war's 'new birth of freedom' in the 1800s to Operation Iraqi Freedom in the 21st century, the concepts of 'freedom' and 'liberty' have long been ingrained in American life and policy.

Count Casimir Pulaski, the Polish nobleman who fought with George Washington against the British in the American War of Independence, arrived in the United States and declared: 'I came here where freedom is being defended, to serve it, and to live

15

or die for it.' Pulaski died for the cause after being shot at the Siege of Savannah and became an American hero in the process.

His battle cry has echoed down the centuries. The victory of Washington's army over the colony's British rulers secured the first and most important freedom of all: freedom from British rule. The 'No taxation without representation' struggle achieved American independence from this far-off country whose society was class-ridden and where liberty was defined largely by social status.

In the USA, defining freedom has been tricky to say the least; this is after all a country that fought a civil war over the right of white men to keep black slaves, and that passed a law forbidding its citizens the right to drink alcohol. But whatever the rights and wrongs, the Statue of Liberty stands in New York Harbour as America's statement of enlightenment to the world.

The fascination with all things military is far easier to understand and explain. The relatively short history of modern America has been characterised by warfare: the Revolution, the Civil War, two world wars, the Spanish-American War, Vietnam, Iraq and a myriad of conflicts in between. Add to that the violent days of the Wild West with gun-toting outlaws like Billy the Kid, and the gun and the uniform became symbols of America as surely as its patriotic statues and memorials, providing an inextricable link between patriotism and militarism.

The men and women who serve in the army, navy, air force, marine corps and coast guard hold a special place in the hearts of all Americans – and the country does not take kindly to anyone who disrespects them. An attack on the military is often seen as an insult to America itself. During a concert in London, the country band Dixie Chicks publicly criticised America's 2003 invasion of Iraq. The American people responded by boycotting their concerts, sending death threats and destroying the band's CDs. The Dixie Chicks may have thought they were simply expressing their right to free speech, enshrined as it is in the First Amendment of the American Constitution, but a large section of the public gave them both barrels, metaphorically speaking.

Imagine how much worse the reaction would have been if the offender had been a crooked politician who had defrauded some of the neediest and most desperate war veterans in American history out of millions of dollars, denied them medical care and used his power and influence to pocket

Charles Forbes with members of Veterans Bureau - Library of Congress

much of the ill-gotten gains. The memory of such a person would surely live on in the annals of treachery. The reviled individual would have his place in America's version of a Rogues' Gallery, and his name and his dark deeds would to this day be etched in the nation's consciousness.

All of which begs the question – why have so few people ever heard of Charles Forbes? His crimes, which included all of the above, were committed relatively recently, in the 1920s, and they had a dreadful effect on thousands of ex-service personnel who were looking to him for help and comfort. His response was to ignore their plight as if they did not exist. He conspired with a small band of like-minded petty crooks and fleeced the veterans whose care he had been entrusted with.

In a country that respects its military so much, Charles Forbes should be a top-drawer, class A American villain. But for some reason his despicable and cowardly deeds, directed against some of the most vulnerable people in society, barely register as a footnote. Only scholars of the 'Roaring 20s' – and in particular the corruption-riddled presidency of Warren G. Harding – are aware of Forbes and the scale of his dastardly behaviour.

His story is as bad as any told in this book. Charles Robert Forbes, who left his native Scotland at the age of six, was as slippery as an eel and had few redeeming qualities. He was a shyster and a conman, a swindler and a two-bit huckster, a playboy and a cheating womaniser, an army deserter and a jailbird. To make matters worse, many of the military veterans he ripped off were former army colleagues he fought alongside during the First World War. His pathetically short jail sentence must have seemed a mere smack on the wrist.

Yet this was America in the 1920s, when the country was experiencing massive social upheaval. The country was recovering from its participation in the war; one of the final acts of the outgoing Woodrow Wilson administration had been to impose Prohibition on the nation; violent gangsters led by Al Capone were trading in bootleg liquor; dance halls rocked to the Charleston and the Breakaway; trendy young women wore 'flapper' costumes; families for the first time had cars, telephones, electricity and access to the movies; and the Wall Street Crash and Great Depression were just round the corner.

Into this maelstrom of change was thrown the rather hapless figure of Warren Gamaliel Harding, a small-town newspaper editor-cum-poker player-cum-politician who had somehow risen through the ranks to become the Republican Party's presidential candidate. His friends and associates, many of whom he rewarded with public office, became known as the 'Ohio Gang' – a byword for corruption.

His shambolic and scandal-ridden reign spawned two new English dictionary entries before it was even under way. His choice as presidential candidate had been finalised in Room 404 of the Blackstone Hotel, Chicago, prompting a United Press reporter to use the term 'smoke-filled room' to describe the allegedly shady and underhand process. Then, during Harding's campaign he promised what he described as a return to 'normalcy'. He insisted he had seen the word in his lexicon but it was generally believed he intended to say 'normality'.

Harding once made the startling admission, 'I am not fit for this office and should never have been here'. Had it not been for the president's generally-accepted incompetence, his crony Charles Forbes would never have been put in charge of America's inaugural Veterans' Bureau. Forbes was a barefaced crook and was presented with a gilt-edged opportunity to embezzle more money than he ever thought possible; the betrayal of the country's war heroes in the process seemed of little consequence to him. The swindling Scotsman conned America out of an estimated 250 million dollars. The equivalent in 2015 would have been a staggering 3.5 billion dollars.

It has been said in Harding's defence that he wasn't a bad man, rather an individual lacking control. But Harding the incompetent begat Forbes the con-merchant, and Forbes, for all his fading into obscurity, was one of the biggest scoundrels the American government has ever had the misfortune to encounter.

Charles Forbes was born in 1877 in the village of Glenluce in Wigtownshire, 10 miles east of the bustling ferry port of Stranraer. By 1881 the census shows the family had moved from Wigtownshire to Cathpair Lodge, just outside the Midlothian village of Stow. Charles was four and had an older sister Mary Jane, an older brother George and two younger sisters, Christina and Emelina.

His father, also Charles, was a coachman, and the census gives his place of birth as Ireland. However, in all subsequent census forms in the United States, Forbes senior lists his birthplace as Scotland. His wife Christina Nichol was originally from Aberdeen.

The next available census record is from the United States in 1900. Charles and Christina senior were then living in Somerville, Massachusetts, a suburb of Boston; Charles senior worked as a golf instructor. Five years later the couple, along with son George, were living in Manhattan, New York, where Charles senior was an elevator operator.

As for young Charles, he had already left the family home and married the first of his three wives. In 1898 at the age of 22, he tied the knot with Sadie Markham, daughter of a brickmason, in her home town of Pittsfield, Massachusetts. The couple's first child, Mildred, was born four months later.

He had been educated at some prestigious seats of learning, including the privately-funded Phillips Exeter Academy in New Hampshire and the Cooper Union Institute in New York. He went on to study engineering at Columbia University and Massachusetts Institute of Technology. His involvement with the military had started at the relatively tender age of 16, when he joined the marines as a musician and was stationed for a time at the Washington Navy Yard in the nation's capital.

In 1900 Forbes joined the army. Within weeks he had disappeared from his base and was classed as a deserter. In the first decade of the 20th century the desertion rate in the U.S. Army was between seven and fifteen per cent. In most cases the grim reality of army life coupled with disillusionment and boredom caused serving soldiers to seek an escape route. There are no records of why Forbes deserted but he was missing for more than three years before being captured and sent back to his unit. As in the majority of cases, no disciplinary action was taken against him; he was restored to duty and ordered to serve out the remainder of his enlistment.

To be absolutely fair to Forbes, his desertion was the only stain on an otherwise distinguished army career. In fact, his military service seems to have been the one time in his life when he appears to have demonstrated decent and at times heroic behaviour. He served for a few years in the Philippines, achieved the rank of sergeant, and was honourably discharged in 1908. During the First World War he was to attain far greater levels of distinction. Forbes seems to have been a capable and reputable soldier; it is a great pity his conduct in civilian life failed to match up.

The events in Forbes' life between 1908, when he ended his first spell of army duty, and 1917, when he signed up for war service, were crucial to everything that followed. He developed a reputation as a ladies' man and his first marriage to Sadie Markham ended in divorce. In 1909 he married again, this time to magazine writer Kate McGogy. Her father, Isaac, had been a lieutenant in the Indiana Infantry during the Civil War and had fought with the Union side. The two men may well have shared a few stories of their military exploits.

Forbes and his new wife moved to the Pacific north-west and settled in the Seattle area. He practised as a civil engineer and dabbled for the first time in the murky world of local politics. There was plenty of opportunity for the glib-talking ex-soldier to make contacts, witness deals being done, mix with the movers and shakers and gain a first-hand education of the black arts of politics and big business. He became a classic schmoozer among Democratic Party circles in Washington.

In 1912 Forbes was given a plum job in Hawaii, at that time a United States overseas territory. A major expansion of the naval station was about to be built at Pearl Harbor on the island of Oahu, and Forbes, perhaps with the help of some of his new political connections, was among the engineers appointed to oversee its development.

Life on the Pacific Ocean archipelago was good for Forbes and his wife; the couple's daughter, Marcia, was born there. Forbes not only had a responsible, well-paid job, he was also carving out an image as an important public figure. He became a socialite, a raconteur, a man who enjoyed drinking and gambling and who thrived in the company of others – he was now a big fish in a small Hawaiian pond.

In his book *High Treason: The Plot Against the People*, Albert E. Kahn describes Forbes as 'a ruddy-faced, hard-drinking, swaggering adventurer, with a penchant for spinning extravagant yarns and an easy way with members of the opposite sex'. It may not have been the classic description of a dashing womaniser, but those characteristics were to be invaluable when V.I.P. visitors came calling in 1916.

Warren Harding and his wife Florence arrived on Hawaii on a congressional junket. He had been an Ohio State Senator since 1900 and a U.S. Senator since 1914, and the couple both came from the small town of Marion, Ohio, where Warren owned the *Marion Star* newspaper. Florence was known as 'The Duchess' and was generally recognised as the brains behind her husband's business success. She was also perfectly aware that Harding was enjoying dalliances with other women.

When the senator and his wife met the smooth-talking Forbes at a social function in Honolulu they were 'instantly charmed' by him. The two men shared many common interests, not least of which were poker and women, and struck up an immediate friendship. Forbes was engaging, he told the tallest of tales, his wife and Mrs. Harding got on well together, and by the time the junket was over Forbes and Harding had become close bedfellows.

For Forbes this new connection was a personal triumph. At last he had a chum with serious political clout, a man who had access to the wheelers and dealers in the nation's capital. Even though Harding was an old-school Republican, he was determined to keep him as a close friend. Little did Forbes know then how much influence Harding would eventually wield and how much he would stand to benefit from the cosiness of the relationship.

The friendship between Forbes and Harding was forged in Hawaii over drinks, poker and ribald story-telling. They thought of each other as kindred spirits, cut from the same cloth, and over the years they championed each other's causes and rewarded each other with favours. For the two men, it was good while it lasted, but thanks to Forbes' chicanery and Harding's gullibility, it was short lived and ruinous for them both. For America, it truly was a match made in hell. It cost the United States millions of dollars in public money and it caused untold misery and hardship for tens of thousands of desperate citizens who were crying out for help.

A year after their meeting, America was belatedly plunged into the First World War. The president, Woodrow Wilson, had resisted calls to become involved since the outbreak of war in 1914. It was seen very much as a territorial conflict between the major powers of Europe – Great Britain, France and the Russian, German, Austro-Hungarian and Ottoman Empires. To America, thousands of miles away across the Atlantic Ocean, it must have seemed as though Europe was self-destructing. The country chose to remain isolated and strictly neutral.

One good reason for this stance was the continuing flow of immigrants from all over Europe to the United States. Many were from Germany and Austria; many others were from Britain, France and Russia. So the question of which side the U.S. would back if it did enter the conflict was vexed to say the least. Heavy pressure was put on the United States by Britain, one of its closest trade partners, although there was little appetite for war among the American people.

What turned the tide of public opinion was a series of German submarine attacks on passenger liners including the Clyde-built *Lusitania,* which was sunk off Ireland with the loss of 1198 passengers, 128 of them American. On 6 April 1917, America officially entered the war.

Forbes was a member of the Territory of Hawaii National Guard, and on America's entry into the war, became a signalman in the 33rd Infantry Division, American Expeditionary Forces, with the rank of major. He fought with his colleagues in France, where trench warfare was at its most brutal and deadly. It is to his credit that he emerged with an exemplary war record that saw him promoted to lieutenant-colonel and decorated with the award of the Distinguished Service Medal by the U.S. Government and the Croix de Guerre by the French.

His DSM citation read: 'The President of the United States of America, authorized by Act of Congress, July 9, 1918, takes pleasure in presenting the Army Distinguished Service Medal to Lieutenant Colonel (Signal Corps) Charles R. Forbes, United States Army, for exceptionally meritorious and distinguished services to the Government of the United States, in a duty of great responsibility during World War I. As Division Signal Officer of the 33rd Division, Lieutenant Colonel Forbes performed his duties with marked distinction, maintaining communication at all times within the division, with adjoining units, and with the higher command. His ability and untiring devotion to duty were great factors in insuring the successes achieved by the Division.'

Forbes must have been justifiably proud at his military achievements. Such awards in wartime are never given out lightly, and he was perfectly entitled to describe himself as a war hero.

The presence of the American troops on the front line of battlefields such as Ypres and the Somme helped win the war for the Allies, but at a tremendous human cost. Soldiers of all nationalities were unprepared for the horrors of modern warfare; certainly the American troops had witnessed nothing like it. During the Spanish-American War of the 1880s they had still been using cannons, rifles, muskets, revolvers and even cutlasses.

By 1914 20th century technology had transformed the weaponry available. In France and Belgium heavy artillery fire rained down on the men in the trenches. Planes and tanks were used in warfare for the first time, and machine guns and bolt-action rifles, which could deliver devastating blows to the enemy from long distance, were weapons of choice. However, the most horrific 'weapon' was the use of poison gas. Shells containing mustard and/or chlorine gas were fired into the trenches, killing and disabling thousands of soldiers.

When they arrived back in the United States, many thousands of the surviving troops were in dire straits. They were having nightmares about the horrors they had witnessed; countless could not stop shaking; some were unable to control their bowels; a condition newly-described as shell-shock was commonplace; the brave young men who had marched off to war returned home as physical and psychological wrecks, some unable to talk, walk or sleep, their symptoms typified by the 'thousand yard stare'.

Medical help was practically non-existent. America had never been faced with traumatised or 'insane' military veterans on such a scale and was wholly unprepared for dealing with the problem. The American Legion had been lobbying hard for government help since the days of the civil war, and the organisation became a strong campaigning voice after 1918.

Psychiatrist Thomas Salmon, a member of the Legion's Commission for Mental Hygiene, warned that, unless there was a massive increase in medical facilities to treat the veterans, hundreds would be 'doomed to permanent insanity'. He added: 'No blacker reproach to the honour and humanity of this country exists today than the practical abandonment by the richest nation on earth of more than half its ex-servicemen who are afflicted with insanity.'

It was clear something had to be done. When the time came the two men who stepped into the breach were none other than Warren Harding and Charles Forbes.

After the war Forbes returned to Seattle. He, Kate and Marcia made their home in the affluent village of Burton on Vashon Island, a 20-minute ferry trip from the city. His civil engineering career was flourishing and he worked his way up to vice president of Hurley-Mason Construction, a firm based in the city of Tacoma. He was put in charge of the Spokane division so his job entailed considerable travel throughout Washington State and possibly beyond.

Meanwhile the U.S. was gearing up for the presidential election year of 1920. The nation had grown tired after eight years of Woodrow Wilson's Democrats and the national mood was for change. It was obvious that the Republican nominee would be a shoo-in for president but the party was in disarray, unable to decide who to select as its candidate.

Party kingmakers looked around for a compromise candidate that could unite the warring factions. It was at this point that Warren Harding's crooked poker-playing cronies known as the 'Ohio Gang' came into play. Chief among them was a shady lawyer and local politician by the name of Harry Daugherty, who had become one of the ablest political 'fixers' in the country.

His skillful manipulation propelled Harding from anonymous Ohio senator to presidential certainty by exploiting the divisions in the Republican Party. He was the central figure in the smoke-filled room in Chicago and served as Harding's campaign manager. When Harding won a landslide victory, ironically against another Ohio newspaper editor James Cox, Daugherty was rewarded with the post of attorney general.

Harding, tall with striking features, may have looked like a president, but he was an individual with many character

Harry Daugherty - Library of Congress

flaws and a host of highly dubious friends. After his election one of his long-standing mistresses had to be bought off when she threatened to publicly expose his infidelity.

His cabinet included some impressive political figures, including future presidents Calvin Coolidge and Herbert Hoover, who served as vice president and secretary of commerce respectively. He also appointed former president William Taft to the position of chief justice. But others, including Daugherty, Edwin Denby as secretary of the navy, and Albert Fall as secretary of the interior, were there as a result of blatant cronyism.

There were many challenges facing the new administration, not least of which was how to deal with the poor shambling wrecks who had come home from the war and were in urgent need of medical help. In August 1921 the United States Congress approved the creation of a new agency, the Veterans' Bureau, and charged it with the task of building hospitals, providing adequate medical care and helping the thousands of wounded and disabled veterans find employment. The move was a reaction to the criticism from the American Legion and an effort at streamlining by effectively merging three existing agencies, including the Bureau of War Risk Insurance.

Harding didn't have to look far for the person to head up the new body. The good friend whose acquaintance he had made in Hawaii had gone on to campaign effectively for him in Seattle and he had been anxious to properly reward that loyalty. Forbes had already been appointed to the War Risk Insurance Bureau at a salary of $10,000 a year. Now the ex-pat Scotsman, with no record of high political office and with a growing reputation for dodgy dealings, was given one of the most powerful positions in post-war America.

He was put in control of an annual budget of $500 million. The old rogue could scarcely believe his luck. It was a recipe for absolute and total disaster.

He had now moved from the relative remoteness of Washington State to his own plush set of offices in the nation's seat of power, Washington DC. His new job gave him direct access to the White House and to his friend, the recently-elected president. Harding, in turn, was delighted with the appointment. He was convinced his friend, furnished with impeccable war credentials, was up to the task. In Washington circles, Forbes was unquestionably one of Harding's favourites.

The appointment also thrust Forbes into the public limelight. This was a high-profile position and many newspaper column inches, not to mention congressional and senatorial utterances, had been devoted to the plight of the veterans. He was initially given a positive welcome. After all, here was a man who had fought in the war himself, who had seen the horrors that had turned some of his comrades into human shells. If anyone could empathise with, and help ease, the anguish these souls were enduring, then surely it must be one of their own, a man who could boast war service decorations to his name.

Forbes gave himself the nickname 'The Colonel', but his arrival in Washington was not greeted with universal approval. The men who were the power behind the Harding throne – the Ohio Gang – detested him. He was viewed as an outsider, and certainly not as a 'gang' member; his only influential friend in the capital appears to have been the president. Daugherty openly disliked him and the others regarded him with suspicion and found him a slippery, evasive character who was not to be trusted.

From the word go, Forbes set about blowing his budget – but not on the needy veterans it was intended for. He established a network of 14 regional Veterans' Bureau offices across the country and employed 30,000 staff, many of them old friends and cronies who were as unscrupulous as he was. The offices were bulging with employees and some staff members were finding it difficult to justify their jobs and their inflated wages.

What followed was, as one historian put it, tantamount to Forbes establishing an 'opportunistic patchwork of individual bribery and greed'.

His job description included the management of all veterans' hospitals, the building of new hospitals for war veterans, and the disposal of wartime medical supplies and equipment. Yet the 'wide boys' and 'chancers' who populated the Bureau offices were spending weeks travelling coast-to-coast, ostensibly examining potential hospital sites, while in reality staging wild booze-laden parties in defiance of the country's Prohibition laws.

One field agent, R.A. Tripp, wrote to his superior in Washington that he was 'soused to the gills' most of the time and added, 'To hell with the central office work, the fun is in the field'. Tripp ended the letter by writing, 'Let me know when Forbes is going to sell by sealed proposals, then's when I get a Rolls Royce'.

Whether Tripp ever got his Rolls Royce is unknown, but what is certain is that Forbes was up to his neck in dizzying levels of corruption, promising private construction firms land and building contracts in exchange for kickbacks worth thousands of dollars. To make matters worse, he had grown indiscrete and was running his mouth off to anyone who would listen. Heavy drinking parties, all on Bureau expenses, became the norm and Forbes even boasted that he would soon be promoted to the President's Cabinet where more 'opportunities' would present themselves.

Among those given jobs in the Bureau was Carolyn Votaw, the president's sister, with whom Forbes was said to have formed an 'intimate relationship'. He was seen as a playboy in the capital and was captivated by Katherine Mortimer, the wife of middleman Elias Mortimer. Mort, as he was known, was acting on behalf of the Thompson-Black Construction Company of St Louis. He and his bosses had shown great personal interest in contracts for building new hospitals for the veterans. Also on board were Forbes' old bosses at the Hurley-Mason firm in Tacoma.

In the spring of 1922 Forbes embarked on a nationwide trip along with the Mortimers to undertake a survey of construction sites. While in Chicago the party met with John Thompson, director of Thompson-Black who gave Forbes a $5000 cash gift. In return his firm was awarded hospital contracts. Part of the deal was that Forbes would receive thousands of dollars plus a percentage of the company's profits on the deal.

He alerted the companies to rival bids by surreptitiously opening the sealed bids of the other contractors and leaking the details to Thompson-Black and Hurley-Mason.

Everybody was a winner. It was all too easy. The colonel became a wealthy man and turned his eyes to another straightforward money-making scam. He had inherited massive government warehouses in Maryland that were stacked to the rafters with surplus medical supplies like pyjamas, gauze, bandages, sheets, soap and medicine. Truckloads of the material left the warehouses bound for a Boston firm. They were sold off at ridiculously low prices; at a time when V.A. hospitals throughout America were short of equipment, Forbes sold nearly $7 million of medical equipment to private interests for a mere $600,000.

While Forbes and his hangers-on were bleeding the Bureau dry, the veterans were being all but ignored. More than 300,000 US soldiers had been wounded in combat during the First World War, yet only 47,000 of them had their claims for disability insurance approved. Thousands of others had their applications turned down by the Bureau for reasons described as 'hair-splitting'.

More scandalously, Forbes had not even opened 200,000 pieces of mail received at his office from veterans. He was obviously too busy with other things to be bothered with such mundane matters. A columnist for the *American Mercury* newspaper later wrote, 'Congress little realizes that its creature, the Veterans' Bureau, has probably made wrecks of more men since the war than the war itself took in dead and maimed'.

Of course it couldn't last. Forbes may have been defrauding the government right, left and centre but he was not a smart crook. He had failed to cover his tracks and, perhaps more importantly, he had made too many enemies.

Votaw had been furious when Forbes swanned off on a lengthy trip without her. Mort had discovered Forbes in compromising situations with his wife during the road trip and believed he had seduced her; he was now a deadly enemy and ready to blow the whistle. Word had reached Daugherty and other Ohio Gang members of misdeeds in the Bureau. The writing was well and truly on the wall for Forbes.

Warren Harding was quite possibly the last person in the administration to get wind of the scandal. In Daugherty's 1932 book *The Inside Story of the Harding Tragedy* he recalls telling the President there were 'strange goings-on' at the Bureau. He told Harding, 'It is hard for you to believe evil of a friend but there are limits to the application of this principle and you have reached the limit in this case. You are walking on the crest of a volcano'.

Daugherty, who by his own admission disliked Forbes in-tensely, added, 'I think nothing in Harding's life ever cut him so deeply as this man's betrayal of the trust he had placed in him'.

Warren Harding -
Library of Congress

In early 1923 Forbes had just awarded a major hospital contract to Hurley-Mason – but the game was up. Harding summoned him to his office and Forbes at first denied the charges. However, when the evidence against Forbes became concrete, a passing newspaperman in the White House witnessed the 6ft-plus Harding with his hands round the bare throat of Forbes 'shaking him as a dog would a rat'. He was yelling at his one-time friend, 'You yellow rat…you double-crossing bastard'.

It is perhaps typical of Harding that he refused to sack Forbes on the spot. Instead, he allowed him to leave the country and go to Europe, ostensibly to settle family matters, with the proviso that he resign. Forbes mailed his resignation letter to the President on 15 February 1923.

It was not the only major scandal to rock the administration. The Teapot Dome scandal saw Secretary of the Interior Albert Fall sent to jail for leasing navy petroleum reserves in Wyoming and California to private oil companies at low rates without competitive bidding.

Nathan Miller, in his book *Star-Spangled Men*, said Harding 'drifted lazily over the bubbling morass of corruption like a hot-air balloon in Macy's Thanksgiving Day Parade'. The most memorable quote attributed to Harding was: 'I have no trouble with my enemies. I can take care of my enemies in a fight. But my friends, my goddamned friends, they're the ones who keep me walking the floor at nights.'

Before Forbes or Fall would go to trial, the stress took its toll on Harding. The tall, handsome man who had become president only three years earlier was now a pale shadow of his former self. After a gruelling trip to Alaska, he died at the Palace Hotel in San Francisco.

Forbes was charged with conspiring to defraud the United States government. It was estimated his activities had cost the country as much as $250 million. Mort was happy to tell the authorities everything; he sang like a bird about Forbes accepting bribes and bedding his wife. The Federal Court found him guilty and sentenced him to a $10,000 fine and two years in jail.

Forbes entered Leavenworth Federal Penitentiary in Kansas on 21 March 1926. He was prisoner number 25021 and he served one year, eight months and six days of his sentence. His cellmate was another fraudster, Dr. Frederick Cook, who years earlier had claimed to have reached the North Pole before American explorer Robert Peary.

A news report stated that Forbes had been put in charge of the prison's construction work and that he was 'supervising the erection of new buildings'.

His second wife Kate had divorced him in 1923 on the grounds of negligence and cruelty. On his release the old charmer soon found himself with a third bride, Katherine Tullidge, a widow 19 years his junior. The 1930 census records the couple living in rented accommodation in Pasadena, California, with Forbes listed as a gas station proprietor. Ten years later they were living in Washington DC.

The jail sentence seemed pitifully short for a man whose crimes were committed at the expense of the country's returning heroes – including men he served alongside.

These men and women had put their lives on the line for their country's freedom. They were heroes, in dire need of psychological and specialist medical care. They answered the call in America's time of need and expected that their country would support them in return. They had fought to liberate their allies in Europe but returned home to find they were being treated as little more than cheap tools in a conman's get-rich-quick scheme, abandoned and deceived by a greedy ex-comrade in the name of the U.S. government.

There is a final twist to this sorry tale. Arlington National Cemetery in Virginia is the resting spot for many thousands of U.S. ex-servicemen and women who have known the pride of serving their country. Since the days of the civil war, it has been a burial place for hundreds of thousands of heroes and a symbol of the nation's pride.

Charles Forbes, a former lieutenant-colonel in the army, a signalman who had received the Distinguished Service Medal, died on 10 April 1952. He callously ignored the pleadings of thousands of his former colleagues and pocketed money earmarked for their recuperation, yet Forbes lies buried alongside America's heroes at Arlington.

His tombstone epitaph reads: 'Charles Robert Forbes, Lt Colonel. United States Army. Feb 14, 1877 – Apr 10, 1952. Distinguished Service Medal.'

3

Thomas Cream

Daniel Stott. Died June 12, 1881. Aged 61 Years.
Poisoned By His Wife & Dr. Cream

– INSCRIPTION ON A GRAVESTONE IN GARDEN PRAIRIE CEMETERY, ILLINOIS

Early in the morning of Tuesday, 15 November 1892, before dawn had even broken, Dr. Thomas Neill Cream, a serial poisoner of prostitutes on the streets of Victorian London, was escorted from his cell in the city's Newgate Prison and led to the gallows.

He looked tired and scruffy but composed as he climbed the wooden steps. The piercing black eyes which had once captivated unsuspecting female victims had dimmed since his capture, trial and inevitable sentence. That grey London morning was to be his last – and no-one who had crossed the good doctor's path would shed a tear.

Only a handful of public officials were with him as he calmly read out a short statement thanking his prison guards for looking after him so well in his final days. He kept it matter-of-fact; there was no expression of sorrow or regret from the man dubbed 'The Lambeth Poisoner'.

Less than a month earlier, Cream had been convicted of murdering four women and attempting to murder a fifth over a seven-month period. The trial judge, Justice Henry Hawkins – known as Hanging Hawkins – told the 42-year old that 'his willingness to murder was so diabolical in its character, fraught with so much cold-blooded cruelty, that it could be expiated only by death'.

True to form, Judge Hawkins had sentenced Cream to hang. Public executions were a thing of the past, but even by the standards of crime-ridden 19th century London, Cream's offences were notorious. On the appointed day, a crowd approaching 5,000 gathered outside Newgate Prison walls.

A good hanging was just cause for rowdy public celebration in those days. Press reporters were there to monitor proceedings and police officers struggled to keep the revelry under control. Most of those present constituted the 'great unwashed' of grimy old London, including many of the city's prostitutes who had been terrorised by Cream's unquenchable bloodlust.

Inside the purpose-built execution shed in a Newgate Prison yard, a hood was placed over the head of Thomas Cream. The noose was then slipped round his neck by hangman James Billlington, the 16ft drop was carefully checked and the rope measured before the prisoner was dispatched.

But Cream was not going quietly. A split second before Billington pulled the lever and released the trap-door, Cream uttered the words: 'I am Jack the......'

He was unable to end the sentence but the four mumbled words, heard by those closest to him, were to keep his name and his dark deeds uppermost in the annals of London criminality. An industry has grown up around the possible identity of Jack the Ripper and Cream's last words have ensured he remains at the heart of it.

The crowd outside Newgate knew nothing of what had been said. All they saw was the black flag being flown from inside the courtyard signifying the prisoner had been successfully executed. They drank and sang and danced in celebration.

Cream's capture and demise was a huge relief for London. Even by Victorian standards, the exploits of the Lambeth Poisoner had struck terror into those who occupied the pitiful underclasses of the sprawling city. He is no footnote in history; he deserves his prominent place among Britain's worst serial killers. To this day, whenever a new Jack the Ripper theory is advanced, Thomas Cream's story finds its way into the media.

London was Cream's most celebrated stomping ground. The deranged, deluded and opium-addled doctor possessed a pathological hatred of women in general and prostitutes in particular. He stalked the filthy slums to the south of the city, directly across the River Thames from the grandeur of the Houses of Parliament, Westminster Abbey and Buckingham Palace. Victorian London was at the centre of the biggest empire in the world yet tens of thousands of its citizens lived in poverty and squalor. Their houses were no better than cesspits and bred deadly diseases like cholera and tuberculosis.

But London was only one part of the Thomas Cream story. His expertise as a poisoner of women did not develop overnight; he had spent years perfecting his skills and techniques. His early life was so bizarre it could almost be written off as some fanciful tale of how a killer escaped justice over and over again. In truth, Cream should have been caught and executed long before his grisly reign of terror on the streets of London.

Thomas Neill Cream was born into a working-class family in industrial Glasgow in 1850. Clyde shipbuilding was in its heyday and Glasgow was the thriving, bustling 'Second City of the Empire'. He was the eldest child of shipping company clerk William Cream and his wife Mary Elder. When Thomas was four, the family left Scotland and sailed off to a new life in the Canadian city of Quebec.

It was as a young man growing up in Canada that Cream began to exhibit odd personality traits. He qualified as a doctor of medicine in Montreal and his fellow students remembered his fascination with the anaesthetic properties of the drug chloroform. He also found himself linked for the first time to the deaths of young women – one of whom he had been forced to marry at gunpoint. No evidence was found against him but uncomfortable questions were being asked. Cream had to beat a hasty retreat from Canada and moved across the border to the United States.

Having effectively evaded the law in Canada, and imbued with a certain cockiness, he headed for the seedy back streets of 1880s Chicago. By now Cream was gaining a reputation as an abortionist, specialising in 'helping' low-life hookers and the 'soiled doves' of society. Chicago and its burgeoning red light district offered him no shortage of clients, and it was here, a decade before his London poisoning spree, that he honed his skills as a ruthless killer.

There was, of course, no shortage of people prepared to kill – many for a living – in 19th century America. Much of the country's Wild West history was still being written when Cream found himself in Illinois. Gun-toting frontier outlaws and professional hitmen were a deadly mix, and there were many unsavoury and bloodthirsty characters – far too many to count. Survival, in certain parts of the United States, could never be taken for granted.

Thomas Cream brought something quite different to the party. On the surface he appeared a respectable medical professional; however, underneath that façade lurked a sleazy, calculating and deeply disturbed individual. Cream was, to put it bluntly, a lunatic. In time his oddball tendencies gave way to depravity, drug-taking, blackmail, pornography and what seemed a remorseless thirst for killing. Psychologists nowadays would have a field day with him; he has been described as a pathological narcissist by some and a homicidal maniac by others. Cream was simply a monster.

When Cream entered the world in Scotland, the eldest of seven children, his mother and father doted on him. His birth announcement in 1850 was filled with hope and optimism, as one might expect from devoted parents. It read, 'William Cream, clerk, 60 Wellington Lane, and Mary Elder had a lawful son, their first child, born 27 May 1850, named Thomas Neill'. The witnesses were William's brothers George and Robert Cream and the birth was registered at Glasgow's Barony Parish.

William Cream was an Irish immigrant, and by all accounts, an honest and hard-working man. His wife Mary had been brought up in Glasgow's tough Gorbals area and the couple wed in June 1849 in Gorbals Parish Church. When the 1851 census was taken, William's job had changed from a clerk in a shipping office to a collector with the Glasgow Gas Company.

Wellington Lane, where the young family lived, was then a narrow, dingy back alley running between Hope Street and Blythswood Street, west of where Glasgow Central railway station now stands. Life for the working-class population of the city was harsh and, for the Creams, as with many other young couples, bringing up a child in what was a typical Glasgow slum made life that bit tougher.

But William and Mary were resourceful and had their eyes on a better life. They saved their hard-earned cash and planned their escape from dreich old Glasgow. In 1854, along with Thomas and his younger brother Daniel, they set sail for the Port of Quebec on the St. Lawrence River in eastern Canada.

Quebec City was a boomtown back in the 1850s. Almost 100 years earlier it had been the scene of the Battle of the Plains of Abraham, when the British, under General James Wolfe, defeated French forces under the command of the Marquis de Montcalm, a victory which allowed Britain to take control of Canada. The city's position on the St. Lawrence made it one of the most important seaports in North America, particularly for the transfer of furs and timber. Vessels packed with immigrants from Scotland, Ireland, France and other parts of Europe were also a regular feature of the city's harbour.

The Cream family appeared to settle well in their new home. William was employed as a manager by the lumber and shipbuilding firm of Gilmore and Company. Thomas and Daniel welcomed five new siblings, Rachel, Mary, William, Robert and Hannah. Census records show that their neighbours were mostly Scots or Irish immigrants, so there was no shortage of Celtic company to keep any homesickness at bay.

At this point there seemed nothing unusual about Thomas Cream, certainly nothing to suggest he would go on to become a brutal killer. He was described as an average student and even spent several years as a Sunday school teacher. However, it does seem that, in his father's eyes at least, Thomas could do no wrong. The youngster appears to have been, to an extent, pampered, as William found him a short-lived job in a shipbuilding firm then employed him when he set up his own lumber company. Then again, Thomas did not relish the hard physical work, and after three years he decided his future lay in medicine.

In his book, *Monsters of Medicine: The Lives of Five Serial Killer Physicians*, William Colliflower wrote that Cream seemed a 'very spoiled and undisciplined child' and that he was 'more concerned with his appearance, his clothes and his 'toys' than any meaningful activity'.

At the age of 22 Cream enrolled at the college of medicine at McGill University in Montreal, an institution that had been established by fellow Glaswegian James McGill, one of the wealthiest men in Canada, in the 18th century. Cream cut quite a dash as a student, elegantly dressed in the style of a 'dandy', and sporting a bushy dark moustache and sideburns. His student lodgings were in well-off quarters in the city's Mansfield

Street and some reports suggest he travelled to and from the university in his own horse-driven carriage. Everything, of course, provided by his doting father.

Commercial production of chloroform had not long begun when Cream was studying at McGill and it was perfectly natural to expect a young man studying medicine to show an interest in a new drug. Cream, however, was said to have had a 'morbid fascination' with it and other anaesthetics. He did at least put his new-found knowledge to good academic use by writing his thesis for his doctor of medicine degree about chloroform and its qualities.

Shortly after his graduation in 1876, a fire broke out in his lodgings in Mansfield Street. It was serious enough to cause some structural damage and arson was suspected but never proved. Cream made a claim for loss of property and emerged with $350. No-one could prove how the fire started and Cream may have been 100% innocent of any wrong-doing, but it was the first time the law had come sniffing around his neighbourhood, and the shifty doctor had proved elusive.

It is impossible to explain what came over Cream and why, at this stage in his life, he went so badly off the rails. He was 26, armed with a doctorate from a prestigious university and appeared to have a bright future ahead of him. However, apart from the few years in his father's employ, he had never had what could be called a 'real' job. While he was a striking young man to look at, he had a noticeable squint in his left eye which one author described as 'wonky'. The worst that can be said at this point was that he had some mildly unusual character traits – certainly nothing to suggest 'serial killer' tendencies.

His university graduation coincided with him capturing the heart of a rather naïve and innocent teenage girl called Flora Brooks from the nearby small town of Waterloo. Love blossomed and the couple was soon engaged. Equally soon, Flora, unknown to her domineering and protective father Lyman, became pregnant. Weeks later Flora took badly ill and her father called for a doctor to examine her, only to be told she had recently had an abortion. Flora blurted out the truth – that the frightful deed had been performed by her newly-qualified doctor fiancé.

Lyman Brooks, a respectable hotelier, was outraged. He rounded up an armed posse and travelled to Cream's lodging house in Montreal. The doctor was hauled back at gunpoint to Waterloo and five days later he 'agreed' to marry Flora in a private ceremony.

If the family thought they had done the right thing by their daughter and solved an embarrassing problem, they were gravely mistaken. One morning Flora awoke to find a note on her pillow. Her new husband had gone to England to further his education and would be in touch. He never was.

Poor Flora did not recover from what was a highly dangerous – not to mention illegal – procedure. Less than a year later she died, and while her official cause of death was given as consumption, the old medical term for tuberculosis, there is no doubt that Thomas Cream's bungled abortion had played a major part in her illness.

Cream's name was mud in the eyes of his in-laws. Not only had he brought disgrace on the family by impregnating their teenage daughter, he had aborted his own child in a procedure so botched that it had almost certainly led to Flora's death. This was no suspected arson attack; this time Cream had the blood of his young wife on his hands. But so much time had passed since the operation that there was no proof and the law was never involved, despite the deep suspicions of Flora's family doctor.

Yet again he gained financially. As if Lyman Brooks was not suffering enough from the death of his beloved daughter, Cream rubbed salt in the wounds by claiming $1,000 from him through an unknown clause in the wedding contract. The men eventually settled on a payment of $200.

Abortion in the 1870s was forbidden and very much a back-street business. Terminations were carried out under awful conditions. Most practitioners used the old-fashioned remedies of bloodletting and purging; there was little in the way of sterilisation, and there were no antibiotics. Many women died from the procedure, but for the abortionists it was a lucrative trade.

While Flora Brooks lay ill in Canada, her husband was once again enjoying life as a medical student, this time at the famed St Thomas' Hospital in London. He took lodgings in Lambeth Palace Road and his two-year stay seems like an unintended reconnaissance mission for the killing spree of later years. This time round he was quite the womaniser, and spent many hours in the company of prostitutes on the streets he was to go on to terrorise. There was even a suggestion he contracted a dose of syphilis while in England.

His fornicating lifestyle clearly interfered with his studying, and after a year he failed his entrance exams to the Royal College of Surgeons. The following year, 1878, his academic work improved; he became an accredited midwife and passed an exam that qualified him for membership of the Royal College of Physicians and Surgeons in Edinburgh.

If there were any 'unfortunate accidents' involving young women during his time in England then they are not recorded. Who knows if he practised his dodgy abortion techniques on any of the miserable streetwalkers who frequented Lambeth? What is certain is that he returned with a heightened interest in chloroform coupled with a new fascination – the rat poison strychnine.

In May 1878, Cream sailed the Atlantic again, this time from one London to another – he swapped London, England for London, Ontario, a town in the south-west of the Canadian province, midway between the Great Lakes of Erie and Huron. The Flora Brooks affair had, in his mind, died down, and he felt free to set up a medical practice in his new home town. The surgery in Dundas Street was to last less than a month before yet another scandal erupted.

One morning a child made the gruesome discovery of a teenage girl's body lying beside a shed at the back of Cream's surgery. The victim, later identified as Kate Hutchinson Gardener, had scratches on her face and a bottle of chloroform lay by her side. She had worked as a chambermaid at the nearby Tecumseh House Hotel, and a police investigation revealed an overdose of chloroform as the cause of her death. It quickly emerged that Kate had recently become pregnant and had visited Cream to ask for an abortion.

This time police were immediately suspicious and a coroner's inquest was opened into Kate's death. It was revealed she had been having affairs with at least two wealthy – and married – businessmen. Both, not surprisingly, denied they had had anything to do with her. Cream claimed that Kate had come to his surgery and offered him $100, a princely sum, if he would perform an abortion. He said he rejected her request and suggested to the inquest that the girl might have committed suicide as a result.

On the other hand, medical evidence revealed that Kate had been strangled, and the notion that the victim could have killed herself using a rag soaked with chloroform was ridiculed. The inquest's verdict was murder caused by an overdose of chloroform at the hands of a person unknown. It was a damning verdict for Cream, but as the evidence was mostly circumstantial, he could not be charged.

Yet again he had escaped, this time by the skin of his teeth. Of course, had the police carried out even a modicum of detective work at his alma mater, McGill University, they would have found a proven link between Cream and chloroform. They might even have been able to stop him in his tracks. Instead he was a free man, although his business and reputation were in ruins. This most recent scandal had been a close call and brought an effective end to his practice in Canada, so he decided to up sticks and head across the border for a new life in the 'Windy City' of Chicago.

If Cream was yearning for the thrill of the big city then he had landed in the right place. Chicago in 1879 was one of the most rapidly developing and exciting cities in the world. A disastrous fire eight years earlier had caused massive destruction, but now Chicago was being rebuilt in spectacular fashion. The world's first skyscrapers were being constructed there; it had become the most important hub in the American railroad system, and it was becoming a haven for the country's nouveaux-riches.

Between the 1860s and the late 1880s the population of Chicago rose from 109,000 to more than 1,000,000. The city overtook Philadelphia as the second most populous in the United States. Jobs a-plenty were available at major industrial sites like the Union Stockyards meatpacking factory and the South Works steel mill, and a mass of new immigrants poured into the city.

But it was developing another less welcome reputation for lawlessness. Gangsters and racketeers were endemic, and it was said that every politician elected in Chicago had his dodgy friends to thank for getting him there. The streets of the great city were violent and dangerous, and the murder rate was high. Conditions were ripe for the seeds of organised crime and the rise of what became known as the Chicago Mafia.

In his 1904 book *The Shame of the Cities*, American journalist Lincoln Steffens described Chicago thus: 'First in violence, deepest in dirt, lawless, unlovely, ill-smelling, irreverent, new; an overgrown gawk of a village, the "tough" among cities, a spectacle for the nation.'

Thomas Cream was not by any means tough; he was certainly no match for the streetfighters and thugs who had been drawn to his new home. Still, Chicago held a particular appeal for him. Hand in hand with the mass influx of workers and the population explosion, there had been an invasion of a certain type of 'street people' with whom Cream was very familiar. Prostitutes had become a feature of the expanding new city and the good doctor was in town to minister to their every need.

He set up a medical practice in a rented house in West Madison Street, close to the city's red light district, and it was common knowledge that a large part of his work consisted of performing abortions. Cream was not the only one involved in the illegal trade; the authorities knew perfectly well what was going on yet chose to turn a blind eye. Policing in Chicago had become a necessity after large-scale riots and strikes by immigrant workers. The city's force was considered reasonably well-organised, although officers received little in the way of training.

Those employed in the police force of 1880s Chicago were not regarded as enforcers of the law. They were seen as agents of big business and the city elite, and enemies of the working-class. Much of their work was taken up with apprehending low-life drunkards and street beggars, dealing with saloon bar brawlers, and enforcing the city's liquor licensing regulations. There was plenty to keep them occupied in the violent and impoverished neighbourhoods, so the activities of a backstreet abortionist did not warrant their attention. And of course most cops, like everyone else in authority in Chicago, were corrupt.

All of which played perfectly into the hands of Cream. He was able to carry out his 'medical' business largely unhindered, and as a professional man with a university degree, he was a cut above many of the shady fly-by-night merchants plying a similar trade.

Angus McLaren, in his book *A Prescription for Murder*, wrote that a census at the time revealed more than 3,500 women working the Chicago streets and charging a going rate of 50 cents a customer.

In a city with such a bustling red light district, and in an age when there was little meaningful form of contraception, there was good money to be made for someone with Cream's credentials. His business was booming and would have continued to do so had he been able to keep his nose clean – but that was too much to ask. Within a few short months of arriving in town, a major scandal again broke out around him.

Cream used a number of young women as midwives. Their job was to mix with the prostitutes, round up potential customers who had fallen pregnant, and arrange an appointment either at Cream's surgery, a brothel, or the house of a midwife, for the procedures to be carried out. The operations were gruesome and painful; Cream was able to put his expertise with chloroform to good use as a means of keeping the poor women sedated.

One of his so-called midwives was a young African-American woman called Hattie Mack. She lived in an apartment in West Madison Street, not far from Cream's surgery, and her home was used occasionally by Cream to carry out abortions. In early 1880 neighbours noticed a foul stench coming from the house; when police broke down the door, they found the decomposing body of Canadian-born prostitute Mary Anne Faulkner.

At first Hattie Mack was charged with Mary Anne's murder; however, she then proceeded to tell police everything she knew about the activities of Thomas Cream. Not only that, she repeated the stories he had told her; his boasts about the hundreds of abortions he had carried out and his dislike of prostitutes. More importantly, she claimed she was not with Cream when he operated on the victim.

Cream was now the one facing a murder charge. He gave police his side of the story but it was less than convincing, and he was thrown in jail awaiting trial. His cellmate was notorious Chicago abortionist Charles Earll – an unqualified 'quack' – who had been arrested many times in the previous few years.

While Cream was awaiting trial, the *Chicago Tribune* – in a lengthy and moralising editorial – waded into the abortion argument by calling for the two men to face the death penalty.

The article, published on 9 August 1880, referred to Earll as a 'professional butcher'. It said of Cream: 'The evidence points to an equally incompetent, unscrupulous and callous practitioner with previous experience in this worse than brutal pursuit.'

The paper added that the jailing of abortionists for one or two years was 'mere trifling'. It stated: 'It amounts to positive encouragement for the practice of abortion. What is needed is *hanging*. The law provides the extreme penalty in every case where the death of the mother results from the crime... The hanging of one or two abortionists would make the regular vocation of abortionist as rare as that of the professional and hired assassin.'

In thunderous tones, it concluded: 'Let the law then be invoked to its utmost limit. If Earll and Cream be the guilty persons, as seems to be the case from all the evidence at hand, *let them hang!*'

It was powerful stuff from one of the best-read and most influential newspapers in the land. But while there was no doubting the *Tribune*'s moral argument was watertight – and it must have made uncomfortable reading for Cream – the doctor knew he had two crucial weapons in his defence armoury.

In the first instance, he had plenty money to hire one of the many influential and flamboyant legal counsel only too willing to take on a defendant in a Chicago show trial. Secondly, and an equally important factor in 19th century America, the young woman about to testify against him was black.

On the morning of 16 November 1880, an all-male, all-white jury was sworn in to hear the murder case in front of a packed courthouse. The presiding judge was Joseph

S. Gary, and Cream's attorney was the well-known and theatrical Alfred Samuel Trude, who in an ironic touch was for 27 years used as a defence lawyer by none other than the proprietors of the *Chicago Tribune*.

Cream for his part was groomed and dressed impeccably, and looked every inch the upstanding gentleman doctor as he stood in the dock.

There was only ever going to be one verdict. Hattie Mack's murder charge was dropped in exchange for her testimony, and while she may not have been the best-dressed person in court, she gave her evidence to the best of her ability. Trude, in his address to the jury, referred to her disparagingly as a 'frowsy little negress'. At the end of the day the decision for the jurors was whether to take the word of a white man or that of a black woman. After only 15 minutes of deliberation they found Cream not guilty of the murder of Mary Anne Faulkner.

So the unfortunate Mary Anne joined Flora Brooks and Kate Gardener on the growing list of suspicious deaths linked to Thomas Cream. Yet again he had managed to escape conviction; in spite of a public call for his hanging, he still walked free. He was fast becoming the 19th century equivalent of Teflon Man and seemed to be relishing the attention.

Instead of keeping his head down and letting the publicity blow over, Cream went straight back to his work – as boastful and arrogant as ever. His criminal repertoire grew arms and legs; he graduated from the illegal but possibly accidental killing of prostitutes to poisoning and blackmail. It was as though, emboldened by his seemingly charmed life, he was playing a deadly game of 'catch me if you can' with the authorities.

The dictionary definition of narcissistic personality disorder describes someone who has an 'exaggerated sense of self-importance' and 'a preoccupation with grandiose fantasies concerning the self'. It also states that such a person deals badly with rejection and failure and responds with feelings of 'rage, shame, humiliation or emptiness'.

William Colliflower, in describing Cream's unquestioned narcissism, suggests the doctor may have been impotent and 'unable to perform' while with prostitutes and that this defect may have led to rage and feelings of hatred and destruction towards the women. Whatever was going on inside Cream's head, he appeared to believe he was bombproof and was goading the police at every turn.

Barely a month after his trial – in December 1880 – another pregnant street girl who had gone to him for help was found dead. Ellen Stack had been prescribed abortion pills by the doctor; they were made up by a highly respected local pharmacist Frank Pyatt then sent back to Cream. By the time Ellen Stack swallowed them they were laced with strychnine poison and she suffered horrific convulsions before dying.

Cream then decided he would attempt to blackmail Mr. Pyatt. He wrote him a letter warning that a prosecution was being prepared and his business was in danger. The pharmacist, in the certain knowledge he had done everything above board, went straight to the authorities. An investigation was carried out but it was inconclusive; the worm, once again, wriggled off the hook.

Spare a thought for Cream's hard-working and industrious father William, who was still in Quebec with several of his other children. His wife Mary had passed away and he was discovering that the son on whom he had lavished love, attention and money had turned into a seedy abortionist. William's health was suffering and there was every reason to believe that his eldest son's activities were causing him stress from which he would never recover.

In 1881 Cream was to be the central figure in one of the most sensational criminal trials Illinois has ever witnessed. However, before it played out he discovered that blackmailing was not as easy a game as he had thought; in fact it landed him back in a prison cell.

A Chicago furrier called Joseph Martin had not paid his medical fees. Cream wrote to him demanding $20 and threatened to make it publicly known that Martin had infected his wife and children with venereal disease if he did not pay. When he refused, Cream sent a series of libelous poison-pen letters which Martin took to the police. Cream was arrested but released on bail of $1,200 thanks to the intervention of a woman called Mary McClellan who believed Cream had become engaged to her daughter.

By this time a couple by the name of Daniel and Julia Stott had entered Thomas Cream's life. Daniel, an agent with the Chicago and North Western Railroad, was 61, while his very attractive wife was 33. They lived comfortably in the village of Garden Prairie, in Boone County, Illinois, about 67 miles from the centre of Chicago, and were popular and respected people in the community.

Daniel suffered from epileptic seizures, and early in 1881, heard of a 'foolproof' remedy for the condition concocted by a Chicago doctor called Thomas Neill Cream. He travelled to the surgery, was given a prescription, and he sent Julia back to see Dr. Cream to have it renewed each time the medicine ran out. But Julia frequently stayed overnight in Chicago, and she and the doctor were soon having a full-blown affair.

Much appears to have been discussed between the two, including the possibility of purchasing an insurance policy on Daniel's life. They may well have discussed killing him. If Julia was not 'in' on the plot, then Cream certainly had plans of his own for her unfortunate husband.

On 12 June 1888 Julia prepared a dose of Cream's elixir for her husband. Within 20 minutes of taking it, Daniel Stott suffered a massive fit and died. In the tight-knit community of Garden Prairie, his death raised few eyebrows, since it was known he suffered seizures. The cause of death was given as an epileptic attack and he was buried in Garden Prairie Cemetery. Julia was every inch the grieving widow, dressed in black and weeping as she rode in the funeral procession.

What happened next seemed, on the face of it, bizarre. Cream had in truth just got away with committing the perfect murder. However, his narcissism would not let matters

Garden Prairie Cemetery, Illinois.

rest. He proceeded to send a series of telegraph messages to the local coroner and the district attorney claiming that Stott had died of strychnine poisoning administered by a highly respectable pharmacist. He also tried to collect damages from the chemist on Julia's behalf. A lawyer was summoned and traces of Cream's medicine were found in the Stott house. It was fed to a stray dog which died of convulsions within minutes.

When Daniel Stott's body was exhumed it was found to contain enough strychnine to kill six men – the quantity of the poison was 30 times greater than the prescription had called for. A coroner's inquest was held and ruled there was enough evidence to charge both Cream and Julia Stott with premeditated murder.

In quiet, rural Garden Prairie, a few miles from the city of Rockford, the case was causing a sensation. The widow Stott became a reviled figure, with most villagers believing she was a co-conspirator and the one who had mixed the fatal dose. Murder carried the death penalty in Illinois, and local residents erected a gallows outside the village before the trial even started.

Cream knew his blackmail scheme had misfired badly, and he could feel the net closing in around him. Without warning he jumped bail and headed back across the border to Quebec. However, he had reckoned without the tenacity of the Boone county sheriff, who tracked him down to the remote territory of Belle-Rivière. On 27 July 1881 the front page of the *Chicago Tribune* was dominated by the stories of Cream's capture and the shooting of Billy the Kid by Pat Garrett.

Before the trial started at Boone County Court in Belvidere, Cream learned his father had disowned him and would not pay for a defence lawyer. He had to make do with a public defender, although there was even worse news awaiting him. Julia Stott had decided to turn state's evidence in exchange for the charge against her being dropped.

The doctor still believed he could get away with it. In his evidence he painted Julia Stott as a seductress and claimed she had asked him for the strychnine to poison her husband. The *Rockford Journal* summed up the distaste in the locality for Mrs. Stott in an editorial that branded her a 'she-fiend of the most aggravating order'. The paper claimed she was 'probably responsible for much or all of the heinous and sickening things that have been held chargeable to the doctor'.

But the jurors were not swayed by what they read in the paper. Three hours after the edition hit the streets, the jury found Thomas Cream guilty of murder. Finally, his incredible run of luck had come to an end. Yet the jury spared him the noose, possibly because of the part Julia Stott may have played in the crime. Instead, he was sentenced 'for the term of his natural life' at Illinois State Penitentiary in the city of Joliet as inmate number 4374.

And that should have been the end of the story. In America, after all, life means life. Then again, this was Illinois, where anything – even a prison sentence – was negotiable if the bribe was high enough. The prison in Joliet was notoriously corrupt. It was a filthy place with no toilets or running water and was described at the time as 'rotten to the core'.

Cream spent more than nine years in jail, during which time his father passed away. The old man left behind a considerable estate which he divided among his children – even some for the errant Thomas. Daniel Cream was the only family member who had remained loyal to Thomas, and he used some of the cash to make a case for his brother's release.

Incredibly, he was able to persuade Illinois Governor Joseph W. Fifer to announce in 1891 that Cream was a 'fit and proper person for executive clemency'. The murdering doctor, who had deliberately poisoned a patient by lacing his medicine with strychnine, and who had been responsible for the deaths of four women, was set free. There was no question that a considerable sum of money had changed hands in high places in order to achieve such a spectacular result.

But if Daniel Cream and his band of supporters thought justice had been served they would have been horrified when they saw the shambling figure that emerged from the Illinois Penitentiary. Cream had changed beyond recognition; the dapper figure with a shock of dark hair was now a scruffy, balding old man. He was showing signs of serious drug abuse and his behaviour led some to believe he was insane.

When he returned to Canada to collect his $16,000 inheritance, his family was shocked to the core. He was dirty and foul-mouthed, and Daniel's wife found him a threatening presence in the house. There was some relief when he said he was taking the money and heading to London.

Thus began his final murderous rampage that should never have been allowed to happen. Cream should either have been executed or locked up for life long before he boarded the SS *Teutonic* in September 1891. It is to the eternal shame of the authorities in Canada and the United States, in particular the corrupt politicians who ruled the roost in Illinois, that he was set free to kill again. Without the bare-faced greed of the individuals who profited from his release, there would have been no Lambeth Poisoner and at least five young women would have been spared horrible deaths.

By the time Cream arrived back in his old haunt of Lambeth he was a man out of control, a killing machine. He seemed permanently high on drugs and was always in possession of pornographic material – and of course he now had plenty money to buy large quantities of strychnine. It was not enough that he poisoned the women, causing them to suffer violent convulsions before they died; he also followed up every kill with an attempt at blackmail.

As in Chicago, if he had kept quiet, he would have remained undetected for longer and many more London prostitutes would have lost their lives. But his egotistical craving for attention got the better of him. He sent dozens of anonymous letters to the police, in a bid to blackmail fellow doctors and even a member of the British aristocracy. It was as though, despite the obvious consequences, he could not stand the thought of no-one knowing that he – Thomas Cream – was responsible.

The end of Cream's reign of depravity was long overdue. There was no future in the way he was behaving. It was almost as though he wanted to get caught – and perhaps in a bizarre way he did. His entire adult life had been an endless procession of killings, and the blackmail threats, which were all traceable to him, may have been his way of bringing an end to the debauchery.

Police in London eventually shadowed Cream and uncovered his previous record in America. At least four prostitutes had died at his hands on the streets of London and he paid the ultimate price on the gallows.

As for his apparent claim to have been Jack the Ripper, that too was almost certainly a narcissist's fantasy. The Ripper crimes had been committed while Cream was incarcerated in Joliet and the two men had very different modus operandi – Cream poisoned while the Ripper mauled his victims. The clear disparity has not stopped Ripperologists dreaming up weird and wonderful possibilities to prove that Cream was in fact Jack, although it seems extremely unlikely to say the least.

Back in Garden Prairie there was an unusual postscript to the sensational murder of Daniel Stott and the ensuing trial. Stott had been a member of the Masonic Lodge in nearby Belvidere and his brother Masons had no doubt who shouldered the blame for the death of their colleague.

Shortly after Cream had been jailed and Julia Stott given her freedom, a

Inscription on Daniel Stott grave - Garden Prairie Cemetery, Illinois

group of Masons walked to Garden Prairie Cemetery under cover of darkness. They erected a tombstone with the epitaph, 'Daniel Stott, Died June 12, 1881; Aged 61 years. Poisoned By His Wife & Dr Cream'.

More than 130 years later the stone is still standing in the well-preserved little cemetery. There cannot be another headstone like it anywhere in the world.

4

William Stewart

He seemed to be filled with an insane desire to slaughter as many as possible, and he hewed them down without the least mercy.

– FELLOW MORMON SAMUEL KNIGHT ON WILLIAM STEWART

From the 17th century onwards, the boatloads of emigrants who left their homelands in Europe and sailed to the New World of America did so for a multiplicity of reasons. Many, like the tragic victims of Scotland's Highland Clearances, and the tens of thousands of Negro slaves kidnapped from their homes in West Africa, simply had no choice in the matter.

Of those who went to the U.S. voluntarily, most wanted to better themselves; to escape the drudgery of the smoky industrial cities of Scotland's central belt, the north and midlands of England, and the Ruhr area of Germany. Famine forced tens of thousands of Irish to make the journey in the 19th century. On the other side of the class divide, wealthy businessmen descended in droves and amassed fortunes in vast tobacco and cotton plantations. The country also attracted the European aristocracy, with many idle sons treating the land as nothing more than a giant playground.

If there was one common thread that defined American immigration it was religion. From the earliest days of the Pilgrim Fathers and the Puritans, the crossing to America was, for tens of thousands of people, an escape from the horrific excesses of religious persecution that had blighted centuries of turbulent European history.

Down through the ages, the continent had been scarred by innumerable wars and conflicts fought by one religious group against another; millions had died in the name of God and religion. Catholics and Protestants seemed to be engaged in an eternal and bloody battle for supremacy; Jews were slaughtered throughout Eastern Europe in the pogroms of the Russian Empire and in countries such as Romania, Poland and Germany; adherents to 'new religions', the Quakers of England, and the Amish and Mennonites from Central Europe routinely suffered and died for their beliefs.

The dominant creeds in Europe – Catholicism and Protestantism – wanted uniformity of religious worship in their countries, and were fanatical and brutal in their methods of stamping out non-conformity. Religious opponents, including women and children, were tortured and killed in horrifying ways. Some were burned at the stake or hanged like common criminals, others had body parts cut off before being slain or were hunted down and executed like the Presbyterian Covenanters of 17th century Scotland.

Europe was no place for someone whose religious convictions did not fit the established norm, so when America was opened up by the Pilgrim Fathers, themselves escaping persecution, it was as though a lantern of hope had at last been lit. This new frontier promised a long awaited refuge, a place where so-called religious dissidents could practise their faiths in peace and safety. It was a land where people could worship God however they chose and establish their individual religious communities in the manner of the pioneers who sailed on the *Mayflower*. Most importantly, it held out the promise of a land free from the shackles of intolerance.

Of course the dream was all too good to be true. Those who escaped the brutality of Europe found that religious persecution and intolerance were alive and kicking in the United States. The Puritans of the Massachusetts Bay colony would not brook any conflicting religious opinions; they tortured and hanged Quakers who preached in the streets of Boston. The new country's seat of power, Virginia, was in the grip of 'Protestant militants'.

One reason for the turmoil was that many of those who landed in America were as zealous about their religious beliefs as those who had persecuted them in Europe. Puritan leader John Winthrop spoke of his desire to establish a Christian Utopia – his 'city upon a hill' – in New England. But in the Puritans' wake came many more groups, each with its own Utopian ideals and breed of fanaticism. All too soon the religious scene in the sprawling lands of America became swamped with a bewildering array of creeds and doctrines, and with them came the sectarianism, bigotry and strife that had beset Europe.

Scottish Anglican minister Rev. George Aeneas Ross, who preached in Wilmington, Delaware, regarded the spread of Quakerism in the 1700s as 'pernicious heresy' and 'subversive of patriotic principles'. Benedict Arnold, the man regarded as the most notorious American traitor, claimed one of his reasons for betraying George Washington and going over to the British side during the War of Independence was America's alliance with Catholic France, a country he described as 'the enemy of the Protestant faith'.

The massive influx of Irish fleeing the Great Famine led to an anti-Catholic witch hunt, culminating in riots in Philadelphia in 1844. Former president Millard Fillmore fought the 1856 election on behalf of the American Party, the political arm of the fiercely anti-Catholic Know-Nothing movement – and gained a respectable 873,000 votes.

The increase in immigrants saw a greater spread and diversity of faiths and denominations to the new land and more challenges to the religious establishments.

If America was finding it difficult to tolerate the Catholics and the Quakers, the Baptists and the Methodists, it was convulsed with a frenzied hostility when a new and 'blasphemous' doctrine emerged in its own back yard, attracting thousands of followers. The messages preached by leaders of the Church of Jesus Christ of Latter-day Saints – or Mormons – were seen as menacing and counter to traditional American values.

Mormons spoke of joining God after death in a 'celestial kingdom' and condemned all other forms of Christianity as false. They were viewed as a demanding, mysterious, secretive and violent cult. But most shockingly to American society, church members were encouraged to practise plural marriage, a form of polygamy, in which select Mormon men could take multiple wives.

The early Mormon Church met the full force of American intolerance. The country knew only one way of dealing with a group of people perceived as 'un-American'. Just as the Catholics, Freemasons, Native Americans and blacks were persecuted, so too the Mormons. By the mid-1800s they had been chased out of three states – Ohio, Missouri and Illinois – their founder and leader had been murdered, houses had been burned and property and belongings destroyed.

There was, however, no stopping the tide of recruits to the new religion. Young male Mormons travelled overseas – including Scotland – on missionary work to recruit church members. When the church left its home in Illinois, tens of thousands of the faithful made the long trek west to the mountains of what is now Utah. There they established America's Mormon State – a religious Utopia unequalled since the days of the early settlers.

But for all the brutality meted out to the 'saints', as Mormons called themselves, it was a group of the Church's own followers that carried out one of the most cowardly and barbaric massacres of defenceless men, women and children ever witnessed on American soil.

Mormons felt they had been so harshly dealt with that they had set up militia units to protect themselves against attack from outsiders. In truth the Mormon organisation was a church complete with its own private and well-trained army. The militia's purpose was supposedly to defend the church from its enemies, never to kill innocent people.

Yet in a remote part of southern Utah, at least 120 emigrants on a west-bound wagon train were lured to their deaths by members of a Mormon militia. These members were armed to the teeth, and many had their faces painted to make them look like Indians.

The Mountain Meadows Massacre occurred on 11 September 1857. It was America's first 9/11, an inhumane act of murderous violence, and at its heart was a man from the Scottish Highlands, William Cameron Stewart. His actions during the killing were animalistic in their brutality. He went on a sadistic and feral rampage that stands comparison with any American outlaw.

Mountain Meadows - Library of Congress

Stewart showed his victims not a single ounce of mercy, even as they pleaded with him for their lives. Of all those who participated in the butchering of the defenceless homesteaders, multiple witnesses described him as the most bloodthirsty.

William – or Bill – Stewart, who ironically spent part of his childhood in the Lochaber area of the Highlands, just miles from the site of the infamous Massacre of Glencoe, entered the record books of shame that day. Yet it is only among Mormon historians in Utah and the families of the 17 massacre survivors that his name and crimes live on. In his native land his despicable deeds are unknown.

Whatever the mitigating factors that led to the attack on the wagon train, there can be no justifying such a wholesale slaughter, nor the heartless and hateful part played by Stewart. He is said to have relished the killing and encouraged others, even young boys, to join in the carnage. He then looted the bodies as they lay on the ground.

In his book, *Blood of the Prophets*, Will Bagley quotes an Indian tribesman who witnessed the events as saying, 'Many a little girl pleaded with Stewart not to take her life. Catching them by the hair of the head, he would hurl them to the ground, place his foot upon their little bodies and cut their throats'.

It is incredible to think that wanton killing on this scale and of this brutality was carried out by men who had devoted their lives to God and their church. This was not the work of a small band of desperadoes, it was a well-orchestrated and calculated slaughter perpetrated by armed militia men. Almost 70 individuals have been identified as participants in the massacre. The atrocity at Mountain Meadows was the work of an entire Mormon community; everyone knew what had happened and everyone knew who had been involved.

Yet to the eternal shame of the Mormon Church hierarchy, it tried to hush up the macabre events of that day. It attempted to blame the local Paiute Indian tribe, and then spent many years in various stages of denial. As for William Stewart, he compounded his awful crimes by becoming a fugitive from justice and fleeing to a Mormon colony in Mexico.

So what was it that turned men who had been God-fearing, law-abiding, hard-working citizens, devoted churchmen, and civic and religious leaders into a depraved fraternity of cold-blooded murdering savages? What prompted them to wipe out an entire party of emigrants and leave the mutilated bodies of their victims scattered in a barren valley in America's Wild West?

The answer is a combination of hysteria, revenge, hatred and fear born out of the belief that Mormonism, an institution only 27 years old at this time, was under attack from the entirety of mainstream America. A siege mentality had taken hold in the communities of devoted church followers in Utah. Allied to that was the unshakeable belief that God spoke directly through the Mormon prophets, and that the church's home in Utah was, in fact, the Kingdom of God on earth.

To this day, accusations of brainwashing are levelled at Mormon teachings and Mormon leaders. Fairly or otherwise, it has been that way since the church's earliest days. Mormonism, with its social order led by a Prophet and Council of Twelve Apostles, and its family structure once rooted in the practice of polygamy, has come to be generally regarded as a cult, and its teachings outlandish and bizarre.

Yet its success in attracting new adherents has been breathtaking. Within 15 years of its foundation in 1830 it boasted 40,000 followers. By 2014 it was one of the fastest-growing religious organizations in the world with more than 15 million members, slightly less than half of that number in the United States. The American state of Utah was effectively transformed into a Mormon kingdom with Salt Lake City as its headquarters, and the church boasted a bank account of staggering proportions. Whatever its critics might think, the Church of Jesus Christ of Latter-day Saints did something right.

It was in the early 1820s that Joseph Smith, a poor farmer from upstate New York, claimed to have received visitations from an angel directing him to an ancient book of golden plates. The book, he said, was delivered to him by the angel and he and a close body of associates translated it into what became known as the *Book of Mormon*.

By 1830 he was confident enough to launch his new religion on America, a country in the midst of a spiritual revival known as the Second Great Awakening. Smith, who was being compared by his followers to Moses, led his flock to the town of Kirtland, Ohio, which he proclaimed the 'new Jerusalem' and to Independence, Missouri, which he christened the 'centre place' of Zion.

But America was quite simply not ready to embrace such a profound alternative to its long-standing spiritual beliefs; it could not cope with a movement quite this radical. As more and more zealous converts followed Smith to his settlements, Americans reacted with predictable violence. In Kirtland, Smith and one of his fellow leaders were beaten to a pulp, tarred, feathered and left for dead.

In Missouri, at that time a frontier state, the reception was even more hostile. The Mormons let it be known they belonged to the 'only true and living church upon the face of the whole earth' and established themselves in closed communities set apart from their neighbours. Tension was never far from the surface; Missourians waged a campaign of persecution against the Mormons, burning their homes and property and attacking them at polling stations.

With Smith preaching aggression, armed Mormons retaliated. After a series of confrontations the situation came to a head when 17 Mormons were killed by a 55-strong militia unit in an incident known as the Haun's Mill Massacre. This massacre followed an order by Missouri Governor Lilburn Boggs that Mormons be 'exterminated or driven from the State'. One militiaman justified the killing of a 10-year old boy by saying, 'Nits will make lice, and if he had lived he would have become a Mormon'.

As a result of the attack the followers of Smith surrendered, forfeited their goods and left for a new home in Illinois. However, the memory of Missouri would never be forgotten. It was a hard lesson and instilled in those who lived through it a sense of alienation and a burning desire for revenge.

In 1839 Smith led his flock to a patch of land on the banks of the Mississippi River, where he established the city of Nauvoo, Illinois. There a grand temple was built, and the construction of a university was authorised. He began to reveal the doctrine of plural marriage, and with the blessing of the state of Illinois, he set up the Mormon Church's own militia unit which he called the Nauvoo Legion. Prior to the civil war it was one of the largest bodies of armed men in the country.

Yet Smith was never far from controversy, and as his power and profile increased, so did opposition to his preaching, both inside and outside his church. The people of Illinois, who had initially welcomed the Mormons, grew alarmed and suspicious as thousands of converts poured into Nauvoo.

In 1844 Smith decided to run for president of the United States, but he did not live to see the election. He and his brother Hyrum were arrested for treason and detained in jail in the town of Carthage. While awaiting trial the prison was stormed by a mob and the two men were murdered. It was yet another shocking event in the tumultuous early years of Mormonism, another reason for its followers to fear and distrust the outside world.

The slaying of the church's founder was enough to convince the Mormon hierarchy that its future lay not in the hostile lands of the increasingly populous American Midwest, but in the more remote and uncharted parts of the far west. Led by Smith's successor Brigham Young,

Brigham Young - public domain

thousands made the perilous 1,200-mile trek – either on foot or by covered wagon – to the Great Salt Lake Basin of Utah. There were very few 'white settlers' to bother them; this time their only neighbours were tribes of Native Americans.

By now the ranks of the faithful had been swollen by European converts, impressed by the teachings of the missionaries who had been sent abroad. Scotland, especially the industrial Central Belt between Glasgow and Edinburgh, had proved a fertile recruiting ground. During the first few decades of Mormon presence in Utah, the British-born population averaged around 22%, a large proportion of which were Scottish.

Many of the Scots who were converted were a product of dirty factories and dingy towns and cities. They were crying out for an escape and the early Mormon missionaries gave them a belief that there could be something better. By the end of the 19th century almost 10,000 people in Scotland had signed up as members and almost half that number made their way to America.

William Stewart was not the typical Scottish Mormon convert. His early life was spent in the farms and the wide open glens of Highland Scotland, far from the grimy industrial towns and cities. The most authoritative books on the subject place his age at the time of the massacre as 30, meaning he would have been born around 1827.

Details of where he spent his early life are conflicting, but it seems that, for at least a few years, he was living in the west Highlands, possibly around the Spean Bridge area of Lochaber. There are also suggestions that he either lived or was born in Glen Lyon, Perthshire. It is perfectly possible he spent some of his youth in both places. In either event he would certainly have been brought up on stories of the 1692 Massacre of Glencoe, in which members of the Clan Campbell enjoyed the hospitality of the MacDonalds of Glencoe before killing 38 of them, one of the most shameful episodes in Scottish history.

Little else is known of Stewart's upbringing, although it seems certain that he worked on a farm and was something of a handyman. During his time in Utah he was listed as a farmer and a carpenter and seems to have been a 'Jack of all trades'.

Stewart converted to Mormonism in the late 1840s or early 1850s. It may be he left the Highlands and travelled to the Central Belt where he heard the preaching of the Mormon missionaries, or he may have heard stories from men returning from the south. In the early part of 1853, suitably captivated by what he had heard, Stewart sailed from Liverpool to America to throw in his lot with Mormonism.

It is likely Stewart disembarked at New Orleans then sailed up the Mississippi River to Iowa. There, like most of the tens of thousands of Mormon pioneers, he set off on the long westward trek. The journey crossed what are now the states of Iowa, Nebraska and Wyoming and into northern Utah. The Overland Trail, as it was known, was a dangerous route, not for the faint-hearted, and many perished through illness, extreme cold, starvation or Indian predations.

Records show him as a member of the Appleton M. Harmon company – consisting of 200 individuals and 22 wagons – that left Keokuk, Iowa, on 15 June 1853. A month later the wagon train crossed the Missouri River. Stewart was described as single and captain of 10 people. On 22 July he left the train and travelled the rest of the way with a Colonel Ross and his company.

Stewart arrived at a time when the church and the U.S. government were at loggerheads over the future of the Utah Territory, which was almost exclusively Mormon. Young wanted it introduced into the Union as the State of Deseret (a word meaning honeybee in the *Book of Mormon*). Young was immensely powerful; he was the territorial governor as well as the leader of the church. But the taboo surrounding the polygamy issue was a major barrier to acceptance by the rest of the country.

In 1855, Stewart married Mary Ann Corlett. She and several members of her family had left the working-class town of Salford in Lancashire, where her father James was a joiner, to join the Mormons. The couple were wed and settled down in the small settlement of Cedar City, 250 miles south of Salt Lake City and remote from the seat of Mormon power.

Cedar City, in Utah's Iron County, had been founded in 1851 by church pioneers from nearby Parowan and an ironworks was established there. Most of those who settled in the town were from Britain and had experience in heavy industries such as smelting or coal production. The Deseret Iron Company, as the Cedar City works were called, was dogged by problems from the outset, mostly related to the extremes of weather which often left the nearby creek flooded.

In 1857 Stewart is known to have spent days working on the duct carrying water from the creek to the steam engine boiler. He also worked on the steam engine stack, the engine cylinder and performed many carpentry tasks. These men worked closely together; it was a case of all hands to the pump; they lived and worked 'out of each other's pockets'.

Of course the practice of plural marriage meant that in a few short years, many of the men and women in such a small, close-knit community were related to one another.

It was a tough life for everyone – men, women and children alike – in pioneer Utah. However, their unswerving faith helped sustain them during periods of drought and the skirmishes with the Paiute Indian tribe. Of all the Indian people who populated Utah, the Paiutes were among the most deprived and poverty-stricken, reduced to eating lizards and snakes to keep themselves alive. Attacks on humans were uncommon but they often stole horses and cattle from passing wagon trains for food and clothing.

The Mormon social order has been described as a theocratic democracy. It effectively removed any distinction between the priesthood and the laity. All adult males over the age of 12 were considered part of the priesthood and could ascend to the highest rank. Many of those who worked with Stewart in the smelters and furnaces of Cedar City were high-ranking priests and bishops – and many were among the leading massacre planners and participants.

The men in southern Utah bonded well partly because so many were from Britain. The back-breaking toil in the ironworks was also a factor in their close connection. Still, there was another reason for their kinship. These men were all part of the local militia, and in 1857 Mormon-held Utah was in a state of siege and paranoia. The local companies of the Nauvoo Legion were preparing to repel their borders by force if necessary. The men of the Iron County Militia were armed and ready to fight to the death.

Young had put his troops on guard. The Gentiles of the outside world were about to encroach on Utah just as they had in Missouri and Illinois. An army of government soldiers had been dispatched by President James Buchanan, who was exasperated at the hostility and resistance Mormons were directing at his officials and representatives in Utah.

In early 1857 Buchanan said, '...all the officers of the United States, judicial and executive, with the single exception of two Indian agents, have found it necessary for their own personal safety to withdraw from the territory, and there no longer remains any government in Utah but the despotism of Brigham Young.'

The news of an oncoming army was met with horror by the Mormons of Utah. For the most part, they wanted nothing to do with government by the United States; they wanted to be governed only by their own church leaders. Young took to the pulpit, proclaimed a state of martial law and put his people on a war footing.

There was one more incident in May 1857 that added to the sense of resentment among the Mormon population. Parley P. Pratt was a Mormon Apostle and one of the leading lights of the early church. The great-great grandfather of future Republican presidential candidate Mitt Romney, he had taken 12 wives and fathered 30 children.

Pratt's problem was his twelfth wife, Eleanor McLean. She had left her husband Hector to follow Pratt to Utah and taken her children with her. In Salt Lake City the pair were 'sealed in celestial marriage' by Young. Hector McLean, however, was outraged, and took Pratt to court in Arkansas claiming he had kidnapped the children.

McLean lost the case and afterwards attacked Pratt, stabbing him to death near the Arkansas village of Van Buren. The loss of another prominent leader shook the church. The state of Arkansas was blamed and it quickly joined Missouri, Illinois and Ohio on the Mormon tablet of revenge. Woe betide anyone from these 'enemy' regions who dared venture across the Utah border; a wartime 'bunker mentality' enveloped the resident Mormons, and bloodlust was in the air.

William Stewart had arrived in 1853. He had experienced nothing of the viciousness suffered by his brothers and sisters in the Midwest and had obviously never set eyes on Joseph or Hyrum Smith. To an iron worker in Cedar City, Parley Pratt would have been a distant figure, albeit a man who commanded respect bordering on reverence. It is highly unlikely Stewart ever met him.

Like everyone, he would have been alarmed at news of the approaching army troops, although quite why he went on such a maniacal murderous rampage of the wagon train party is a mystery. He had no known personal grudge or vendetta against anyone; he simply seems to have enjoyed the thrill of the slaughter.

Springtime heralded the annual departure of dozens of wagon trains heading across the plains to the 'Golden Lands' of California. In 1857 one of the largest and wealthiest bands of emigrants ever assembled was heading west. It had covered wagons, travelling carriages, a herd of at least 1,000 cattle and a number of fine horses.

Those making the crossing were unaware of Young's martial law declaration and as they headed through Nebraska, some emigrants left the group while others joined them. The leader, Captain Alexander Fancher, was a former soldier, an experienced traveller and an upstanding pillar of the community. He had his route planned down to the last detail, to Salt Lake City then south along the Old Spanish Trail to California. It was a course that would take the party past Cedar City and into the pass known as Mountain Meadows.

In the panic-stricken communities of Utah, gripped by hysteria and reprisal, people were aware of the Fancher wagon train – for one obvious reason. The men, women and children all came from the north-west of Arkansas, where Pratt had been knifed to death. A rumour had also spread like wildfire that the main group had been joined by a rowdy band of emigrants from Missouri who called themselves the 'Missouri Wildcats'.

As the train headed south through Utah there were reports of clashes with local Mormons. One emigrant known as the Dutchman is said to have shouted at Mormons that he had 'the gun that killed Joe Smith' and that it was 'loaded for Old Brigham'. When they reached Cedar City there was another seemingly drunken confrontation between emigrants and local people.

The vast majority of those heading west were perfectly reasonable and polite, but in such a fevered atmosphere the travellers quite simply stood no chance. Up to 140 emigrants – men in their 50s to children as young as eight months – were walking to their deaths.

Four heavily-armed Mormon battalions made up the Iron County Military District under the direction of Colonel William Dame. He commanded the first battalion which drew on men from in and around the village of Parowan, a few miles from Cedar City. Dame was the man in charge of military operations in the area, but he and his battalion were not present during the massacre.

The second battalion was commanded by Major Isaac Haight, the mayor of Cedar City, the stake (or diocese) president and a director of the ironworks; the third battalion, also based around Cedar City, was under the command of Major John Higbee, a counsellor of Haight in the town's stake presidency; and the fourth battalion was based in outlying villages like Fort Harmony and Santa Clara and was commanded by John D. Lee. All the battalions were divided into companies and platoons.

Haight, Higbee and Lee, along with the Mormon bishop of Cedar City, Philip Klingensmith, were the men who bore the greatest responsibility for the planning,

Isaac Haight

John D Lee

Philip Klingensmith

ordering and execution of the tragic events at Mountain Meadows. Stewart was a second lieutenant in one of the Cedar City platoons; had it not been for his gung-ho attitude to murder, the massacre may well not have happened.

The first indication of Stewart's hard line towards the wagon train came the day after the disturbance at Cedar City at a specially-convened meeting, led by Haight, to decide how to deal with the homesteaders. Most wanted to attack them but one man, Laban Morrill, disagreed. As Morrill left the meeting to head home he was followed by Stewart and another Scotsman, Daniel MacFarlane from Stirling, with the intention of waylaying him. However, Morrill took an alternative route home and so avoided an attack.

Stewart was a relatively young and physically strong man. He had a long flowing beard and a stern countenance that made him appear rather fierce. In short, he was not the type of person you would willingly pick a fight with. However, he also appears to have been a devout churchman and a caring husband and father to his seven children. In the book *Massacre at Mountain Meadows*, authors Ronald Walker, Richard Turley and Glen Leonard describe Stewart as 'a good man in normal times'.

These of course were not normal times. Young had sown the seeds of utter paranoia among his flock in Utah and hysteria was described as being at 'fever heat'. Since word had been received of the approaching army detachment, he had ordered that no Mormon should sell any food or provisions to passing wagon trains. He had also, over the years, forged an alliance with Indian tribes on the basis that they were both minorities persecuted by the 'white man'.

On Monday 7 September, the day after the Cedar City meeting, the Fancher wagon train was encamped at Mountain Meadows, about 35 miles beyond the town. Suddenly, at daybreak, a band of Paiute Indians attacked, killing seven and wounding another 15. The emigrants, many roused from their sleep, quickly wheeled their wagons into a corral and barricaded themselves inside.

However, this was no ordinary Indian raid. It had been orchestrated by Lee and was the first part of a calculated and quickly-moving Mormon plan to eliminate the train and place the blame squarely on the Paiutes. It was as though the people of the remote towns and villages of Southern Utah were taking it upon themselves to gain revenge for the events in Arkansas and Missouri.

Stewart was dispatched to Mountain Meadows along with fellow militiaman Joel White. Word reached them that a number of emigrants had left the corral and were looking for stray horses on the meadows. Stewart then asked to borrow two pistols and said he would 'fix' the men.

Two days after the initial attack, at a spot called Leach's Spring, Stewart and White came face to face with two emigrants, 19-year old William Aden and another believed to be the quarrelsome character known as the Dutchman. Aden was from Tennessee and had just joined the wagon train at Salt Lake City.

Stewart asked if he could have a drink of water from a tin cup that was hanging from the back of Aden's saddle. The teenager agreed and as he reached for the cup, Stewart pulled out one of the borrowed pistols and shot Aden through the head, killing him instantly. The Dutchman somehow managed to escape and fled the scene on horseback and in a state of terror.

It was the first killing of a wagon train member directly attributable to a Mormon. More importantly, the fact that an emigrant had witnessed it and taken news of the grim deed back to the corral meant the Indians could no longer be blamed. Stewart had given the game away.

The homesteaders now knew they were being attacked by Mormons as well as Indians. If the emigrants were allowed to reach California and report the Mormon attack, there would be immediate military reprisals. The militia leaders in Cedar City decided there was only one course of action open to them – the extermination of the entire train.

Having started the job on the Monday, the Paiutes suffered losses, and many lost their appetite for killing. Without hesitation the Mormon civic, religious and military leaders in Cedar City decided they should finish matters. With a small band of Indians still onside by Friday 11 September a number of Mormons readied for the action with their faces painted like tribesmen.

The elimination plan was cool, clinical, brutal and stomach-churning in its savagery. The Mormons were to promise the emigrants safe passage through the Meadows then, at a given signal, kill every man, woman and child, except those too young to remember.

The night before the massacre, the Mormons prayed on the Meadows. In *The Mountain Meadows Massacre*, a scathing account of the event, author and one-time Mormon Josiah Gibbs described the scene: 'Under the blue vault of heaven, from which the angels must have looked down with infinite sorrow on the hellish scene, those wretched victims of unquestioning obedience, superstition and fanaticism, knelt in the form of a prayer circle with heads bowed in abject servility to an alien god.'

On the morning of the 11th a handful of Mormons rode up to the emigrant corral brandishing a white flag of truce. They told the emigrants they could guarantee them safe passage through the valley and past the Indians on the condition that they hand over their weapons until safety had been reached. The wagon train members, by now extremely hungry, fatigued and desperate, agreed.

Under instruction by the Mormons the wagon train was separated into three columns. At the head were wounded adults and small children led by Lee; some distance later the women and children; and bringing up the rear were the uninjured men, each walking with an armed Mormon militiamen by his side. Half a mile separated each column.

Believing they were at last being allowed to continue their journey to California, the emigrants cheered their 'saviours' as they set off through Mountain Meadows. Then suddenly a cry of 'Halt' was heard. Uttered by Higbee, it was the signal for the carnage to begin.

Lee and the Indians immediately turned their guns on the sick and wounded, mostly farmers and their wives from Arkansas. Orders had been given to spare the young children but several were caught in the crossfire and became 'collateral damage'.

Lee testified that a Mormon militiaman called Samuel McMurdy clambered into a wagon full of injured people and shouted, 'O Lord, my God, receive their spirits, it is for thy Kingdom that I do this'. He then shot dead two men who were huddled together.

Women and children were screaming, men were running for their lives but were brutally cut down. Those who were not shot dead had their throats cut. Young girls pleaded for their lives but were ruthlessly murdered. Most of the men at the back were shot in the head at point-blank range by their Mormon escorts. It was a scene of horror.

Stewart and his colleague White had been detailed to chase and kill anyone who was left alive after the initial volley of shots. To say he acted with enthusiasm would be a gross understatement.

In *Massacre at Mountain Meadows*, Walker, Turley and Leonard state that some of the Mormons refused to kill and fired their rifles in the air. They added, 'Others made up for it, out of duty or conviction or because once the killing began they lost control of themselves.

'William "Bill" Stewart – the man who killed Aden – and Joel White, his accomplice, took out after the few emigrant men spared in the fusillade who were now running for their lives. The two Mormons nearly got themselves killed by running into the line of fire. Their act helped earn them the reputation for being the "most bloodthirsty" men on the field.'

Mormon participant Samuel Knight years later described Stewart's conduct: 'He seemed to be filled with an insane desire to slaughter as many as possible, and he hewed them down without the least mercy.'

Another account tells of how Stewart ordered a young boy to kill an injured woman who was recovering consciousness. When the youngster said he did not want blood on his hands, Stewart waited till the woman tried to stand then 'drove a bowie knife to the hilt in her side'.

The Scotsman also boasted that he had taken 'the damned Gentile babies' by the heels and smashed their skulls against the tires of the wagons. He went on what can only be described as a murderous orgy. The number who lost their lives to him could easily have reached double figures, a massacre in itself.

Within five minutes the killing was over. The lush grassland of the beautiful mountain valley was now scattered with the broken bodies of at least 120 innocent and defenceless souls. The bodies were stacked together; no attempt was made to bury them. Only 17 children had been spared. One would later recall how he saw the Indians wash their faces in a stream and 'then they were white'.

The looting began once the massacre was complete. Stewart, along with Klingensmith and Higbee, were seen searching the bodies for money, watches and jewellery. They reportedly asked Lee to hold a hat for them to collect the valuables. The goods were subsequently taken to Cedar City and auctioned.

The same militia leaders who had ordered the massacre then called the men together and told them never to breathe a word of what had happened. In spite of Young and his Mormon hierarchy consistently blaming the affair on the Paiutes word leaked out, sparking a furious anti-Mormon backlash.

Superintendent of Indian Affairs Jacob Forney, who was sent to Utah two years later, wrote that, 'the white hell-hounds…had disgraced humanity by being mainly instrumental in the murdering of at least 115 men, women and children, under circumstances and manner without a parallel in human history for atrocity'.

An investigation into the killings was interrupted by the civil war, and it was not until 1874 that a grand jury returned indictments for murder against nine militiamen, including Stewart. In 1877 he wrote to Young complaining that, since the indictment, he had been an 'outcast'.

He added, 'I am getting tired of being hunted by Government officials. I am not so well off in this worlds goods as many who could stay at home. I would like with your consent to go to Scotland and gather a genealogy of my friends and perhaps do a little good there and also be out of the way until this trouble is over.'

Stewart never made it to Scotland. Along with Haight and Higbee, he fled from justice and remained a fugitive for many years. He spent some time hiding out in Arizona before taking refuge in the Colonia Juarez Mormon colony in the Mexican state of Chihuahua.

In 1895, the same year as the federal indictment was dismissed, Stewart died in Mexico, a year after his wife Mary Ann who had stayed in Cedar City. Only one man, Lee, was tried for his part in the affair. Lee was made the scapegoat and in 1877 was taken to Mountain Meadows and shot dead by a firing squad.

There was one bizarre and slightly chilling twist in the tale. One of the surviving children was 18-month old Felix Marion Jones. His parents, sister and brother, grandmother, aunt and uncle, and five cousins aged between 12 and 25 had all been killed. Felix was the only surviving family member.

Two days after the killing the children were taken to Cedar City and given homes with Mormon families. Felix Jones was taken in by none other than William and Mary Ann Stewart, who looked after him for two years until the youngsters were returned to Arkansas. The boy may have been living in the same house as the man who killed several members of his family.

There is no evidence that Stewart took in the little child through remorse or guilt for what he had done. When Jacob Forney had the children returned home, Stewart told him he had 'paid' the Indians a gun worth twenty dollars and a blanket worth ten dollars in exchange for the child. He also tried to claim $64.50 for 43 weeks bed and board.

The Paiute Indians never had the children and Stewart had never paid a cent for Felix Jones. The butcher of Mountain Meadows was heartless to the bitter end.

5

Robert Millar

...The crowd poured on to the field because of a lack of police protection. Thereafter it was pandemonium on Millar's side of the field.

– NEW YORK TIMES MATCH REPORT, 17 JANUARY 1914

Anyone with even a passing knowledge of the 'beautiful game' they call football – or soccer – has heard the name Eric Cantona. During a dazzling career, the skills of the mercurial Frenchman lit up football grounds across Europe. In a sport where the greatest players are idolised, Cantona achieved godlike status.

Cantona's greatest years came between 1992 and 1997, when he graced the playing fields of England with his sublime artistry. In that five-year spell he inspired Manchester United to four Premier League titles and two F.A. Cups. The supporters dubbed him 'King Eric', and he was voted the club's greatest ever player ahead of the likes of Bobby Charlton, George Best, Denis Law, Bryan Robson and David Beckham.

He was undoubtedly a footballing genius. However, like many blessed with such flair and finesse, he was also a troubled individual. In his native France his disciplinary record was so poor that many clubs regarded him as untouchable. He had punched a team mate in the face, thrown his boots in the face of another fellow player, insulted the French national coach Henri Michel on television, and thrown the ball at a referee after disagreeing with a decision. The French soccer authorities had banned him many times, and on the advice of friends and mentors, he left France to play his football in England.

After a short trouble-free spell at Leeds United, Cantona signed for Manchester United in 1992. He was at the peak of his career, and United fans were treated to some of the most unforgettable displays of football they had ever witnessed.

But Eric Cantona's enduring legacy was shaped by a few seconds of madness on the evening of 25 January 1995, at Selhurst Park, home of London club Crystal Palace. The Frenchman was sent off for kicking out at an opponent and as he trudged off the park a Palace supporter ran down eleven rows of steps and shouted racial abuse in Cantona's direction. When the fan, Matthew Simmons, referenced Cantona's mother, the soccer star snapped.

Cantona heard the remarks and it was as though a red mist had descended. He ran directly at Simmons and, in a moment that has gone down in soccer notoriety, flew at him 'kung-fu' style. The blow hit Simmons in the chest and Cantona followed up the outrageous assault with a few well-chosen punches.

The football world was shocked to the core and television images flashed round the world. It was reported that Cantona had 'flipped' – that he had lost the plot. The authorities banned him for eight months and fined him £30,000. In court he was convicted of assault and imprisoned for two months, a sentence overturned on appeal to 120 hours community service spent coaching soccer stars of the future. Football Association chairman Graham Kelly said the incident was a 'stain on our game'. The reality was that the demons tormenting the Frenchman had long been threatening to boil over. Once the spark was lit the explosion was inevitable.

Regrettably, that is how Cantona will forever be remembered; not for all the virtuoso displays of soccer brilliance but for a crazed 'kung-fu' attack on an opposition supporter. The Shakespearean saying, 'The evil that men do lives after them; The good is oft interred with their bones', is as relevant to Eric Cantona as it was to Julius Caesar.

However, as long as soccer has existed there have been bad guys; men with suspect temperaments and fighting tendencies. Many had little in the way of ability yet made up for it with ample 'brawn'. The football field has never been a place for the faint-hearted.

Scots harbour the belief – perhaps with some justification – that their nation gave football to the world. What is undoubtedly true is that, for such a small nation, we have produced some of the world's finest exponents of the game, players such as Denis Law, Kenny Dalglish, Alan Morton, Alex James, Bill Shankly and Jimmy McGrory. There is a theory that Scottish footballers fall into one of two categories: the skillful 'tanner-ba' player or the snarling hard man. The truth is that many of the greats have possessed both qualities in abundance.

A list of Scottish bad boy footballers could go on forever. Rangers star Duncan Ferguson was jailed for head butting his Raith Rovers opponent John McStay; winger Willie Johnston was banished from the 1978 World Cup in Argentina for failing a drug test; Partick Thistle's Chic Charnley was sent off 17 times in a 20-year career; Derek Riordan was banned from every nightclub in Edinburgh while playing for Hibs.

A fondness for booze caused the downfall of many others, including the wayward Willie Hamilton, who starred for both Hibs and Hearts; Celtic great George Connelly, who walked out on the club at the age of 27 while still in his prime: and 'Slim Jim' Baxter, perhaps the greatest flawed genius of them all.

All had one thing in common. They were supremely gifted players with a self-destruct button that stifled their potential. None of them, however, could lay claim to being the Scottish Cantona; their behaviour never quite plumbed such spectacular depths.

There was though one man who could justly boast of having been the original soccer rabble-rouser. Scotsman Robert Millar – a born and bred Paisley 'buddie' – plied his trade in the fledgling soccer leagues of the eastern United States. He was a class act on the field, a hugely talented forward and record-breaking goalscorer with an old-fashioned 'up and at 'em' mentality.

He was also a firebrand, possessed of a hair-streak temper. In his long, colourful and tumultuous career in American soccer, trouble was never far from his door. A full 81 years before Cantona's 'kung-fu' kick, Millar made all the wrong headlines following an incident that bore more than a passing resemblance to the night of shame at Crystal Palace.

During a game in Brooklyn, New York in 1914, Millar was being subjected to abusive barracking from a section of the opposing fans. He responded by brawling with a spectator on the field of play. As the referee struggled to control the situation other players and fans joined in and the scene soon resembled a 'mini-riot'.

It was a shocking episode but not Millar's only brush with controversy. Seven years later he was banned for 'banjoing' a former team-mate at half-time, and he clashed incessantly with the football authorities. Bob Millar – as he was always known – was without question the *enfant terrible* of the North American Soccer League.

Still, for all he was as hard as nails with a win-at-all-costs mentality, he was also one of the greatest soccer stars ever to grace the American game. He is remembered as a U.S. football legend, one of the men who pioneered the game in the country, yet in his native land the fame and the notoriety he achieved in the States are largely unknown.

Bob Millar was born in May 1889 in Paisley, where his father James worked as a postman. His mother Mary had been born in Ireland and moved with her family to Partick to escape the potato famine. The couple married in 1872 and had nine children, eight of them boys.

The town in which Bob Millar was born had given the world the Paisley Pattern and the Paisley Shawl – famously worn by Queen Victoria – but by the 1890s its celebrated weaving industry was in serious decline. The budding footballer grew up in a heavily industrialised town with shipyards, engineering plants and distilleries among the chief employers of the day. Young Bob would have grown used to the sight of soot-spewing factory chimneys stretching towards the sky.

The Millar family excelled at sports. James Millar was a professional runner and Bob's brother George was the Scottish Welterweight Boxing Champion for two years. Another two brothers, Harry and John, played football in Scotland to a high level. So it was perhaps only natural that Bob, the second youngest of the family, should follow in their sporting footsteps.

In the 1891 census the family was living in the town's Great Hamilton Street, in a row of houses long since demolished. By 1901 they had moved to a tenement flat in Galloway Street, now also knocked down. The street is the setting of a novel, called simply *Galloway Street*, by author John Boyle about life as an immigrant Irish Catholic family growing up in the sectarian divide of the west of Scotland.

It was a tough life in a none-too-prosperous part of town, but the Millars appear to have been hard-working and resourceful. Of the five children still living at home in 1901, Robert and his younger sister Mary were at school while the three older boys all had full-time jobs. James junior, 21, was, like his namesake father, a postman; John, 17, was an apprentice iron-turner; and Matthew, who was 14, worked as a post office messenger.

In 1890, the year after Bob was born, the Scottish Football League was formed, and among the 11 founder members was Paisley-based club St Mirren. Young Bob, like all football-daft boys of that era, honed his skills in kick-about games on the streets near his home. As a schoolboy he was known as a tough and uncompromising competitor, and it was no surprise when St Mirren signed him in 1909, at the age of 19.

He established himself as a fixture in the first team and a regular goalscorer. In April 1910 he wrote his name into St Mirren football history when the club reached the Renfrewshire Cup final against Paisley rivals Abercorn. It was a two-legged affair and in the first match Millar scored the second goal in a 2-0 victory. The second game was drawn and St Mirren won the cup. It was Millar's first taste of big-time football success and he was thirsty for more.

In an interview with the *Brooklyn Daily Eagle* in 1934, after his playing days were over, Millar described the victory over Abercorn as 'the biggest thrill I ever got out of soccer', and revealed he still kept the medal he had won in 1910.

But Scotland was not the only country where football had taken off in a big way. In the industrial towns and cities of north-east America – in states such as Pennsylvania, New York, New Jersey and Massachusetts – organised soccer was attracting thousands of paying spectators. Many Scottish players had crossed the Atlantic to try their luck in the States and Bob was getting ready to leave Paisley for a new life in the U.S.

By now he had a trade and was working as a dyer in a textile factory, and had established himself as a free-scoring striker with one of the leading football clubs in Scotland. He was fiercely ambitious, extremely talented, and was growing restless in his home town. Bob Millar saw his future elsewhere.

There was, however, one matter to be resolved before he left. Bob had met and fallen in love with Paisley lass Alice Courtney. She was 20 – two years younger than him – and on 4 August 1911, the pair were married in St Mirin's Catholic Church, where Bob had been baptised. His address on the marriage certificate was 162 George Street, Paisley, and Alice, a threadmill worker, lived in the town's New Street. Her father Patrick was a farmer.

For a few short months the couple lived together in Glasgow. Then, on 2 December, Bob sailed from Glasgow on the SS *Cameronia*, bound for New York. Alice was expecting a child and did not travel with him. The plan was that she and the baby would make the crossing in due course. Ten days later he arrived in New York, full of hope and excitement for the new life that lay ahead.

It was not long before tragedy struck. Complications set in while 21-year old Alice was giving birth back in Scotland. Both she and the baby died. After less than a year of marriage – and only months after setting foot on U.S. soil – Bob Millar had been left a widower. It was a shattering blow.

Whatever carefully-laid plans Bob Millar had made for a future in America with his young wife were now in ruins. But having come this far, there was no going back. There could be no return to Scotland despite the terrible personal adversity he was suffering. He had been brought up to be resourceful and strong-willed and those qualities were now being tested.

He was a skilled and willing worker and America offered plenty of opportunities and rewards. Equally important for Bob, he could indulge in his abiding passion – football.

The belief that Association Football – or soccer – is a recent addition to the country's sporting landscape is entirely false. Organised regional amateur leagues had been established in the 1850s thanks to the influence of Scottish, Irish and German immigrants. The American Football Association was formed in 1884 in New Jersey, and by the early 1900s national leagues and associations were in place and the game was gaining in popularity.

By way of comparison, the first competitive baseball match had been played in 1846 and the game was regarded as America's national sport. Organised ice hockey evolved around 1880. But it was not until 1920 that American Football's ruling body, the NFL, came into being, and a National Basketball Association was only established in 1949.

A look at the early league tables reflects the importance of the Scottish influence in the early American game. Among the teams were Newark Caledonians, Kearny Scots, Paterson True Blues, New York Clan MacDonald and Campbell Rovers.

For someone with an established footballing pedigree like Bob Millar, there was no shortage of suitors. In 1912 he signed for a team in Philadelphia called Disston Athletic Association. The club, also known as Tacony after the Philadelphia neighbourhood in which they played, was sponsored by the city's Disston Saw Works and was one of the best teams in the country. Millar became an immediate success, his uncompromising style and goalscoring feats endearing him to supporters and helping the team reach the final of the American Cup.

Millar was a tough cookie, of that there is no question. However, at this stage of his career there are no written records of his temper having got the better of him. His years at St Mirren and Disston were notable for their on-field success rather than any fiery outbursts.

That would all change in one shameful scene at a football ground in Philadelphia. Millar's undoubted brilliance as a player made him a target for opposition defenders and supporters alike. It was inevitable that, one day, he would respond to the provocation, that the rage bubbling under the surface would explode. That day was 17 January 1914. It was the day of Bob Millar's 'Cantona' moment.

After his first successful season with Disston, Millar had joined Brooklyn Field Club, a team that competed in the National Association Football League (NAFBL). The quarter-finals of the American Cup saw the two teams drawn against each other with the game to be played at Disston's ground in Philadelphia. For Millar it was a return to his old stomping ground and the fans who had once cheered his exploits. However, many were none too happy to see the prodigal son coming home – wearing the opposition colours.

The *Philadelphia Inquirer* described the game as 'a typical cup match, where none of the players asked nor gave any quarter'. The newspaper said the play was 'mostly of the kick and rush order, Brooklyn showing the better combination, what little was exhibited'. The visitors may have played the better football but they were criticised by

W. Stiles, Sec.; 2, Quinlan; 3, Matthews; 4, F. Heller, Asst. Sec.; 5, Hynd; 6, Adamson; 7, Haughie; 8, Drinkwater; 9, Nichol , W. Monahan, Trainer; 11, Burroughs; 12, Ford; 13, Black; 14, Clark; 15, Knowles; 16, Millar; 17, Shauholt; 18, W. Kirby, Mgr.
BROOKLYN FIELD CLUB TEAM.
Holders of the United States Football Association National Challenge Cup (Dewar Trophy).
Soccer Champions United States, 1913-14; Champions National Association Football League, 1913-14.

Brooklyn Field Club 1913–14. Robert Millar
third from right bottom row wearing number 16

the paper for their roughhouse tactics. The *Inquirer*'s sports reporter said the game was 'one of the hardest and roughest games played at Tacony Ball Park so far this season'.

But while all 22 players may have been guilty of some on-field rowdiness, there was one major moment of controversy in the game. And it involved only one man – Bob Millar. Perhaps the level of provocation became too much, perhaps it was difficult to taste defeat at the hands of his old team. For whatever reason, Millar's volatile temper boiled over. Like Eric Cantona all these years later, he lost the plot.

With the home side winning, a section of the fans began to direct abuse at Millar. The Scotsman gave as good as he got, shouting expletives back in their direction. Then one supporter climbed over the boundary ropes and headed towards Millar. He clearly wanted to get 'in the face' of the player he had once cheered, to make sure his insulting tirade found its target.

But Millar was in no mood to trade insults with the individual. By the time the two men squared up to each other the red mist had descended. Millar took one look at his assailant, drew back his right arm, and then smashed his fist into the man's face.

The punch was the signal for an outbreak of absolute mayhem. Reports at the time said Millar had sparked a 'mini-riot'. More spectators surged on to the field, players from both sides joined in the fighting, and the football pitch became a free-for-all boxing ring. It took several minutes for order to be restored.

The *New York Times* carried a special report headlined 'Philadelphia Crowd Hostile to New York Players in Soccer'. The understated report said, 'The Millar incident was due to some exchange of persiflage between the Brooklyns' inside left and an excited partisan of the Taconys, who lost his temper and jumped the ropes and attempted to strike Millar.'

It added: 'Before blows were exchanged the other players intervened, but meantime the crowd poured on to the field because of a lack of police protection. Thereafter it was pandemonium on Millar's side of the field.'

The *Times* reporter, however, obviously missed the key moment in the incident – Millar's punch. The *Philadelphia Inquirer*, along with other news outlets, made it clear that the offending spectator had been struck a hefty blow by the burly Scot.

It seems amazing that there were no repercussions for Millar or his club following the disgraceful events; a suspension or court appearance was not thought necessary in 1914. Incredibly, Millar was not even ordered off the park. When the riot was over, the spectator was ejected from the ground and all the players – including Millar – were allowed to stay on the field to finish the game, which Disston won 3-1.

It was a bad day all round for Brooklyn Field Club and for Millar. The club had been favourites to win the tie and the Scotsman had written his name in the record books of shame. Brooklyn lodged a protest claiming the match should be replayed because of 'encroachment' by the spectators, but the appeal was thrown out.

Neil Clarke (second left) playing for the USA against Sweden

The man who scored the Brooklyn goal that day was another Scot, Neil Clark, a towering no-nonsense central defender. Like Millar, Clark – whose name was sometimes spelled Clarke – was from Paisley, and had been on the books of Celtic before moving to the States. He was only a few months younger than Millar and the two may well have known each other from playing football games in their home town.

In 1914 Millar and Clark were team-mates and there is no record of animosity or rivalry between the pair. As their footballing lives progressed however, their relationship soured. The next major fracas in the stormy career of Bob Millar involved his fellow Paisley 'buddie'.

Four months after the game of shame in Philadelphia, Millar, Clark and their Brooklyn Field Club colleagues had a chance to redeem their reputations when they took centre stage in America's first National Challenge Cup final. The match was against local rivals Brooklyn Celtic and was played at Coats Field in Pawtucket, Rhode Island.

There was massive interest in the game, as described in the *Pawtucket Times*: 'Long before the captains had met in the center of the field …every vantage point within the spacious enclosure spewed with humanity. The grandstand and bleachers filled like magic; around the field the spectators thronged seven and eight deep. Every automobile was filled to its capacity and even the baseball scoreboard in left field provided a precious foothold for groups of hardy souls.'

It was a momentous day in American football history and this time Millar was the hero. With all the top U.S. soccer administrators in attendance he laid on both goals that saw Field Club win 2-1 and clinch the inaugural trophy. The *Pawtucket Times* singled him out as the game's most instrumental player and reported that he was at the heart of nearly every important moment in the match.

Yet for all his great play there was, it seemed, always a dark side to Millar's performances and those of his team-mates. The paper reported that 'Adamson and Millar tripped with their feet and chopped with their elbows. The rough and tumble play left all the players under heavy scrutiny from referee Creighton, who issued repeated warnings'.

Millar was fast establishing himself as a star of the game in the U.S., albeit a rough diamond. One of the leading soccer writers of the time, Mike Kelly, coined the phrase, 'Where Millar goes the cup goes'. It was a saying that was to stand until the end of his playing career.

In September 1914, along with Clark, he joined Bethlehem Steel, one of the most famous of all the early U.S. teams, who competed in the Allied League of Philadelphia. That season represented the highest point in his playing career. Millar played in 33 league and cup games and scored 59 goals, setting a US record. He scored the first goal as Bethlehem won the 1915 National Challenge Cup, beating Brooklyn Celtic 3-1 in the final.

Off the field his personal life had taken a turn for the better. Since arriving in the States he had worked tirelessly in a number of jobs including an iron worker in the docks, a shipping clerk and a grinder in an engineering factory. The inevitable Paisley connection once again found its way into his life, this time bringing new love and a longed-for domesticity.

Helen Crooks, known as Nellie, had been born in Massachusetts and brought up in Brooklyn. Her father John was an engineer who had emigrated from his native Paisley in the 1880s for a new life in the United States. On 15 November 1915, Bob and Helen were married at St Andrew's RC Church in Bayonne, New Jersey. The following year saw the birth of the couple's daughter Mary Ellen.

But in September 1917 personal tragedy struck for the second time in just a few short years. Back in Paisley Bob's father James had been admitted to the town's Royal Alexandra Hospital for an operation on a chronic duodenal ulcer. The operation was unsuccessful and James passed away without leaving hospital. His death, at the age of 61, was a major shock to Bob.

In the States, Millar had become something of a soccer nomad, moving from club to club with increasing frequency. After leaving Bethlehem Steel in 1916 he joined Babcock and Wilcox and was sent out on loan to three clubs, New York Clan MacDonald, Philadelphia Hibernian and Allentown, before rejoining Bethlehem Steel in 1918.

Exactly why Babcock and Wilcox loaned out their star player not just once but three times is unknown. It does seem surprising to say the least. Perhaps there was disquiet over Millar's on-field temperament, or maybe he was seen as a disruptive dressing-room influence, the latter possibility heightened by the events of 1920 and 1921.

At the start of the 1919-20 season Millar signed for a Brooklyn-based team called Robins Dry Dock. One of his team-mates was his old pal from Paisley, Neil Clark. There is no evidence to suggest the two men were close friends or sworn enemies but they had played a lot of football together; their careers seemed bizarrely intertwined.

Even more remarkably, they had at one point lived only a few hundred yards from each other in Bayonne, New Jersey. Clark stayed with his brother Stewart and his family in Trask Avenue while Millar, his wife and daughter were in a house in West Third Street. By 1920, when they were both playing with Robins Dry Dock, Millar and his family had moved back to Brooklyn to stay with his wife's parents, John and Marian Crooks.

But Millar's stay at Robins was not to last. A few months into the season he quit the team, citing 'significant disagreements' with his team-mates, especially Clark. Whatever the cause of the arguments, the hot-headed Millar was not staying around to let matters fester. He played a few games for Rhode Island team J&P Coats then signed for Erie Athletic Association, a team based in Harrison, New Jersey.

The following season, as fate would have it, Erie and Robins Dry Dock were drawn against each other in the National Challenge Cup. The game was played in January 1921. It was an early opportunity for Millar to exact revenge against his former colleagues and he was itching to prove a point. Tension was in the air even before the first whistle sounded.

There was almost an inevitability that this was going to end badly. Millar and Clark lined up in direct opposition to one another, Millar as a centre forward with Erie and Clark as a centre back for Robins Dry Dock. Both men were tall, well-built and capable of 'putting it about' on the field and, during the first half, there were apparently plenty 'verbals' exchanged between them.

When the half-time whistle was sounded, the two were still cursing at each other. Then, as the other players left the field, the two Paisley men squared up. Once again a cloud of red mist coloured Millar's judgment and he reacted exactly as he had in Philadelphia seven years earlier. He clenched his right fist and punched Clark in the mouth.

It was another disgraceful episode and this time there was no escaping punishment. Millar could not lay the blame at the door of an over-zealous spectator; he had quite simply had a rush of blood to the head and thumped an opposition player. He had let down himself and the Erie team, who lost the match 5-3. The National Cup committee members suspended Millar for two months, a lengthy ban for such a star player and one that spelled the end of his involvement with Erie.

The *Bethlehem Globe* reported that 'Apparently the friendship that is usually prevalent among stable-mates no longer exists between Neil Clark and Bob Millar, both former players with Bethlehem Steel and later with Robins Dry Dock'.

The paper added: 'This was revealed when other matters were brought up before the National Cup committee at its special meeting on Saturday night and Millar was suspended for two months for striking Clark. The fracas for which sentence was imposed occurred during the interval of the Robins-Erie game when Millar took a swing at the Robins' center halfback.

'This conduct somewhat indicates that despite the success of the Robins' campaigning last season, dissention exists among the players, Millar finally leaving or being forced to leave, and the blow he is alleged to have struck was in giving vent to his feelings against his former teammate.'

Millar resumed his soccer wanderings, playing for club after club, often for only a few months at a time. He was 30 at the time of the Neil Clark incident but was still fit and skilful enough to continue playing at a high level for a further seven years. In 1925 he won two international caps for the United States, both times against Canada.

In August of the same year he took up a player-coach position with the New York-based club Indiana Floorings, a team later renamed the New York Nationals. In 1928, in one of his last outings as a player, he led the Nationals to victory in the Challenge Cup. Not surprisingly, the replayed final was not without incident.

The Nationals were up against Chicago Bricklayers and Masons at the city's Soldier Field, now home of the Chicago Bears American Football team. The first match had been drawn 1-1 and there was unquestionably ill-feeling between the two sets of players. The Nationals won the second game 3-0 but by all accounts it was memorable not for the quality of its football but for the violent conduct exhibited by the players.

Millar, despite being 37, was still very much at the centre of the controversy. A report in the *New York Post* detailed the shocking scenes near the end of the match: 'The game threatened to end in a general riot in the second half, when Tom Scott, the powerful right back of the Western finalists, kicked Bob Millar, the Nationals' manager . . . Thousands of spectators surged onto the field of play, and peace was only restored, and the game allowed to proceed, by the timely arrival of a large force of police.'

This time it seems that Millar was the victim but yet again he had been directly involved in a major incident that could have had serious consequences. Millar was no shrinking violet and it is highly unlikely that he was just a hard-done by, innocent party. More likely, as in the Neil Clark incident, there had been a bit of 'previous' between the two players.

Although a victory for the team, it signalled the end of Millar's involvement with the Nationals. Internal politicking was being played out in the boardrooms and administration offices of American soccer. In 1928 'soccer wars' raged with the upshot that the American Soccer League, of which the Nationals was a member, was ruled an 'outlaw' league.

In typical headstrong fashion, Bob Millar delivered a strongly-worded letter to his employers. It read: 'I hereby advise you that I must refuse to continue as playing manager of the New York Nationals Football Club. I hereby tender my resignation, because to engage further in unsanctioned soccer football will materially endanger my status in organized soccer and will thereby affect my future livelihood as a professional soccer player. You have not lived up to the terms of my contract, which call for me to play and manage under the rules and regulations of the United States Football Association, and by forcing me to engage in outlaw soccer, you are breaking my means of gaining a living. I am compelled to seek a position in organized football.'

Millar moved to the New York Giants but played only 14 more games before hanging up his boots. He had enjoyed a long, highly successful and incident-packed career, although arguably his greatest achievement in the U.S. game was still to come.

In 1930 Millar was named as the coach of the U.S. national team competing in the first soccer World Cup in Uruguay. The 16-strong squad that set sail from Hoboken, New Jersey for the Uruguayan capital, Montevideo, included five who had been born in Scotland: Jim Brown, Jimmy Gallagher, Alex Wood, Andy Auld and Bart McGhee.

Not one member of the American media went to Uruguay to cover the event and the soccer public was denied some incredible stories. The U.S. team won both their group games against Belgium and Paraguay; Bart McGhee scored only the second goal in World Cup finals history; goalkeeper Jimmy Douglas recorded the first World Cup shut-out in the 2-0 win over Belgium; and Bert Patenaude scored the first hat trick in finals history in the match against Paraguay.

The U.S. reached the semi-finals where they were trounced 6-1 by Argentina, a game marred by the dirty play of the South Americans. They kicked, stamped, gouged and employed every dirty trick in the book. Auld had smelling salts thrown into his eyes by an Argentine player, leaving him temporarily blinded and the U.S. team was left with only nine fit players.

But finishing third in the tournament was a great and unexpected achievement and cemented Bob Millar's place in U.S. soccer folklore.

Millar lived the rest of his life in the New York area. He stayed in the city's Bronx district for a number of years and in the 1940s moved into the bar tendering business, running Bob Millar's Café and Restaurant in Brooklyn's Fifth Avenue.

His sister and eight brothers all died before him, and in January 1967 Bob passed away at his home in Staten Island. He was buried at New York's Oceanview Cemetery.

Millar's career was tumultuous and uncompromising at best, violent and disgraceful at worst, but his unexpected success at the 1930 World Cup made him a hero in the eyes of the American soccer authorities and the indiscretions of his playing career were all but erased.

In 1950 he was paid the ultimate accolade. The man who had sucker-punched a spectator, walloped an opponent, instigated a pitch invasion and been a thorn in the flesh of the authorities was inducted into the U.S. Soccer Hall of Fame. Bob Millar, Scotland's answer to Eric Cantona, the *enfant terrible* of American soccer, had truly come of age.

6

David Jack

If you don't make good that amount of damage to each and every one of us ...inside of ten days, you son of a bitch, we shall suspend your animation between daylight and hell

– Letter from the Executive Committee of the Squatters League of Monterey County to David Jack

It is a staple of restaurant menus throughout the U.S.–high-class hotels, downtown burger joints, roadside diners, bars, cafes, even the seedy fast-food vans Americans call 'roach-coaches' share a common larder item – Monterey Jack cheese.

The white and creamy dairy product – along with its spicy variant Pepper Jack – is up there with ranch dressing, Reuben sandwiches, fried green tomatoes, cornbread, grits and Buffalo chicken wings as uniquely American restaurant fare. In modern culinary terms, Monterey Jack is as American as apple pie, perhaps even more so.

The origin of the first part of its name is straightforward. In the 18th century, when what is now California was part of the Spanish Empire, Franciscan missionaries founded the Mission San Carlos Borromeo de Carmelo and endeavoured to convert the local Indians to Catholicism. They began producing an old Spanish type of cheese known as queso blanco (white cheese) or queso del pais (country cheese). The site of the Mission is now the California city of Monterey.

But exactly how the word 'Jack' came to be added has been a matter of dispute for more than a century. There are some who claim it derived from a dairyman who lived in nearby Carmel and who dried out the cheese by pressing it in an implement known as a 'house jack'.

It is a theory many citizens of Monterey cling to, perhaps because of its simplicity and relative innocence. They take comfort in the belief that the genesis of Monterey Jack was part of the area's Spanish and Mexican heritage, that it predated the American 'conquest' of California and that it represents something wholesome and ethical. The cheese has put the city on the map and a cosy explanation for the name is preferable to one with even a hint of controversy.

Deep down, however, Montereyans know that the truth is dishearteningly different. There is romance in the centuries-old history of the soft queso blanco cheese allegedly used to feed the armies of Julius Caesar. However, the attachment of 'Jack' is entirely unromantic and unwholesome. It is tied to the hard, earthy and businesslike demands of marketing, self-promotion and naked capitalism.

That an intrepid Scotsman was the person responsible should come as no surprise. Our small nation has, after all, produced hard-headed entrepreneurs who have for centuries exploited such opportunities the world over. In this case the son of a Perthshire farmer saw potential in the Monterey area, took over the cheese-making enterprise, and as one author said 'marketed the hell out of it'.

David Jack succeeded beyond his wildest dreams. He was the man who put the 'Jack' into Monterey's cheese and gave the city the brand name and the product that defines it to this day. In the process he became a multi-millionaire, achieving the riches so many emigrants to America yearned. Today – although few people realise it – his memory lives on through the taste buds of restaurant-goers and grocery shoppers throughout the land.

Thanks to Jack's resourcefulness, a foodstuff regarded as quintessentially American is actually the brainchild of a born and bred son of the Strathearn soil. It is one of those quirky historical facts of which Americans and Scots alike are blissfully unaware. At face value, it is a triumph of Scottish business acumen, an entrepreneurial tour de force, a classic tale of the little man striking it rich.

If only Jack's legacy ended with the creation of Monterey Jack cheese then Scotland could take pride in him and celebrate his achievements. After all, there is nothing we Scots enjoy better than raising a toast to one of 'oor ain'. Our kinsmen invented the television and the bicycle, the telephone and the steam engine. Surely the popularising of a simple, well-marketed cheese is something else worth beating the drum over?

Unfortunately, the brutal truth is that the country has no reason whatsoever to be proud of David Jack. There was a lot more to the man than a sharp business sense and the promoting of a dairy product – and none of it was good. In fact we should, in many ways, be ashamed to claim him.

Jack was a ruthless and unscrupulous individual. He is remembered in California not for his cheese-making exploits but as 'the man who stole Monterey'. He amassed his fortune as a 'land-grabber' – a man who callously and without pity preyed on the property of others. Hundreds of people suffered terrible hardship, including the loss of their homes and livelihoods, at the grasping hands of David Jack.

There is nothing to suggest that Jack ever acted illegally or that any of his business dealings contravened the letter of the law. Instead, he bent and twisted the legislation of the day to suit his devious and covetous ends, acquiring vast amounts of land by employing techniques that were dubious in the extreme.

California in the 1850s was in a state of social and political upheaval. The Mexican-American War had ended in 1848 with victory for the U.S. and the ceding of California and other territories to America. One of the most contentious and largely unsettled issues concerned the question of land grants by the Mexican Government to rancheros and other landowners. In some areas, including Monterey, there was precious little documentation in existence to establish who owned what; the system was one of chaos.

It was open season for rapacious chancers to 'grab' as much land as they could legally lay their hands on – and Jack was a king among scoundrels. Certainly, there were other dodgy characters behaving in much the same way. But few, if any, operating in California at that time accrued such vast acreage and attracted such venom as the young man from Scotland.

For many years Jack was so despised in the Monterey area that he had to travel with bodyguards because of threats on his life. Potshots were frequently aimed at him by dispossessed rancheros. At one point, the story goes that his wife had to make his lunch every day because of dark murmurings that, if he bought food, it would be poisoned.

A more illustrious fellow Scotsman, writer Robert Louis Stevenson, spent time in Monterey while Jack was there. Stevenson was a man with a moral compass and he wrote of Jack that, 'the man is hated with a great hatred'. The author also recorded that Irish-born union leader and rabble-rouser Dennis Kearney, a controversial figure in California, had counselled the people of Monterey to 'hang David Jacks'.

Naturally, in a country where the spirit of free enterprise is positively encouraged, Jack had his defenders. The noted American historian Hubert

Robert Louis Stevenson

Howe Bancroft said of him that 'he whose deeds and successes are a reflection on the indolence of others will always be a subject of diatribe'.

Bancroft also shone a light on what drove Jack. He added: 'Mr Jacks came into possession of his estates, on the whole, by fair dealing, through the force of that good fortune, business judgment and character which are very generally admitted to be the birthright of the Scotch. It may perhaps be true to say, though not miserly, he was fond of money, and that it was his strongest ambition to purchase every rod of land to which he could see his way.'

At his height Jack – who became known as Jacks after his move to America – was reputed to have owned a staggering 90,000 acres of land in what is nowadays one of the most desirable parts of California.

The entire city of Monterey belonged to him, as did the land that now houses the affluent resort cities of Pacific Grove, Seaside and Del Rey Oaks; the famous Pebble Beach golf course; the army post of Fort Ord, now a National Monument; and parts of the cities of Carmel-by-the-Sea, where Clint Eastwood would be mayor, and Salinas, home of the author John Steinbeck.

There was a flip-side to Jack's financial dealings. After earning a fortune he turned to benefaction. His Presbyterian upbringing never left him, and later in life, he donated land and many thousands of dollars to religious groups. He also sat on the board of the University of the Pacific in the city of Stockton and his largesse helped the institution stay afloat through difficult times. His 'good works' have been recognised by his adopted city.

It is often said of the billionaire Scottish businessman and philanthropist Andrew Carnegie that he gave away much of his fortune to 'buy back his soul'. Perhaps a similar charge can be levelled at David Jack?

The story of David Jack began in April 1822, in the bustling market town of Crieff. His father William Jack had nine children, and David was the first of three by his second wife Janet McEwan. William had come to Crieff from the nearby village of Muthil and is known to have worked in various manual labouring jobs in the surrounding countryside. In the 1841 census he is listed as a farmer.

David grew up with his family in the town's Burrell Street, one of the main thoroughfares. His early life was, by all accounts, one of poverty. In his teens he worked as a handloom weaver, and there is a suggestion he considered joining the clergy as a Presbyterian minister. His schooling, however, had given him a good head for figures and a keen sense of wanderlust. The young David Jack obviously saw his future far from his home town of Crieff.

Jack's great-great-great-great nephew, Kenneth Jack, wrote an account of his ancestor entitled *Land King: The Story of David Jack*, published by the Monterey County Historical Society. He wrote, 'In his early years he was said to be a somewhat solitary youth who had few friends. This may have been an indication of his independence and single-mindedness that would reveal itself in later years'.

The town Jack was preparing to leave had a history dating back to the 13th century. It also sat amid stunning scenery. In his 1884 *Ordnance Gazetteer of Scotland*, Francis Hindes Groome described Crieff as 'this Montpelier of Scotland' and added that 'from every street…a landscape of rare sweetness and beauty is disclosed'.

Whether David Jack appreciated the beauty of his natural surroundings is doubtful, growing up as he did in relative poverty. Three of his elder brothers, Peter, James and John had left for America and established themselves as storekeepers in Long Island, New York. Peter had returned to Perthshire, no doubt telling tales of the opportunities that awaited adventurous and enterprising Scots on the other side of the Atlantic.

David grew determined to leave behind his stagnant life in Crieff. He saw little future in the town and was anxious to try his luck in the New World. On 30 August 1841, at the age of 19, he sailed from Liverpool to New York on a packet ship of the famous Black Ball Line.

On his arrival he swapped an historic Scottish town for an historic American town, heading for Williamsburg, the former colonial capital of Virginia. There he worked as an army contractor before returning to New York, where he was employed by a wheelwright at the Fort Hamilton army base in Brooklyn.

At the same time, an up-and-coming officer was installed by the U.S. Army as post engineer at Fort Hamilton. Robert E. Lee, who went on to become the most celebrated general in the Confederate Army during the civil war, served there for five years and was a frequent visitor at the store where Jack worked. The two men were said to have got along well and Jack commented on Lee's 'nobility of character'. Lee was later to distinguish himself in the Mexican-American War, the conflict that changed Jack's fortunes.

As the 1840s drew to a close, news began to filter from the west coast of a sensational discovery. Within weeks it had the nation in the grip of hysteria. Newspaper headlines across the country screamed one word – gold. The California correspondent of the *New York Herald* reported that even children were picking up gold in the 'treasure streams'. He wrote that, in comparison 'the famous El Dorado was but a sandbank, the Arabian Nights were tales of simplicity'.

The California Gold Rush was well and truly on and thousands of prospectors – Argonauts as they were called – swarmed westwards like biblical locusts upon the earth. Jack, by now in his mid-20s, had dollar signs in front of his eyes. He quit his job at Fort Hamilton to become a 'forty-niner' and prepared for the long, arduous trip west. Before leaving New York, however, he took the bold step of investing all his savings – $1,400 – in revolvers, figuring that people in California, law-abiding or otherwise, would pay good money for them. It proved to be a shrewd financial move.

There was no easy or quick route to California from the east coast. Jack found a job as a sutler (a civilian who sells goods to an army) with the 3rd Regiment of Artillery and sailed with them from New York, round Cape Horn, to the port of San Francisco, on a voyage lasting 138 days. It was April 1849 when he set foot on Californian soil, and the Gold Rush was in full swing.

Jack's first move was to sell off his estimated stash of 80 guns and make a return on his investment. It was hardly a difficult task. Within 48 hours the revolvers had been snapped up for $4,000 – a tidy profit of $2,600. The Scot had bought them for close to $18 each; he marked the price up to $50 when he got to San Francisco. He was unconcerned whether they were sold to lawmen or outlaws, as long as he made a decent profit. It was his first step on the capitalist ladder, and two days after arriving in the boomtown of San Francisco, Jack was a relatively wealthy young man.

Heavy rain and flooding in the goldfields of the Sierra Nevada were apparently what persuaded Jack there were easier ways of seeking his fortune. He worked as an inspector in the San Francisco Custom House, earning $100 a month, an excellent wage at that time, and began to loan quantities of his $4000 'gun money' at the rate of between 1.5% and 2% a month.

Jack found out quickly that, from the comfort of his office, there were surefire ways of making money from the prospectors without having to risk life and limb – not to mention financial ruin – in the headlong clamour for gold in the 'badlands' of the Sierra Nevada mountains.

Although San Francisco was in the grip of Gold Rush fever, it did not hold Jack's interest for long. In late 1849, eight months after arriving, he left the city and sailed 100 miles south to Monterey Bay. He arrived with all his worldly belongings on New Year's Day 1850, in a city that, like his old home town of Crieff, was steeped in history and clothed in natural beauty.

No-one paid any heed to the young immigrant Scottish office worker when he stepped off the boat at Monterey Harbour. His arrival went unnoticed and unheralded. But little did the citizens realise how drastically he would change their lives, and the dramatic effect he would have on the future of the old Spanish city.

Monterey had been the capital of the Spanish and Mexican territory of Alta California. Before the late 1840s it had been a world removed from the wealthy and populous American state into which it has evolved. Rather, it was a pastoral and sparsely-populated land inhabited by Native Americans, farmers and rancheros. The official non-Indian population of California in 1840 was only 8,000. Sadly, its laid-back way of life would prove its undoing.

When the Mexican-American War ended in 1848, parts of what are now California, Utah and New Mexico were ceded to the United States. However, when gold was discovered the same year, everything changed. Hundreds of thousands of immigrants from the east coast and abroad flooded into the towns and cities. The non-Indian population of California rose from 18,000 to 165,000 in two years, the economy boomed out of all recognition and the crime rate shot through the roof.

It was the normal practice for ceded land to go through a period of 'territorial' status before being granted full U.S. statehood. In this case though, California was suddenly awash with money and gold, and on 9 September 1850, it became the 31st state and expanded American influence to the Pacific Ocean. The dominant political issue of the time was slavery and California was admitted as a free state – one where slavery was prohibited.

In Monterey David Jack had found himself in the employ of a gentleman called Joseph Boston who ran a general merchant's store in a building known as Casa del Oro – the House of Gold. This was the place where the prospectors would bring their gold for storage in Mr. Boston's safe. It also doubled as the county tax depository and Jack soon gained intimate and invaluable knowledge of the prompt payers and, more importantly, those who were tardy.

Jack stayed in a room in the house but within a year had formed a partnership with fellow Scotsman James McKinlay. He had emigrated from Stirling, only 23 miles from Crieff, and he operated a money-lending and merchant's business from an office in Monterey's Pacific House. McKinlay was almost 20 years older than Jack and became something of a mentor figure. Very soon, Jack was lending out money on his own behalf and imposing healthy rates of interest.

The 'somewhat solitary youth' who had left his family in Crieff had grown into a dour, almost reclusive young man. His life as a clerk was spent poring over ledgers, registers and balance sheets, work that came easily to someone with his mathematical mindset. He had also developed a fastidious attention to detail; his diligent bookkeeping methods involved dotting every 'i' and crossing every 't'.

Jack prospered under the tutelage of McKinlay, and he was becoming skilled in the dark arts of real estate. His personal wealth increased, as did his reputation among the residents of Monterey as a dodgy dealer. But Jack wanted more than simply money. He wanted land, every square inch he could lay his hands on, by fair means or foul. It became an insatiable lust that would overwhelm him and consume his every waking moment.

In his book, *Storied Land: Community and Memory in Monterey*, John Walton states: 'Jacks was a dour man – serious to a fault, hard to like, a caricature of the tight-fisted Scot, devoted to church and family, and easily the most despised figure on the central coast. His life was threatened repeatedly, if never seriously, and his severe control of the local property market was a rallying cry for political movements in the 1870s and 1880s.'

By 1852 Jack's money-lending enterprise was in full swing. He had been elected treasurer of Monterey County, and thanks to the hours he had spent trawling through ledger details, he knew every detail of every person who was delinquent in paying taxes. Most were rancheros who had been given land by the former Mexican government. He knew how much land they held, how much money they earned, how many family members lived on the property, how many farm animals they kept.

Armed with this information Jack then moved in for the kill. He offered loans to people who had defaulted in their payments; charged a hefty rate of interest, and secured the loans against the land they had been granted. He knew perfectly well who could pay him back and who could not. As soon as repayments slowed down or stopped, he immediately foreclosed and secured title to the land in his name.

In most cases the foreclosure notices were posted in a remote part of the estate. If the landowner was Spanish, the notices were written in English. If the land was owned by an English speaker, then the notices were in Spanish.

By the time rancheros realised what had happened it was too late; not that many of them had the wherewithal to put off the inevitable. Foreclosure was complete, and the property they had been given before the American 'takeover' of California was no longer theirs; it was in the hands of Jack. Left with two choices, the former owners could remain as his tenants or they could clear off. It was that simple and that harsh.

His methods were all perfectly legal, though it was a brutal, heartless and unethical way of doing business. The people Jack was dealing with were poor, some were illiterate, and most were lacking in any business sense.

In his position as county treasurer, Jack was now mixing with the movers and shakers of Monterey's new society. California, since the end of the war, had progressed from what one author described as 'Spanish pastoralism to Yankee efficiency'. At the heart of that transition lay land use and a new culture and approach to land ownership.

By the early 1850s Jack had confined himself to the land owned by rancheros, other Hispanics and some English-speaking incomers. With the help of some new-found cronies he was ready to take his land-grabbing antics to greater heights. In fact, by the end of the decade he would have pulled off what must go down as one of the most audacious and spectacular land coups in American history.

Jack had formed business alliances with two gentlemen in particular: Delos Rodyn Ashley was a young lawyer from Arkansas who had been appointed Monterey's district attorney, and Matthew Collins Ireland was a farmer from Ohio who sat on the city's Board of Supervisors. All three were incomers to Monterey and they had one desire in common – to line their own pockets at any cost.

The California Gold Rush is often portrayed as one of America's most glamorous and exciting chapters, a time when many thousands of people made their fortunes. However, the reality for the poor and ethnic people of towns and cities such as Monterey was grim. They had been hard-working, upstanding citizens, yet they were being conned out of everything they owned by an influx of rogues and shysters.

Robert Louis Stevenson, during his stay in Monterey, wrote, 'Alas for the little town! It is not strong enough to resist the influence of the flaunting caravanserai, and the poor, quaint, penniless native

Delos R Ashley

gentlemen of Monterey must perish, like a lower race, before the millionaire vulgarians of the Big Bonanza'.

Jack, Ashley and Ireland may have been the tip of an unethical iceberg in California but they were charlatans. Together they were about to concoct a scheme that would shake the city of Monterey to its core.

Before it could be hatched, Jack returned to Scotland for the first time since he left in 1841. His father had died in 1855 and Jack sailed back to his homeland the following year. For whatever reason, perhaps he felt homesick or perhaps he wanted to escape the glare of public scorn in Monterey, he stayed in Crieff for a year.

He had much to ponder; his dalliances in the world of real estate had left him reasonably cash-rich and with a small landholding, but he had his eyes on much more. While in Scotland the man who was so finicky that he knew the names and even the behavioural dispositions of all his horses and cattle had plenty of time to plot his next money making schemes. Not everything had gone Jack's way in Monterey. He had tried his luck at potato farming and raising hogs, but had lost money to market forces, weather problems, and swindlers. These were mistakes he vowed never to make again.

During his visit to Scotland, he also took time to attend to family affairs. William Jack had been buried in an unmarked grave in Muthil Churchyard. His son, who was making more money in California than his Scottish family could conceive of, made sure that a fine headstone was raised in his father's memory.

Meanwhile, in Monterey, the foundations for the great land-grab were being laid. At its heart was the complex question of how to dispose of what were known as the 'pueblo' lands of Monterey. The pueblo was a Spanish/Mexican tradition of conveniently located land allocated for the use of the community. It often included a town square or plaza, official buildings such as a town hall, jail and cemetery, other municipal property, and lots that were distributed to residents and settlers.

The Monterey pueblo had been established by a grant of 1827 when California was under Mexican rule. It was strictly controlled by Hispanic law dating back to the 1500s. Several other Californian towns and cities had pueblo land for the good of the community including Los Angeles, San Diego, Santa Barbara, Sonoma and the village of Yerba Buena, later known as San Francisco.

Monterey had been the Spanish and Mexican capital of the area, and the pueblo was a vast tract of land encompassing almost 30,000 acres. It was a prize piece of real estate. The city wanted to keep it; the U.S. government had its eyes on capturing it; and speculators and private investors coveted it.

Under the terms of the Treaty of Guadelupe Hidalgo that ended the Mexican-American War, the United States had promised to honour the existing property rights and land grants. That promise was broken. In blunt terms, the American judges and attorneys who encamped in California to settle the issue tore up the terms of the Hispanic law as if it had never existed. What had been community lands were simply privatised.

The relatively peaceful and oft-romanticised way of life enjoyed by the old-time Californios was brushed aside to make way for rampant capitalism and greedy land speculation. In San Francisco, one writer observed that 'the heritage of *all* the people of San Francisco has been divided among a few hundred'. The San Diego pueblo, it was said, had been disposed of 'like a card give-away game'.

A board of three commissioners had been appointed to hear the cases brought by the land claimants. In Monterey Delos Ashley was on the rise and in 1853 he was hired by the Monterey Board of Trustees to press the city's claims to the pueblo land – a total of 29,698.53 acres. One of the trustees who appointed Ashley was none other than Matthew C. Ireland.

Ashley made his case before the U.S. Land Commission in San Francisco on 2 March 1853. He was a thorough and politically-astute lawyer, soon to be elected as a Nevada member of the U.S. House of Representatives. Three years later, on 22 January 1856, the Commission confirmed the city's title to the pueblo lands. It seemed, at face value, that a straightforward deal had been done and that the Mexican community land had been transferred to the safekeeping of the new American city.

Little did the public realise the chicanery and skullduggery that was brewing. After Ashley's work was done he presented the trustees with a bill of $991.50. But by 1856 the city was bankrupt; the trustees had not a cent in the coffers to pay Ashley for all his work. He was, of course, well aware of this. He required payment for his services and he had prepared a meticulous and comprehensive plan to make sure he got what he deserved.

When Jack arrived back in Monterey from Scotland in 1857 he must have been delighted at the turn of events. Jack and Ashley were as thick as thieves and the ambitious plot they had hatched was beginning to show signs of coming to fruition. Ireland was in on the plan, so too were others. The people who stood to suffer – the good citizens of Monterey – were completely in the dark.

Ashley's next move was to amend Monterey's municipal charter. He presented a form to the California legislature giving the city the right to sell off the pueblo land once it came into their possession. The new legislation was passed in 1857.

For the purposes of Jack and Ashley, the wording was perfect. It read, 'The trustees may also pay for the expenses of prosecuting the title of the city before the United States land commissioners and before the United States courts, and for that purpose may sell and transfer any property, right, or franchise, upon such terms and for such price as may by them be deemed reasonable'.

It was an absolute masterstroke, a triumph of sharp practice and double dealing that played straight into the hands of David Jack and Delos Ashley. The city trustees had approved Ashley's bill but did not have the means to pay it. They decided on the only course of action open to them. Bizarrely, in order to pay their own district attorney for securing their own land, they then agreed to sell it at public auction.

The land-grabbing Scotsman must have been positively salivating by this point. All the long days and nights making detailed notes of every aspect of every piece of property in Monterey County were about to pay off handsomely. Jack was set to pull off his biggest stunt – one that would earn him a lifetime of notoriety.

At 5pm on 9 February 1859, on the steps of Monterey's Colton Hall, the public auction for the old pueblo lands was held. It was a bitterly cold winter day and darkness was beginning to fall. Notices advertising the sale had been posted in a handful of inconspicuous places and an advert had been placed that day in the *Pacific Sentinel* newspaper published in Santa Cruz, more than 40 miles away.

By design, hardly anyone was there. However, among the sparsely-attended crowd, two figures stood out – David Jack and Delos Ashley. They were the sole bidders and when the auction was complete, they had bought the lot – every square inch of land. And the price they paid was a mere $1,002.50. It covered Ashley's legal bill of $991.50 plus $11 legal costs down to the last cent.

The two men had got their hands on some of the most valuable lands in California at slightly more than three cents an acre. It was a set-up, perfectly planned and executed. It has gone down in the annals of California history as 'The Rape of Monterey'.

When news of the deed became known, there was outrage in the city. Up to this point Jack had been something of a menace, an underhanded land-grabber. Now he and his scheming cohorts had connived to effectively 'steal' the city – and all without breaking any law. He quickly became the most disliked man in Monterey and the surrounding countryside.

But the Scot could not have cared less. He was emboldened by his stunning feat and, far from being satisfied, went after more and more parcels of land. Nine years later Ashley decided he could not stay in Monterey any longer because of the intensity of the venom. He left for San Francisco and sold his portion of the land to Jack for $500. Now Jack had what he wanted – the entire city.

In 1866 a new Board of Trustees had been elected and declared that the sale of the pueblo land had been illegal. However, Jack's old friend Matthew Ireland was now a state assemblyman and introduced a bill to the state legislature ratifying all land sales made in Monterey before 8 February 1859 – the day before the pueblo sale.

Jack, the humble farmer's son from Perthshire, was by now the wealthiest man in Monterey County, although he had developed an appreciably greater ruthless streak. Next on his strike list were the large ranchos dotted around the peninsula, the owners of which had been recipients of Spanish or Mexican land grants. In some cases they had been farmed by the same family for generations.

Jack did not worry a jot about such niceties. It had been his life's work to plough through the minutiae of every land grant in the area; now he was going to use that knowledge to his advantage. He knew the ranchos were easy prey; there was little if any documentation or paperwork in existence to prove who owned what.

One by one, through whatever legal means available to him, he gained title to the lands. Rancho Aguajito, at more than 3,000 acres, was his for $1,000 thanks to a deal struck by Ireland; Rancho Punto do Los Pinos, which includes present-day Cannery Row, became his; so did the 8,890-acre Rancho Chualar, an extensive chunk of land on which the same families had worked and lived for decades.

Jack wanted these people off *his* land and claimed they were 'alien squatters'. As a result, the Squatters' League of Monterey Council was formed and, in the midst of one legal battle, delivered the following threat, referring to the Scotsman as a 'low lifed son of Birth'.

'Now that this case has been decided in favour of the squatters on that land which you pretend to claim…and you have thereby been the cause of a great deal of unnecessary annoyance to those settlers – some of them you have actually sued for trespass and damages…Now you Son of a bitch if you don't make good that amount of damage to each and every one of those settlers which you sued as well as a reasonable amount of compensation to each of the other settlers – if you don't do this inside ten days you son of a bitch – we shall suspend your animation between daylight and hell.'

The message was signed 'By the Executive Committee of the Squatters' League of Monterey County'.

There were other missives, all in the same vein, and all over Jack's head. In his mind his future was clear and neatly mapped out. Even his wedding day was carefully arranged to maximize a business opportunity.

In 1861 Jack married Maria Christina Soledad Romie in the city of San Luis Obispo, 140 miles south of Monterey. Coincidentally, she was the daughter of a wealthy landowner whose estate, Rancho El Pescadero, he had craved for some time. Not surprisingly, thanks to the union with Maria, he got his wish. The land was his within two years.

Whether he married Maria for love or whether it was a convenient business arrangement will never be known, but the couple remained lifelong partners until Jack's death in 1909. She bore him nine children, seven of whom survived beyond infancy, and she appears to have been unflinchingly supportive despite the considerable malice directed at him. For his part, he was a devoted family man.

That Jack continued to live in Monterey was testament to his ability to rise above the vitriol. He was a relatively small, bookish individual with a beard and receding hairline. In a passport application dated 1896 he is described as being 5ft 4 ½ inches, with blue eyes, a florid complexion and an iron grey beard. He was hardly a menacing figure.

His life was threatened on many occasions; he was confronted in the streets by people who had received legal notices from him; he had to travel with bodyguards because of warnings that he would be injured or killed while travelling; and a posse was dispatched to kill him several times.

'The Old Pacific Capital' was an essay in Robert Louis Stevenson's book *Across the Plains,* and dealt with Monterey as he found it in the late 1800s. In it he professes sorrow for the ending of the Mexican way of life and comments on the behaviour of his fellow Scotsman.

He wrote: 'We have here in England no idea of the troubles and inconveniences that flow from the existence of these large landholders – land thieves, land sharks or land grabbers, they are more commonly and plainly called. Thus the townlands of Monterey are all in the hands of a single man. How they came there is an obscure, vexatious question, and rightly or wrongly, the man is hated with a great hatred'.

Stevenson added: 'His life has been repeatedly in danger. Not very long ago, I was told, the stage was stopped and examined three evenings in succession by disguised horsemen thirsting for his blood. A certain house on the Salinas road, they say, he always passes in his buggy at full speed for the squatter sent him warning long ago.'

The author said Irishman Dennis Kearney, a well-known trade unionist and agitator, had advised the people of Monterey to 'hang David Jacks' and added, 'Had the town been American, in my private opinion this would have been done years ago. Land is a subject on which there is no jesting in the west, and I have seen my friend the lawyer drive out of Monterey to adjust a competition of titles with the face of a captain going into battle and his Smith-and-Wesson convenient to his hand'.

The California and U.S. census records are indicators of the colossal personal wealth that Jack accrued. In 1860, the year after the pueblo land deal, he described himself as a clerk with real estate valued at $20,000 and a personal estate of $23,000. Ten years later, in 1870, the census form lists him as a real estate dealer. The value of his real estate had rocketed to $136,000, although his personal wealth had decreased to $18,450.

From 1880 onwards, he described himself in all official documents as a capitalist. Census forms stopped recording the wealth of individuals but by the end of the century Jack was a multi-millionaire. He spent much of his efforts hiring court lawyers to defend his land dealings. In fact the last appeal against the pueblo land deal was finally settled in his favour in 1903, six years before he died.

He made a fortune selling off land, some of it to the railway pioneers of the Southern Pacific Railroad Company. A devout Presbyterian, he also turned to philanthropy and donated large sums of money to a number of churches, including Methodist and Episcopal. At one point he was a Sunday school teacher in Monterey and many youngsters learned bible study from the man their parents despised.

According to John Walton, the tendency to focus on Jack's good work is an attempt by modern biographers to 'rehabilitate his memory'.

The dairies that produced the cheese operated from the land that Jack took over. There were 14 dairies in all and, as part of a deliberate and aggressive marketing policy, he repackaged the old queso blanco as Jack's Cheese. In time that became Monterey Jack, and the name has remained to this day.

Jack died on 11 January 1909, at the age of 85. His wife Maria died eight years later. The Scot who is remembered by some as the man who 'stole Monterey' and by others as the man who gave the world Monterey Jack cheese was buried in the city's cemetery.

The seven children of the marriage went on to administer the David Jack Foundation and operate the David Jack Corporation. The fortune he left behind was looked after wisely by his children and massive bequests were made to educational institutions in California, including Mills College in San Francisco, Stanford University and the California Institute of Technology.

When Jack was at the height of his power, one of his foreclosure victims was said to have been so displeased with his immoral business practices that he placed an Indian curse on Jack and his progeny. The curse said that 'the seeds of his greed would not spread beyond his children'.

As it turned out Jack had seven children but none of them ever presented him with a grandchild. With the death of his last surviving daughter Margaret in 1962, the line – and all his business ties – died out. Perhaps the Indian curse came true after all.

7

James Callender

I believe nothing that Callender said any more than if it had been said by an infernal spirit. I would not convict a dog of killing sheep upon the testimony of two such witnesses.

– U.S. President John Adams

In 1800 President John Adams was coming to the end of his time in office. It had been a turbulent four years – steering the fledgling nation through its early childhood had tested his diplomatic and political dexterity. Adams, a fussy, pragmatic lawyer and one of the signatories to the Declaration of Independence, had proved a solid, reliable choice; a safe pair of hands following the charismatic George Washington. Adams had piloted the good ship United States of America on a steady course and he wanted to remain at the helm for the next stage of the journey. An election was looming and a second term as president was in his sights.

But there was one formidable obstacle blocking his way. The man who had been his vice president for the last four years, Thomas Jefferson, also had his eye on the top job. Jefferson possessed qualities that Adams lacked. He was a tall, engaging and handsome man, whereas the incumbent president had a pernickety, scolding, school-masterly manner. He was also short and stout and was mockingly called 'his rotundity' by members of Congress.

Jefferson too, had signed the Declaration of Independence; the battle for the presidency was thus a fight between two of America's founding fathers. These were men revered for their intelligence and wisdom, their dignity and foresight, men who had laid the building blocks of what would become one of the world's greatest democracies.

However, the election campaign they fought in 1800 was to go down as the most malicious and poisonous in American history. These two luminaries who had helped the U.S. shake off her colonial shackles engaged in vitriolic personal attacks, dirty tricks and mud-slinging that would make the most hardened modern-day spin doctor blush.

John Adams – Library of Congress

Far from behaving like statesmen, they traded insults like street urchins. It was a disrespectful and slanderous campaign and it brought nothing but shame on the new nation.

Naturally, the two protagonists let others do the dirty work. There were plenty of lackeys and sycophants on either side happy to dish the dirt, and there were newspapers, political pamphlets, bulletins and scandal sheets by the dozen willing to print every grubby partisan word.

The opening salvos had come from Jefferson's men and Adams, to be fair, had initially been thick-skinned enough to let the attacks roll like water off a duck's back Press reports had been scathing, referring to Adams as a 're-pulsive pedant', a 'gross hypocrite' and 'one of the most egregious fools upon the continents'.

Not surprisingly, the president could only take so much. One spring he and his formidable wife Abigail were at Peacefield, their Massachusetts farmhouse, when they picked up and read a pamphlet entitled *The Prospect Before Us*. It contained a description of the serving United States president as 'a hideous hermaphroditical character who has neither the force and firmness of a man nor the gentleness and sensibility of a woman'.

Abigail is said to have exploded with rage. This was an outrageous attack that almost beggared belief. The author had dared to portray one of the most powerful men in the western world as a figure with the sexual organs of both genders. This was one libel too many for John Adams.

Not that Adams was above resorting to personal attacks. One of his surrogates – as the flunkies were referred to – played the race card to devastating effect, embellishing an old claim that Jefferson's parents had Negro and Native American ancestry, and mocking his close relations with France, where he had spent several years as a diplomat.

A story was planted in one paper portraying Jefferson as 'half Injun, half nigger, half Frenchman…born to a mulatto father and a half-breed Indian squaw'. 'The Indian', it said, was 'well-known in the neighbourhood where he was raised'.

The level of character assassination had sunk into the gutter and never rose beyond it. Politicians in later years may have thought they were put through the mill at election time – Barack Obama suffered constant racial abuse amid claims he was born in Kenya, James Polk claimed his opponent Henry Clay had 'slept with whores' and 'broken all of the 10 Commandments', and in 1964 Lyndon B. Johnson ran the famous 'Daisy Girl' TV advert depicting a child dying in a nuclear holocaust if people voted for his Republican opponent Barry Goldwater.

On the other hand, no-one has had to endure the relentless personal battering Adams suffered at the hands of Jefferson. With every headline his chances of winning the election faded. One day he was an 'unprincipled oppressor', the next he was 'a strange compound of ignorance and ferocity, of deceit and weakness'. His administration was a 'continual tempest of malignant passions' while he was 'a wannabe monarch plotting to destroy democracy'.

The principal reason for the mud-slinging was the entry into an American election campaign of competing political parties. George Washington had resisted the temptations of partisanship; 1796 had seen the election of a Federalist president in Adams and a Republican vice president in Jefferson. Yet by 1800 the gloves were off, as old cross-party friendships gave way to the demands of partisan ideology.

For John Adams the 'hermaphrodite' article had been one step too far. However, he had a weapon up his sleeve, and with the prompting of his wife Abigail, he decided to unleash it to its fullest. The Sedition Act was one of the most controversial pieces of legislation he passed. It effectively restricted speech critical of the Government and gave Adams the power to define false, scandalous and malicious writing as 'treasonable activity'.

Opponents claimed it breached the U.S. Constitution's First Amendment – freedom of speech. But Adams had withstood so much abuse that he was a man at the end of his tether. The Sedition Act was on the statute books and he was going to use it to throw the authors of the scurrilous material into jail.

He did not have to look far to find the villain of the piece. There was no secret about the identity of the author of *The Prospect Before Us*. Adams was about to hurl the full force of the law in the direction of the scoundrel, one James Thomson Callender.

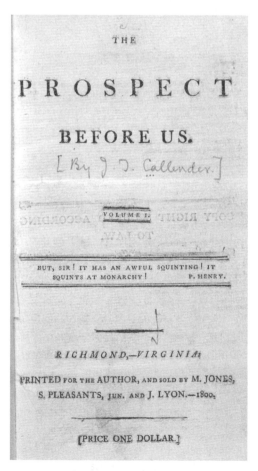

The Prospect Before Us

Callender was a Scotsman who had left his native land under a cloud and carved out a career in America as a salacious journalist. His writing was undoubtedly powerful and eye-catching, although it was filled with personal invective, and he had developed a reputation as a muck-raking guttersnipe.

Even though Adams was aware that Callender had scripted the offending article, he did not know the whole story. Callender – under a variety of pen-names – had been responsible for almost all the shocking anti-Adams propaganda. He was Jefferson's personal attack dog, the future president's 'hired pen'.

Every lie, every libel, every last hurtful insult that dripped from Callender's quill was approved and financed by the great Thomas Jefferson – the man known as the Apostle of Democracy.

When Adams discovered that truth, it hurt him more than any of the press attacks, and drove a wedge between the two men until they died within hours of each other on American Independence Day, 4 July 1826.

The election campaign was Callender's most spectacular offensive. His justification was that, as a hard-bitten hack struggling to earn a buck, he was being encouraged and paid to vent his spleen at an authority figure – and not just any authority figure, the president of the United States.

Callender enjoyed expressing his anger in print; he had been doing it all his life, and it was his way of earning a living. John Adams was only one victim of his pen; he also had the temerity to write disparagingly about the father of the nation, George Washington, another founding father Alexander Hamilton, and then without compunction, he turned the tables and directed his venom with devastating effect at his old friend Jefferson.

The Bill Clinton/Monica Lewinsky affair may have shocked the nation during the 1990s, but the scandal-mongering of James Callender uncovered the first two major sex scandals in United States history. One of his revelations – that Jefferson had fathered a child by a black slave Sally Hemings – reverberates to this day.

Callender had very few commendable personality traits, of that there is no doubt. He slandered, libelled and gossiped with little or no regard for truth or personal injury; in social circumstances he was abusive, drunken and argumentative, and his writing betrayed an anti-Negro racism that was odious even by the standards of the late 18th century.

Nevertheless, many of the scurrilous articles he penned were true – or at least contained sufficient truth to justify their publication. To that extent there is an argument that, despite his lack of finesse, Callender aided the democratic process by revealing corruption and immorality in high places. His scandal rags were early forerunners of the sensationalist yellow journalism of the late 1800s and the excesses of the tabloid press that we take for granted nowadays.

Whatever criticisms can be levelled at Callender's behaviour and the tenor of his writing, he achieved something no journalist has managed to do since – he single-handedly determined the outcome of a U.S. election and thereby altered the course of American history.

Had it not been for Callender and his remarkable attacks on Adams, it is highly unlikely Thomas Jefferson would have won the 1800 election and become the third U.S. president. His time in the White House may never have come and the head of a different American hero would now be gracing the five cent (or nickel) coin.

Callender was born in 1758 and spent his childhood either in Edinburgh, Stirling or the Scottish Borders. There are suggestions his parents may both have died when he was young and his later writings indicate a poor, strictly Presbyterian upbringing which influenced him in adulthood. Nothing, however, is certain about his early life; there are no written records until 1782, by which time he was 24.

Although the whereabouts of his schooling is unknown, his written work is that of a man who was well-versed in classical literature and received a good Scottish education. However needy his early circumstances were, someone was there to ensure he was given the start he needed. Whether that someone was his father, mother, or another relative or guardian is unknown.

Whatever forces were at work during his formative years, Callender emerged as a young man with a fascination of books and authors, especially the Irish poet and satirist Jonathan Swift; a thorough dislike of corrupt practices among those in positions of power; a leaning towards Scottish independence; and a strong Calvinistic sense of right and wrong.

Michael Durey, in his thoroughly researched book *With the Hammer of Truth*, described Callander as having a 'complex and contradictory character'.

He added, 'He was self-righteous, strongly puritanical with regard to personal morals, insufferably proud, with a deep and abiding mistrust of human nature. Yet he became involved with a group who composed bawdy verse, wrote satirical poetry himself, frequently drank heavily, and embraced low tavern life, both in Scotland and in America'.

In 1782 Callender started working as a sub-clerk in the Sasine Office in Edinburgh. It was a dull, menial job that Callender remained in for eight years. An instrument of sasine is a legal document that records the transfer of ownership of a piece of land or building. In the majority of cases – especially in 18th century Edinburgh – these documents would involve the property of the aristocracy and the otherwise affluent and prosperous members of society.

That same year Callender published the first of two pamphlets that, even though they were anonymous, were to gain him a slice of recognition and infamy. He chose an easy target, Dr. Samuel Johnson, one of the most reviled men in Scotland at the time, in an obvious attempt to propel himself up the literary ladder. The tone of his writing was a foretaste of what was to come in the United States.

His first pamphlet was entitled *Deformities of Dr Samuel Johnson*, and in it Callender used sensational and flowery language to tear apart Johnson's scholarly and influential writings. Johnson was an English Tory well-known for his dislike of the Scots and the Jacobite cause – exactly the type of character Callender had grown to despise.

Callender's offering was one long anti-Johnson ramble but the people of Scotland lapped up every word. Johnson and his biographer James Boswell had not long ended a tour of Scotland, during which Johnson had managed to write scathingly about almost every aspect of Scottish life and people.

Of Johnson's account of the Highland journey published in the *Edinburgh Review*, Callender wrote, 'He has furnished his readers with a picture of himself. He has seen very little and observed still less. His narration is neither supported with vivacity, to make it entertaining, nor accompanied with information, to render it instructive. It exhibits the pompous artificial diction of the *Rambler* (a periodical published by Johnson) with the same vacuity of thought'.

Callender was equally trenchant about many of the definitions in Johnson's dictionary and described him as a 'trifling pedant'. He accused Johnson of producing 'enigmatic definitions' of words and phrases 'by which he industriously prevents the reader from knowing the meaning of the words he explains'.

The pamphlet was published in London where, Callender hoped, it would be noticed by men of influence. But there were no takers, and instead of getting a 'leg-up' into literary society, Callender was forced to remain in his job at the Sasine Office. In 1790, after a series of disputes with a colleague over corrupt working practices, Callender was told to leave the job.

By this time he was married with at least two children and living in Edinburgh city centre. He wrote constantly, hoping to find a wealthy sponsor. His efforts were eventually rewarded in 1790 when the eccentric Lord Gardenstone – known for his extreme fondness of pigs – offered Callender his patronage.

As a result Callender secured a job as a messenger-at-arms with an Edinburgh firm of lawyers and saw his poems and articles appear in print, usually anonymously or under a pseudonym, in the many literary magazines. However, his rebellious nature got the better of him; after a series of articles trumpeting Scottish independence and denouncing the Excise Service as corrupt, charges of treason were laid at his door.

In 1792 he published another pamphlet *The Political Progress of Britain*, in which he savagely attacked Britain's empire-building, corruption and warring. He wrote of Great Britain that 'every other nation in the world must have a right to wish that an earthquake or a volcano may first bury both islands together in the centre of the globe; that a single, but decisive exortion of Almighty vengeance may terminate the progress and the remembrance of our crimes'.

The document was outlawed, Callender was arrested in January 1793 and recalls that he escaped 'with some difficulty', before fleeing to Ireland and then the United States to avoid prosecution. He had developed from a humble yet headstrong youth into a fully-fledged radical whose vivid and lurid penmanship had, just as he intended, ruffled the feathers of the political and legal establishment.

However much he had upset the apple cart in Scotland, it was as nothing compared with what he was about to unleash on America, a country which he believed held no such barriers to the expression of free speech

The United States into which James Callender sailed in 1793 was a nation in its infancy and experiencing inevitable teething troubles. Washington had just been sworn in for his second term as president and the men of influence who were later to feel the sharp end of Callender's pen were in positions of power. Adams was vice president, Jefferson was secretary of state and Hamilton was secretary of the treasury.

That year the United States Mint produced its first coins; a yellow fever epidemic killed 5,000 people in Philadelphia, then the nation's temporary capital; John Hancock, the first man to sign the Declaration of Independence, died; and the 37-year old Queen of France Marie Antoinette was beheaded at the height of the French Revolution.

The U.S. nation, described in the 1790s as 'still a fragile experiment in republican government', was already in a state of political conflict. Washington had shunned party politics, preferring the role of unifying presidential figurehead. But partisan politics in the form of the Federalist and Republican parties were emerging, and there were constant fears America would be plunged into war with either France or Britain.

The 1790s was also a boom time for newspapers and political pamphlets. There were publications in every city, town and village and readership exploded. Editors, buoyed by the 'freedom of speech' clause in the U.S. Constitution's First Amendment, were fearless, and began printing opinions in rabid and sensational terms.

Callender, equally bolstered by the reaction to his excessive and overblown attacks on Dr. Samuel Johnson, the Excise Service and the British Empire, had landed in the perfect spot at the right time. If ever a country needed a good scandal-monger it was late 18th century America. There was a host of easy targets, and the Scotsman sharpened his pen for the fray that lay ahead.

Callender needed work quickly; he had a wife and four children to support by this point. After some part-time journalistic work his shorthand skills led to him being hired by the Philadelphia-based *Federal Gazette* to report on what was said during Congressional meetings. Unfortunately for Callender, the job did not last long.

Undaunted, he picked up freelance work here and there and became immersed in the politics of the day. He was a self-confessed Republican, arguing strongly against the leadership of Washington and his chief adviser Hamilton. He subscribed to the common theory that, only years after a long and bloody war had achieved independence from Great Britain, the Washington administration was trying to 'cosy up' to the old colonial masters in preference to America's wartime ally, France.

Only a few veiled press attacks had been written criticising Washington – no one had dared directly lambast the country's greatest ever hero. But in 1795 Callender did just that and opened the floodgates for an outpouring of anti-Washington vitriol.

Writing in the *Philadelphia Aurora* newspaper, a staunchly anti-Federalist publication, Callender wrote: 'If ever a nation was debauched by a man, the American has been debauched by Washington. If ever a nation has suffered from the improper influence of one man, the American nation has been deceived by Washington. Let his conduct then be an example to future ages. Let it serve to be a warning that no man may be an idol, and that a people may confine in themselves rather than an individual. Let the history of the federal government instruct mankind, that the marque of history may be worn to conceal the foulest designs against the liberties of the people.'

It was incredible stuff and shocked America to the core. No-one had dared drag Washington's name and reputation through the gutter in this manner; it was a sensationalist and personal onslaught. Washington's allies were furious. How dare this scoundrel deface the good name of the country's most noble and heroic statesman?

In all fairness to Callender, he had simply articulated what many others were feeling but had been hesitant to commit to words. As in Scotland, his writing betrayed a clear perception of the political world around him and had an eye-catching, populist style.

Other Washington-bashing newspaper men followed, but Callender had been the one who fired the first shot. It gained him a certain notoriety, kept him in steady work and earned him sufficient wages to support his family and his excessive drinking habits.

Whilst many relished his revelations many others despised the mischief-making Scotsman. He was developing a reputation as a diligent but ungracious sot, a man whose company was to be avoided. One rival publication described him as 'an ugly misshapen little man who made a career of spewing venom'.

Venomous or not, Callender had another of the country's founding fathers in his sights. Alexander Hamilton was an enormously powerful figure, the man who George Washington turned to most often for advice and guidance. Hamilton made no secret of his desire to curry favour with Great Britain and improve diplomatic relations between the two countries.

Although he looked every inch the aristocrat, Hamilton had been born on the Caribbean island of Nevis, the illegitimate son of Ayrshire nobleman James Hamilton and his married lover Rachel Faucette. His father left when Alexander was young but he was a scholarly boy who read voraciously. He moved to the colonies just before the Revolutionary War and worked his way up through the army ranks to become George Washington's aide-de-camp.

However, the higher up the political tree they are, the harder and more spectacular are their falls from grace. Callender and his poison pen knew this perfectly well.

In the early 1790s Hamilton, a married man, had conducted an affair with a 23-year old married woman by the name of Maria Reynolds. Far from being an innocent led astray, Mrs. Reynolds had been encouraged by her husband, merchant James Reynolds, to instigate the liaison in the hope of extorting money from Hamilton. By all accounts Hamilton was not the first 'victim', though he was the most high profile.

As one historian put it, 'A plain statement of the facts is that Mrs. Reynolds was a whore, her husband was a pimp and both were blackmailers'.

After a few months the inevitable happened. James Reynolds demanded hush money of $1,000 from Hamilton. He paid it, continued bedding Mrs. Reynolds, and kept making payments to her husband for two years. However, once the money stopped the story leaked out to a few political colleagues; there was even an untrue allegation that the cash payments were part of a scheme to manipulate government securities using insider information.

Amazingly, the story was kept out of the public domain for four years – until James Callender revealed all in a hard-hitting political pamphlet in the summer of 1797. He published private letters that had passed between Hamilton and Mrs. Reynolds, accused Washington's right-hand man of a security fraud and stated, 'So much correspondence could not refer exclusively to wenching. No man of common sense will believe that it did'.

Hamilton, in a pamphlet of his own, admitted the adultery but denied the security fraud. As the central figure in America's first major sex scandal, his influence waned when John Adams succeeded Washington as president, and he never again held high public office. In 1804, he was killed in a duel with Jefferson's former vice president Aaron Burr.

Callender was delighted with the outcome of his publication; Hamilton's exposure as a cad and the humiliating effect on his family meant nothing to him beyond personal celebration and the kudos that came with having hooked a big political fish.

Still, he was not celebrating for long. By 1798 income had dried up and he was forced to seek poor relief, whilst his drinking habits were becoming an increasing cause for concern. His chief patron died of yellow fever and, later that year, his wife fell victim to the same disease, leaving him to look after four children alone.

Then a rival publisher exposed him as the author of a series of anonymous – and highly libellous – articles in the *Aurora* newspaper. The political atmosphere in Philadelphia was feverish and his 'outing' meant that not only could he be jailed under the Sedition Act, but he was also in danger of physical attacks. He left his children with a friend and fled the city for Richmond, Virginia.

Callender's reputation as a polemicist had caught the attention of Thomas Jefferson. The two men had met in Philadelphia and, with an election looming, Jefferson decided

Thomas Jefferson portrait - Library of Congress

he wanted the Republican-minded journalist as his attack dog to maul Federalist rival John Adams. He cautiously provided financial support but, given Callender's debauched lifestyle, kept – or tried to keep – a discrete distance.

The Scotsman was extremely grateful. Although he held a general disdain for authority figures, he admired Jefferson and had placed him on a pedestal. The move to Richmond had brought him closer to Jefferson's Monticello mansion, so the two men could communicate with relative ease.

In return for Jefferson's patronage, Callender promised the future president 'a tornado as no government ever got before, for there is in American history a specie of ignorance, absurdity and imbecility unknown to the annals of any other nation'.

It was a dark warning of what lay ahead. Callender had destroyed Hamilton and now he was about to do the same to Adams, the sitting president of the United States; little did Adams realise the character assassination he was about to endure. Callender was in the mood to repay Jefferson's investment – and then some.

The competition for readership had spawned a breed of hard-nosed newspapermen in the former colonies, each trying to out-shock and out-scandalise the other. And of all the contemptuous hacks that had descended on Philadelphia and Boston, Richmond and New York, James Thomson Callender was the crudest of the lot, the most cavalier with the facts, the most injurious, defamatory and spiteful.

After his articles on Hamilton, a rival Federalist paper, the *Gazette of the United States*, wrote in an editorial that Callender had 'published sufficient general slander on our country to entitle him to the benefit of the gallows'.

Another rival editor wrote: 'In the name of justice and honor, how long are we to tolerate this scum of party filth and beggarly corruption, worked into a form somewhat like a man, to go thus with impunity? Do not the times approach when it must and ought to be dangerous for this wretch, and any other, thus to vilify our country and government…'

So far Callender had written in scandalous terms about the first president of the United States and his chief political adviser. However, he had a lot more ink in his quill…Callender's scurrilous tirades had only just begun.

Bankrolled by Jefferson, Callender in 1799 took up the post of editor of the *Richmond Examiner*, transforming it into a Republican scandal sheet. He kept up a continuous anti-Adams diatribe, insisting that the president was determined to embroil the country in a war with France and, at the same time, form a close bond with Great Britain.

The scaremongering worked. The American people were convinced taxes would rise to pay for John Adams' war and that young men would be forced to serve in the army and navy only years after the American War of Independence had cost so many lives.

In early 1800 the 'tornado' that Callender had promised Jefferson arrived with the publication of his most famous pamphlet *The Prospect Before Us*. It was political dynamite; it savaged John Adams in a way no American politician had ever been attacked before or, arguably, since. Jefferson was sent a copy for his approval and remarked, 'Such papers inform the thinking part of the nation'.

The 187-page document contained 20 separate passages that were found to be libellous. A copy was sent to Adams when he and his family were at home in Massachusetts. What they read horrified them; they knew the election campaign had degenerated but not to this level.

In *The Prospect Before Us*, Callender wrote that Adams, who had led the country since the 1797 election, was 'mentally deranged'. If he was re-elected he would, said Callender 'crown himself king' of the United States and he was already grooming his son, John Quincy Adams, as his successor to the throne. Other examples of Callender's venomous penmanship included:

The reign of Mr. Adams has been one continued tempest of malignant passions. As a President he has never opened his lips, or lifted his pen without threatening and scolding; the grand object of his administration has been to exasperate the rage of contending parties to calumniate and destroy every man who differs from his opinions.

He is not only a repulsive pedant, a gross hypocrite and an unprecedented oppressor but, in private life, one of the most egregious fools on the continent.

Future historians will enquire by what species of madness America submitted to accept, as her president, a person without abilities, and without virtues; a being alike incapable of attracting either tenderness, or esteem.

Take your choice between Adams, war and beggary, and Jefferson, peace and competency.

You will then take your choice between innocence and guilt, between freedom and slavery, between paradise and perdition.

John Adams is a blind, bald crippled toothless man…who secretly wants to start a war with France while he is not busy importing mistresses from Europe.

Callender kept up his attacks in the paper – he called Adams a 'hoary-headed incendiary and a man who had deserted and reversed all his principles' – and he wrote to Jefferson that he was 'now firing through five port holes at once, which is enough for one hand'.

Every insult lowered the president's esteem in the eyes of the nation. The man described as a 'drunken ruffian' had achieved what he set out to do. Adams wheeled out the Sedition Act but it was all too late to save his political bacon.

At a show trial in Richmond, Callender was found guilty of sedition, jailed for nine months and fined $200. However, Jefferson triumphed in the election, and his first act was to pardon and release Callender and a number of other scribes who had suffered the same fate. Both Jefferson and Callender were jubilant at the outcome, although Jefferson could not have guessed at the turn of events that lay ahead.

Two incidents were to turn Callender against Jefferson. First, he made constant demands for money of the new president but received what he considered a paltry amount in return for his services. Jefferson wrote to Virginia Governor and future president James Monroe, 'I am really mortified at the base ingratitude of Callender. It presents human nature in a hideous form'.

Callender then made it clear that, if no more money was to be forthcoming, he wanted to be appointed to the position of postmaster of Richmond. Jefferson refused, saying he was 'unworthy' of holding the post. Incensed, Callender and a fellow editor set up the *Richmond Recorder*, dedicated to the Federalist cause. The Scot had become a mercenary.

Then the Republican machine turned against Callender. A Philadelphia editor gave him a taste of his own medicine, and published an article about Callender's late wife. It read that she was 'overwhelmed by a created [sexually-transmitted] disease, on a loathsome bed, with a number of children, all in a state next to famishing…while Callender was having his usual pint of brandy at breakfast'.

The Scotsman was outraged. This time he was the one feeling the barbs of a personal attack, and he wanted revenge. There was only one man to blame in his mind. Just as Jefferson had formulated the slanders and libels against Adams, now he was responsible for targeting his friend Callender.

Jefferson's wife, Martha, had died in 1782 at the age of only 33, and he had made a solemn promise on her deathbed that he would never re-marry. Of the couple's six children, only two, Martha and Mary, survived to adulthood. They, and a number of slaves, including a girl called Sally Hemings, lived with Jefferson at his estate.

Whatever business Jefferson had been attending to on 1 September 1802, he was stopped in his tracks. The *Richmond Recorder* that day carried what author Si Sheppard, in his book, *The Partisan Press: A History of Media Bias in the United States*, called Callender's 'literary weapon of mass destruction against the President'.

The newspaper report read: 'It is well known that the man, whom it delighteth the people to honor, keeps and for many years has kept, as his concubine, one of his own slaves. Her name is SALLY. The name of her eldest son is TOM. His features are said to bear a striking although sable resemblance to those of the president himself. The boy is ten or twelve years of age. His mother went to France on the same vessel with Mr. Jefferson and his two daughters.'

It added, 'By this wench Sally, our president has several children…THE AFRICAN VENUS is said to officiate, as housekeeper, at Monticello'.

Yet again Callender had succeeded in finding his target by way of a scurrilous rumour. Jefferson had become the third serving U.S. president to be defamed in print by the Scot. Callender continued the onslaught by referring to Sally in overtly racist terms and declaring sarcastically, 'Behold the favourite! The first-born of Republicanism'.

He wrote that Jefferson was 'frolicking with his Congo Harem' and described Sally as 'Dusky Sal' a 'wooly-headed concubine' and 'a mahogany coloured charmer'. In one article he stated, 'If eight thousand white men in Virginia followed Jefferson's example you would have FOUR HUNDRED THOUSAND MULATTOES in addition to the present swarm. The country would no longer be habitable'.

However, it all started to backfire on Callender. Jefferson refused to dignify the allegation with a response, Virginia society closed ranks, and even Callender's Federalist newspaper allies distanced themselves from him. One of the lawyers who had defended him in his sedition trial, George Hay, clubbed him severely in the street.

Hay then persuaded the judicial establishment to close his paper and file charges of libel against him. Callender was jailed again in 1803; this time the world of American politics breathed a sigh of relief.

Ten days after he was released from jail, Callender was seen in a state of extreme intoxication in the streets of Richmond. The following day his body was recovered from the James River. Some said he had fallen into three feet of water and been too drunk to get back up. Others suggested he had committed suicide.

It was a suitably melancholy end to a joyless life, and to a relatively short but bitter and tempestuous chapter in American political history. Callender had been in the country for only 10 years and during that time he had turned his journalistic guns on anyone who crossed his path, especially if he stood to gain financially. Precious few in the U.S. mourned his passing.

From that day to this the story of Sally Hemings – Black Sal as Callender called her – has resounded in the corridors of power of the United States. Despite DNA tests and several witnesses claiming Jefferson as an ancestor, no definitive proof has ever been forthcoming.

Abigail Adams, who had once been beguiled by Jefferson's flirty manner, wrote to him after the Sally Hemings revelation saying, 'The serpent you cherished and warmed, bit the hand that nourished him, and gave you sufficient specimens of his talents, his gratitude, his justice, and his truth'.

Callender, she said, had published 'the basest libel, the lowest and vilest slander, which malice could invent, or calumny exhibit' against her husband. For his part, John Adams said, 'I believe nothing that Callender said any more than if it had been said by an infernal spirit. I would not convict a dog of killing sheep upon the testimony of two such witnesses'.

There are some who feel Callender has a positive place in history, that he published one of the greatest 'scoops' of all time only to be vilified for telling the truth. Most historians, however, regard him as a drunken guttersnipe, lacking any moral fibre, who had simply repeated as fact Virginia bar-room gossip.

The founding fathers Callender vilified wrote a nation's Constitution that is followed more than 300 years later. Every American can quote from it. The bitter vitriol that spilled from Callender's pen has largely faded into obscurity. Yet the trash journalism that he perfected persists to this day.

Decency and political correctness dictate that election campaigns nowadays will never stoop to the same level as 1800. But every U.S. politician now has to endure dirty tricks campaigns, attacks on their personalities and intrusions into their private lives – that is the undying legacy of James Thomson Callender.

8

William Dunbar

Two Negroes ran away but were catched & brought back...Condemned them to receive 500 lashes Each at 5 Dift. Times, & to carry a chain & log fixt to the ankle. Poor Ignorant Devils; for what do they run away?

– Excerpt from William Dunbar's diary.

In the pantheon of scientific greats who influenced 18th century America, the name of William Dunbar shines like a beacon. He excelled in many fields of pioneering study and was widely recognised as a genius by his peers.

As an astronomer and explorer Dunbar ranks among the elite and exotic characters of the Revolutionary era men of science who left an indelible mark on a region of the new land far from the civilised seats of power; an untamed and uncharted wilderness, described by one historian as a 'raw, half-savage world'.

Dunbar's name may not be as familiar as many of his scientific contemporaries but his contributions were spread over several fields of expertise and his home became a gathering place for fellow scholars. Astronomy and natural history were his passions, although he also published works and made advances in the realms of archaeology, hydrostatics, anthropology, linguistics, geography and climatology.

At the behest of President Thomas Jefferson, himself a man of considerable scientific pedigree, Dunbar led a three-month exploration of some of the most rugged and dangerous territory in America, and returned with masses of scrupulous, authentic data including geological surveys and flora and fauna analysis. He was the first man to produce a detailed report of the famed hot springs of Arkansas, the water of which is said to possess medicinal properties and now forms a U.S. National Park.

Dunbar was one of many great minds who came together in America in the latter half of the 18th century. The most influential was Benjamin Franklin whose many inventions included the lightning rod. Dr. Benjamin Rush made great strides in medical science; astronomer Dr. David Rittenhouse built telescopes for the U.S. military during the War of Independence; and Charles Wilson Peale was a natural history pioneer.

Among those with whom Dunbar mingled at his frontier home were the renowned American naturalist William Bartram and ornithologist Alexander Wilson, a Scot who had journeyed to America from his home in Paisley.

Dunbar was elected as a member of the American Philosophical Society. Although he never met Jefferson he corresponded with him for several years. In a letter of introduction, the Irish-born U.S. consul for New Orleans, Daniel Clark, wrote to Jefferson that 'for Science, Probity and general information, he (Dunbar) is the first Character in this part of the World'.

The leading American surveyor Andrew Ellicott, one of the country's foremost scientists of the time, described Dunbar as 'a gentleman whose extensive information and scientific acquirements would give him a distinguished rank in any place or in any country'.

The journey that Dunbar completed before he was afforded scientific recognition was lengthy and arduous. He travelled from his home in the north-east of Scotland to London, crossed the Atlantic and settled for a time in Pennsylvania. He then sailed down the great Ohio and Mississippi Rivers until he reached the Gulf of Mexico. It was there, in the feral and uncultivated lands of the Deep South, that his genius came to the fore.

Dunbar came from a wealthy, landed Scottish aristocratic family whose roots dated to the 10th century. He was a studious child who went on to gain a university degree. He was a true product of the great intellectual, cultural and scientific movement known as the Scottish Enlightenment. When he left his home in 1770 he headed to England and mixed with the young intellectuals of genteel London society.

His achievements in what became an Age of Enlightenment in America should have come as no surprise. He was a highly intelligent and forward thinking individual who left behind a vast body of work. What is perplexing is that the memory of the man and his deeds had, until recently, faded into relative obscurity.

But his scientific prowess was only one side of his personality. There was another side to William Dunbar, a darker side that historical records rarely mention. He was one of many 'gentlemen' immigrants, people of wealth who found themselves in the New World with its developing sense of identity and its newly-founded institutions.

The men who, like Dunbar, gravitated towards America's Deep South, banded together and immersed themselves in plantation society. The vast acres they took possession of were used to cultivate products such as tobacco, rice, indigo and of course cotton. Dunbar's land was on the banks of the Mississippi River and he operated as part of a culture – an institution – that has defined American history since its earliest days: Negro slavery.

One story encapsulates Dunbar's disposition towards slaves. In 1780 he presided over the case of a female slave who had fought with and killed a white girl on a nearby estate. The Scotsman, complete with his enlightened views and university education, decided that as a white female had died at the hands of a black, there should be absolutely no mercy – the girl should feel the full force of planter law.

Cases such as this routinely ended in hanging. However, Dunbar was of the mind that an example should be made of this wretch. His sentence was that the girl, Molly Glass, should 'have her hand cut off and afterwards hanged until she is dead'. In other words, a punishment of 'more than death' was appropriate for a black female killer; she should be made to suffer agonising pain, to be left screaming in anguish, before the rope was tightened round her neck.

Fellow members of his plantation society circle doubtless approved of and applauded Dunbar's sentencing. It was seen as entirely correct to remind rogue black slaves that their wealthy white masters would not tolerate such lawless behaviour, especially if the victim was white. If the method of punishment seemed brutish and repugnant to certain sections of society, then so be it.

The incident epitomises Dunbar's attitude to the slaves who helped him build his plantation empire in the wild lands of Louisiana and Mississippi. He was by no means the worst slave owner in American history, although he regarded the Negroes not as humans but as chattels and pieces of property to be bought and disposed of, to be treated harshly if they stepped out of line.

In his book, *William Dunbar: Scientific Pioneer of the Old Southwest*, Arthur DeRosier writes, 'As one who has studied Dunbar's life and admired his ethical principles, I am surprised at his failure ever to criticise the institution of slavery and his willingness to punish slaves severely.

'He seldom wrote kindly about a slave – even those tending his wife and children – and he never freed one for meritorious service. By the standards of the time, Dunbar did not mistreat slaves, nor did he impose upon them cruel rules to obey. He just did not treat them as fellow human beings'.

Anyone who has seen the film *12 Years a Slave* – based on a true story – will doubtless have winced at the scenes of torture and depravity it contained. To those of us with the good fortune to have been brought up in a comparatively civilised society, it portrays behaviour that is inhuman and barbaric.

The plantations yielded horrific stories of vicious masters who took pleasure in raping and sodomising the slaves who worked for them. They physically abused Negroes, often branding or flogging them. On the other hand, not every slave owner was cruel. There were some who took lovers – in the true sense of the word – from the female slave population, raised children with them, freed them and left them an inheritance.

And not every slave in America was black. White people, many from Scotland, came to the U.S. as so-called indentured servants. Like their Negro counterparts, they were beaten and even forbidden from marrying. However, unlike the blacks, they came with a contract that stated they must be freed once they had completed their term of service. The black people were not so lucky – thousands were slaves for life.

From the surviving records of Dunbar and the plantation owners who made up his inner circle, there seems to be no evidence that they enjoyed or relished the brutal punishment they inflicted on their slaves, or that they could be categorised as sadists. They appear to have believed it was their duty; their way of keeping order in a society largely of their own creation.

There is also no suggestion that Dunbar ever sexually or physically abused any of his slaves, but he was without doubt a hard taskmaster whose punishments were brutal and often exceeded the crime. Written records show that he hanged slaves without remorse, and had them whipped, lashed, and chained or shackled by the hands or feet.

He even had a special wooden structure known as the Bastille built on his property. It was a place of confinement, effectively a dungeon, for errant slaves who were awaiting their fate. Dunbar would leave them there, often in shackles, with little or no food and drink.

For a man of such great intellect, who possessed a logical and orderly scientific brain, his behaviour seems, with the benefit of hindsight, out of place. It seems incongruous – even illogical – that he apparently accepted that a race of privileged and wealthy white people were in every way superior to members of a black society who had been captured and enslaved. Yet in the culture and psyche of southern America where Dunbar found himself in the late 1700s, the belief that black people were inferior in all respects was deeply ingrained. Scientific genius or not, he bought into it.

He was born into immense privilege in November 1749 at Duffus House, his family's ancestral home near Elgin. His father was Sir Archibald Dunbar, 4th baronet of Northfield and Duffus, a man of considerable standing and influence among the landed gentry in Morayshire. There were several strands of the Dunbar family – Sir Archibald originally came from an estate called Kilbuiack – and in the 17th and 18th century they were the principal landowners in the area between Elgin and the coastal village of Burghead.

Sir Archibald's first wife was also his first cousin, Helen Dunbar, the daughter of his paternal uncle. The couple married in 1735, had four children, three boys and a girl, and Sir Archibald became heir to his father-in-law's family seat, Thunderton House in Elgin. The sons, Archibald, Robert and Alexander, were by all accounts typical young aristocrats who enjoyed the pursuits of hawking, fishing, drinking and carousing, much like their father.

The first of several family tragedies struck in 1748 when Helen died. Sir Archibald married again in 1750, this time to Anne Bayne, the daughter of a nobleman from Northumberland. She was more than 30 years his junior and William was the first-born of their children. One of his brothers, Thomas, rose to the rank of major-general in the British Army and served in various parts of the world, including the West Indies.

William was raised at Thunderton House and was a serious, thoughtful and academic child, in stark contrast to his three half-brothers. His father was scornful of the studious boy and did nothing to encourage him, and as a result he became extremely close to his mother. She impressed upon young William that his privileged, upper crust background would count for nothing unless he had a first-class education. She arranged for him to be taught at home by private tutors and it was through her efforts that he gained a place at King's College University in Aberdeen, one of the finest seats of learning in Scotland.

In 1862, when William was 12, his two eldest half-brothers, Archibald and Robert, passed away within a month of each other. Archibald died while serving with the Highland Battalion in Madras, India, while Robert died of an illness at the estate in Duffus. Both were in their 20s, unmarried, and their deaths cast a dark shadow over the family.

The following year William left for university. He was particularly interested in natural history, thanks to the nurturing of his mother, and he emerged four years later with a Master of Arts degree. Life in the city of Aberdeen – just 20 years after the 1745 Jacobite Rebellion – must have been vibrant, invigorating and politically stimulating for a young impressionable student. Elgin, by comparison, must have seemed a small rural market town.

Mid-18th century Scotland witnessed a wave of intellectual, scientific and literary achievements that have never been surpassed. The Scottish Enlightenment saw some of the greatest thinkers, economists, philosophers, architects, sociologists and writers the world has ever produced come together to challenge established authority through rational and intellectual reasoning. It was an era that coincided with the end of the Scottish Parliament in 1707, and the writing and reasoning that emerged continues to have a huge global impact to this day.

The country's university campuses were buzzing with names of the great Enlightenment figures such as physician Joseph Black, philosopher Frances Hutcheson, founder of the School of Common Sense Thomas Reid, geologist and naturalist James Hutton, and architect Robert Adam.

When William Dunbar was studying at King's College, the economic pioneer Adam Smith was preparing to publish his seminal work *The Wealth of Nations*; free-thinking philosopher David Hume had completed his book *A Treatise of Human Nature*; Adam Ferguson's *Essay on the History of Civil Society* was about to hit the streets; and a young Robert Burns was putting pen to paper and producing his early poetical offerings.

Dunbar was at the heart of this great movement as it developed and grew into the most influential period in Scotland's history. He truly was one of the children of the intellectual revolution, a product of the Scottish Enlightenment.

Interestingly – given Dunbar's later connection with the slave trade – the values preached by the Enlightenment's central figures included virtue and 'practical benefit for the individual and the whole of society'.

After graduating from King's College, Dunbar returned to Elgin to continue his studies, but in 1769 his father passed away while visiting London. Sir Archibald's death meant William's surviving half-brother Alexander inherited the rights to all the family estates and succeeded to the baronetcy of Northfield and Duffus.

William had been left only a few hundred pounds in his father's will; he had never been close to Alexander, the new baronet, and as a young man with no shortage of ambition, he saw little point in staying on at the family estate. After bidding his mother a fond farewell he packed up his belongings and headed for London.

As a young aristocrat, Dunbar was undoubtedly made welcome among the London gentry. Not much is known about his stay there, the people he mingled with or how his education was advanced. There is no question, however, that his acquaintances were, like himself, people of privilege, and that he was exposed to a slice of life among the London upper-class. But he suffered from ill-health and decided not to stay long in the city. In 1771, at the age of 21, William Dunbar embarked on a voyage to New York, with the prospect of a new and exciting life ahead.

Upon arrival in New York, Dunbar headed straight for the most important and influential city in the colonies: Philadelphia. There he met with a wealthy merchant and fellow Scotsman, John Ross, and the two formed a business partnership. It may be that the meeting had been pre-arranged through a third party in either Scotland or America; it seems highly unlikely that the arrival of such a well-bred son of the Scottish aristocracy had gone unheralded in America.

Ross, who was 23 years older than Dunbar, had been born in Tain in Easter Ross. He had spent much of his early life in Perth, where he worked as a merchant before making the move across the Atlantic in 1763 and settling in Philadelphia. There he had prospered as a shipping merchant, and with revolution in the air, had espoused the cause of American patriotism.

He was a powerful figure in the city and an excellent contact for Dunbar. Ross was a fervent capitalist and taught the young man many lessons about the hard-nosed world of business – the need for detailed record-keeping and the wisdom of dealing only with men he trusted – which Dunbar never forgot.

While in London, Dunbar had bought goods for trading with the often hostile Indians, and after a long trek he exchanged them in the settlement of Fort Pitt, now Pittsburgh, in western Pennsylvania. But rather than casting their eyes westward, like many people of the generation, Dunbar and Ross were looking south at the riches that lay in the barren and inhospitable lands of what is now Louisiana and Mississippi.

The two men agreed to find a tract of land on which to establish a plantation and the adventurous Dunbar was perfectly happy to make the long journey. He set off from Fort Pitt on a flat bottomed boat and sailed along the Ohio River until it joined the Mississippi in southern Illinois. He then headed south towards New Orleans and the Gulf of Mexico. Within two years of arriving in America, the quiet, bookish, well-heeled Scot was proving to be not just an intellectual with a head for business, but also a daring and intrepid individual, and a force to be reckoned with in colonial America.

Dunbar selected a piece of land near the mouth of the Mississippi River as the spot for his new plantation. The area was then part of British West Florida, and the site he chose was close to a settlement then known as Fort New Richmond. Today it is the Louisiana state capital of Baton Rouge. It showed wise and considered judgment on Dunbar's part, for the Mississippi River and the relatively fertile land on both banks were to provide an ideal base for his business enterprises and his scientific studies.

He then travelled to the city of Pensacola where the governor of British West Florida, Peter Chester, granted him permission to settle the land he had chosen. However, the next stage of his journey took him away from the American mainland and introduced him to the murky world of slave trading. Dunbar sailed to Jamaica, home to hundreds of thousands of black African slaves and dozens of huge sugar plantations, many of them owned by wealthy Scottish merchants such as Archibald Campbell from Argyll, Charles Stirling from Glasgow, and George Forbes of Aberdeen.

Dunbar sailed back to his new estate with a 'large number of slaves' who were said to have come 'direct from Africa'. There is no account of him ever having fretted in any way about his involvement in slavery; in fact, everything points to him having taken to the business like a duck to water.

The slaves who laboured in the fields of Jamaica were treated notoriously badly, and in recent years Scotland, in particular Glasgow, has been forced to confront its involvement in the episode. Not only were Scots among the most brutal of plantation owners, but Scottish vessels sailed from Glasgow and elsewhere, collected slaves from West Africa and delivered them to the Caribbean or the east coast of America.

Dunbar, as an intelligent man, was by now perfectly well aware of the slavery issue. Yet he never questioned the need for slaves or suggested an alternative; he seems to have regarded slaveholding as something of a privilege. As DeRosier writes, 'The sad truth is that William Dunbar, one of the leading lights in the Mississippi Territory, was not an anti-slavery leader…slaves were property to be bought and sold, with no more rights than cotton gins, scientific equipment, or land'.

Historian Bernard Bailyn echoes the sentiment in his book *Voyagers to the West*. He writes: 'In July 1776 he [Dunbar] recorded not the independence of the American colonies from Britain, but the suppression of an alleged conspiracy for freedom by slaves on his own plantation.'

In 1776 Dunbar's meticulously-kept diary records that he had 14 slaves – seven men and four women working in the fields, and three women in the house. The outdoor work was gruelling; most of the slaves were employed working with timber and producing thousands of wooden staves every week to be shipped to the sugar plantations of Jamaica. The others planted crops including indigo, corn, rice and peas.

The climate was hot and humid in the summer and endlessly cold in the winter, yet the slaves were kept out in all weathers, often becoming sick. They were plagued by mosquitos, and the swamps they worked in were infested with alligators and snakes. It was a marginally better life than the brutal regime of Jamaica but it was still a desperate and hostile place.

That year (1776) two female slaves, Bessy and Ketty, ran away from Dunbar's estate. He wrote that they had 'received a little correction the former evening for disobedience'. Ketty returned the following day, having found conditions too rough in the wild, although Bessy was missing for a week before arriving back at the plantation. Whether she was captured or came back voluntarily is not known.

Dunbar was furious with Bessy. He decided she had to be severely punished for having the audacity to desert her duties and her master. His diary records that he 'ordered the Wench Bessy out of Irons & to receive 25 lashes with a Cow Skin as a punishment & example to the rest'.

A cowskin, or rawhide, whip was a barbaric instrument and the 'weapon of choice' among planters and their overseers in the fields. It was generally three feet long and one inch thick, tapering to a point and made of untanned dried ox hide. The first blow resulted in the skin being left gashed and bleeding and every blow thereafter simply lacerated the skin deeper and deeper. Slaves were left in unspeakable agony, and many suffered shock, infection and internal bleeding. They bore the scars of their beatings, externally and internally, for the rest of their lives.

The African-American social reformer and statesman Frederick Douglass, who was born into slavery in Maryland, described the cowskin as 'a terrible instrument'. He added, 'I think this whip worse than the "cat-o'nine- tails". It condenses the whole strength of the arm to a single point and comes with a spring that makes the air whistle.'

The 25 lashes that poor Bessy received was not regarded as excessive – some male Negroes were whipped 100 times in one 'sitting' – but it must have been a hellish ordeal for her. She would have been stripped either naked or to the waist, her hands tied before her with a rope. The rope would have been passed over a beam and drawn up until she was standing on her tiptoes, and her legs would then have been tied together.

In most cases the plantation overseer administered the flogging, which was invariably a 'public event', intended to dissuade other slaves from straying out of line. The slaves compelled to watch were forbidden from raising a word in protest or a hand to help the wretched victim, even when they were cut from the whipping post and left writhing on the ground in agony.

After 25 lashes of the whip, Bessy's body would have been a mass of scars, slashes and welts, with cuts and lesions so deep that blood would have been flowing in streams down her back and legs, forming in pools at her feet. The woman's flesh would quite simply have been torn to shreds and her screams must have pierced the air. It was a harsh and inhuman physical and mental torture.

This was how the intelligent, university-educated young aristocrat from Morayshire responded when one of his chattels dared to defy him. Another slave 'challenge' tested his resolve that same year, the 'alleged conspiracy' referred to in Bailyn's book.

In mid-summer, Dunbar had just returned from a three-week long trip when he was given a piece of news that 'appalled' him. Fellow planters informed him that a slave rebellion was being planned, and that three of the conspirators were slaves on Dunbar's estate at New Richmond. He wrote in his diary: 'Judge my surprise! Of what avail is kindness & good usage when rewarded by such ingratitude.'

When his errant slaves were identified, Dunbar wrote a telling sentence, one that gives an insight into the treatment a slave on his plantation could have expected. It read, 'Two of the three had never before misbehaved and never once received a stroke of the whip'. The implication was clear: the whip was a common instrument of punishment on the estate.

 Two other rebellious slaves were identified – the informers were slaves belonging to another Scottish planter and close neighbour of Dunbar, Alexander Ross – and they were rounded up for what would loosely be described as a trial. It was to be held at a plantation in Natchez, a few miles up the Mississippi from Baton Rouge.

Dunbar described in his diary how he was helping transport one of the slaves by boat. The man had his arms and feet bound, he was sitting at the bottom of the small vessel and according to Dunbar 'stung with the heinousness of his guilt, ashamed

Left: Sketch of Natchez, Mississippi, as it looked in the 1850s
Right: Marker in Natchez commemorating Dunbar's scientific achievements

perhaps to look a master in the face'. When the boat was in the middle of the river, the slave suddenly threw himself overboard and drowned in the strong currents.

That, at least, was the official version. Dunbar recorded in his diary that the slave's actions were 'sufficient evidence of his guilt'.

The four remaining rebellion leaders were all hanged after a 'solemn' trial. A number of others who had been on the fringes of the conspiracy were given floggings upon returning to their plantations. In a demonstration of how skewed Deep South society was in favour of the landed white man, the owners who had 'lost' the hanged slaves were all given compensation of no more than £100 per felon by an official known as the receiver-general.

Slaves who ran away were often given extremely harsh sentences, sometimes hanging. In May 1777, two of Dunbar's workers escaped but were captured and returned by a hunting party.

This time he wrote in his diary: 'Two Negroes ran away but were catched & brought back...Condemned them to receive 500 lashes Each at 5 Dift. Times, and to carry a chain & log fixt to the ankle. Poor Ignorant Devils; for what do they run away? They are well dressed, work easy, and have all kinds of Plantation produce at no allowance...After a slighter Chastisement than was intended they were set again at liberty and behave well.'

To even think of sentencing them to 500 lashes could hardly be described as the act of an enlightened man. Rather, it was the betrayal of an ingrained attitude that regarded slaves as less than human, objects to be ill-treated at will. The 'slighter chastisement' he wrote of likely involved fewer lashes of the whip than originally envisaged. Five hundred strokes of the dreaded cowskin could have – and frequently did on some plantations – lead to death.

Dunbar's protestation that his slaves were reasonably well-clothed and fed had some substance to it. He provided each slave with a small plot of land, Negro men got a pair of shoes, a pair of trousers and a jacket, and women received a pair of shoes, a petticoat and a jacket.

His diary entries, however, reveal that he constantly referred to them in disparaging terms. Often he called them 'ignorant savages' or 'stupid savages' and 'a set of worthless servants'. He never showed any concern for their well-being or compassion when one died, instead lamenting the financial loss. It was a matter of regret that the slave could no longer be traded for whatever he or she was thought to be worth.

In 1780 a slave called Cato, described as 'the most likely negro upon the plantation', died from severe colic pains after working outside in bad weather. Dunbar treated the death as though he had lost a valuable possession. He wrote that 'a new negro being a Natural died' and added that he would have fetched a good price at market.

Dunbar was by all accounts a very sociable man whose company was regularly sought by his planter companions. He is said to have possessed a 'wry sense of humour, jokes, and a convivial manner', and was one of the mainstays of a frontier social club whose members dined alternately at each other's homes. The men of wealth would 'get merry by the moderate use of madeira and claret'.

Alcohol was, however, out of bounds to the slaves on Dunbar's plantation. In 1777 a Negro called Adam was found in a drunken state. Again Dunbar was furious and resolved to make an example of the man, he wrote: 'Adam was found to be drunk upon which I ordered him to be confined in the Bastille, Ordered him 500 lashes next day, in order to draw a Confession from him how he came by the Rum.'

When Adam sobered up he admitted he had stolen the rum. He didn't get 500 lashes, he most likely got a few whips of the cowskin across his back, but he was left in the Bastille in chains until his leg became so swollen he was unable to work. Dunbar then took him to market and sold him.

For 10 years Dunbar stayed at the New Richmond plantation, but when the Spanish reclaimed West Florida in 1783 as part of the Treaty of Paris that ended the American Revolutionary War, he found his land was under Spanish rule. He moved to the city of Natchez in what is now Mississippi, where he purchased a 1,000-acre plantation he named The Forest.

In 1785 he married Dinah Clark, from Whitehaven in the north-west of England, and the couple raised nine children. As Dunbar was away so often on field trips and scientific explorations, his wife was left for long spells to take control of the plantation in Natchez.

Dunbar was developing a reputation for his scientific achievements among his friends in the Deep South, and turned his hand to invention. In 1800 he finalised the invention of a screw press for the square baling of cotton. It was, at the time, an incredible piece of technology and it had the effect of cementing cotton as Mississippi's 'white gold', and ensuring that the slave trade endured for several decades longer. This followed the invention of the cotton gin, a machine that separated cotton fibres from their seeds, by American Eli Whitney in 1793, which had already revolutionised the cotton industry and led to a massive increase in the slave trade in places like Mississippi and Louisiana.

The city of Natchez became part of the United States in 1798, meaning that since arriving in America, Dunbar had lived under three flags – those of Britain, Spain and the U.S. During the plantation era the city was home to more millionaires than anywhere else in the country, including Philadelphia, Boston, or New York. That wealth was generated almost exclusively from cotton and the slave trade.

Dunbar became the 'most extensive and successful planter' engaged in the cotton trade in Natchez. He wrote that cotton was by far the 'most remunerative staple' that had been raised in the country. His success as a plantation owner and his growing renown as a scientist made him one of the most respected members of Natchez society.

From the early 1790s onwards he devoted himself more and more to scientific work and undertook a dazzling array of projects. As well as astronomy and the natural world he also studied Indian sign and tongue languages, fossilisation, and meteorology. He even reported the possible sighting of a UFO near Baton Rouge in 1800. He had one of the first telescopes in Mississippi and near his Natchez home he built an astronomical observatory.

In 1804 Thomas Jefferson asked him, along with fellow Scot George Hunter, to lead a scientific expedition up the Red River as part of the exploration of the recently-acquired Louisiana Purchase from France. Trouble with the Osage Indian tribe led to the trip being shortened, although a great deal of scientific data was still collected during the three months the party was away.

But his treatment of slaves never improved as he aged. In 1807 he wrote to a fellow planter that a runaway slave called Aquilla would receive a 'severe chastisement' when he was recaptured. He stated that Aquilla was a 'finished rascal' and added, 'I will make him declare under the lash what he has done'.

Right up until his death at The Forest in 1810, a month short of his 60th birthday, Dunbar was still buying and selling slaves, a process that meant individual slaves were sold to the highest bidder, with the inevitable break-up of Negro families. He was even instructing merchants the specific African tribes from which he wanted his slaves to have originated.

There is no question William Dunbar was a brilliant man. His achievements were incredible and it is right that he is remembered as one of the most remarkable and ingenuous pioneering Scots that ever made it to the New World. One historian described him as 'a renaissance man in the image of Benjamin Franklin' while another classed him as 'a giant in an age of giants'.

There are many other sentiments in a similar vein, all suggesting a man who has perhaps become a forgotten intellectual. Yet it is equally without question that Dunbar's legacy is stained by his acceptance of slavery and treatment of the Negro slaves under his control.

Perhaps his aristocratic birth and upbringing in Scotland had taught him to look down on those less fortunate than himself; it may be that he simply 'followed the crowd' when he arrived in America, a country where the ownership of black slaves was routine; or perhaps his business mind recognised that cheap black labour would increase the likelihood of profits.

There is one other theory for what drove Dunbar to treat slaves the way he did. In Scotland he was the fourth son of an aristocrat, and as such was highly unlikely to inherit anything. It left him as something of a blue-blooded misfit, without any locus in the high society circles he craved. However, as a young patrician transplanted to America in the 1700s, no matter how far down the pecking order he was, commanded instant respect and awe.

Bailyn, in *Voyagers to the West*, suggested that Dunbar was 'feeling within himself a sense of authority and autonomy he had not known before, a force that flowed from his absolute control over the lives of others, he emerged a distinctive new man, a borderland gentleman, a man of property in a raw, half-savage world'.

In other words, he went from aristocratic Mr. Nobody in Scotland to a figure at the epicentre of a powerful societal structure in the American Deep South. It was a society that he, as a man of privilege, helped create and one that was in his interests to help sustain. The fate of his slaves – his human chattels – was no more than a matter of collateral damage.

Dunbar's treatment of slaves is told in his own hand, by the entries in his diary documenting life on his plantations. He was by no means the worst slave master in America or even the Mississippi region. There were many Scottish plantation owners, slave traders and overseers who were far more brutal. But the fact remains that as a man of intelligence and with a scientific brain, he might have been expected to have acted with more compassion.

DeRosier, in *William Dunbar: Scientific Pioneer of the Old Southwest*, wrote: 'I have tried to understand his unqualified acceptance of an institution other educated southern men questioned during the period of his rise to economic power…but one reviewing the life of William Dunbar should not confuse any of his habits with democracy or a love for people…Dunbar never gave a thought to the less fortunate. He wore his standing in society as a badge that rightly belonged to him.'

It seems that Dunbar was content to turn his brilliant mind to some of the most complex scientific and mathematical questions of the day without ever considering the morals and ethics of his own behaviour, even as he ordered his slaves to be beaten, chained, hanged, or bought and sold like pieces of meat.

The truth is that William Dunbar, product of the Scottish Enlightenment, frustrated aristocrat turned successful cotton planter and slave owner, cared not a jot for the welfare of the pitiful, wretched African Negroes who came into his possession. They were simply belongings to be disposed of when they had outlived their usefulness.

9

Mary Garden

Suffice it to say that Mary achieved the success I predicted for her but her head was turned and she became almost inhumanly ungrateful

–Miss Garden's benefactress Florence Mayer

In the upper echelons of late 19th century Chicago society, Mrs. Florence Mayer occupied an elevated position. Her husband David had helped establish one of the grandest department stores in the rapidly-expanding and blossoming city, and the couple's residence was an elegant mansion set back from the shores of Lake Michigan. She was surrounded by the trappings of wealth.

The Mayers were part of the nouveau riche class which had established itself as a prominent feature of Chicago life while the city was being extensively rebuilt in the aftermath of the Great Chicago Fire. The blaze in October 1871 killed more than 300 people and was one of the worst disasters in American history. Most of the buildings in the densely-populated areas of the city were wooden and the inferno simply consumed them block by block. By the time the flames started to burn themselves out 24 hours later, the once bustling city resembled a wasteland.

Days later a city preacher, the Rev. Robert Collyer, stood among the ruins of his church building and told his congregation, 'Nature called the lakes, the forests, the prairies together in convention long before we were born, and they decided that on this spot a great city would be built'.

Mary Garden –
Library of Congress

The rebuilding effort was instant and revolutionary. Some of the era's greatest designers, including Frank Lloyd Wright and Louis Sullivan, transformed Chicago into one of the most modern and architecturally-ambitious cities in the world. It was the beating heart of the American industrial revolution, a centre of shipping, meat packing, mills and lumber yards, the biggest transport hub in the U.S. with more than 30 railroad lines entering the city, and the centre of the nation's advertising industry.

Thousands of enthusiastic and resourceful young men and women descended on Chicago in the wake of the fire, sensing opportunity. The dingy housing precincts that had been burned down were being replaced by affluent neighbourhoods and exotic homes. In 1873 the millionaire railroad engineer George Pullman had a mansion built to resemble the Palais Garnier Opera Theatre in Paris.

The tallest skyscrapers in the world were built to house stores and office buildings in 'new Chicago', and the city was dubbed the 'birthplace of modern architecture'. It was exciting, vibrant, the happening place to be for anyone possessed of an entrepreneurial spark.

For young ambitious David Mayer the Great Fire heralded great prospects. He had been born in Roth, a town in Bavaria, Germany, and was only an infant when he emigrated to New York with his parents and three older siblings. After spending six years in Richmond, Virginia, the family moved to Chicago when David was 13.

His father Henry was a relatively wealthy store owner and other family members were high achievers; David's brother Levy became one of the best known and most controversial lawyers in Chicago history. As a teenager David started work as a clerk in his father's company, and by the time he was 21 he had partnered with another German immigrant Leopold Schlesinger to establish a dry goods (or department store) business known as Schlesinger and Mayer.

In 1892 David married young society beauty Florence Blum in her home city of New York. He was 41; she was 20, the daughter of a French-born shirt manufacturer called Gottlieb or Gotcho Blum. He was a partner in the firm Moses, Blum and Weill that in the 1870s had patented 'The Best One Dollar Shirt in the United States'. Gotcho may not have been as wealthy or successful as the Mayers but he certainly knew how to market himself, and he must have been delighted at his daughter's marriage into such a prestigious Chicago family.

By the time he married Florence, David Mayer's firm owned one of the most upmarket department stores in downtown Chicago, and he was an extremely wealthy man. The couple lived in a large mansion house in the exclusive Kenwood neighbourhood in the south side of the city; they were an upwardly-mobile couple, and she was an intelligent, enchanting and charming member of the city's cultured elite, one of the belles of Chicago's fashionable society.

Florence threw herself into upper-class Chicago lifestyle with ease. She bore her husband three sons and a daughter. The 1900 census records that her widowed mother Nettie, sister Adele and brother Walter were living with her and David. The Mayers also had six servants from various parts of the world including England, France, Sweden and Finland.

Chicago in the late 19th century was a theatre-lover's paradise. One of the joys of David and Florence Mayer's lives was to encourage young singers and musicians and help them reach their full potential. Florence in particular became a noted patron of the Chicago arts scene and lavished money on budding young musical talent.

Among Florence's closest acquaintances was the noted Chicago theatre impresario Will J. Davis. He told her of a young red-haired female concert singer who he had heard performing after a dinner at Chicago's Union League Club. She had sung *My Old Dutch*, a Cockney vaudeville music hall song written in 1892 by Albert Chevalier. Afterwards, Davis approached the rather shy young woman and half-jokingly told her that if she put on a coster suit (worn by fruit and veg sellers in old London) she would be a great vaudeville success.

Florence, who was still a relative newlywed, was persuaded to hear the young woman sing at the rooms of her musical tutor Sarah Robinson-Duff. It was made clear that if she was to progress up the musical ladder, the girl needed financial support.

When Florence Mayer heard the girl's voice she was utterly enchanted. She told her husband that nurturing such a talent would not only be a wonderful investment opportunity, it would also thrust upon the world stage a classical singer in the mould of Dame Nellie Melba and the 'Swedish Nightingale', Jenny Lind, two of the 19th century's towering operatic stars.

As talent-spotting decisions go, it was a judgment that turned out to be absolutely flawless, for the singer in question was Mary Garden, who would go on to have a glorious career as one of the greatest operatic divas in American history. The Mayers saw Mary as their protégée, a talent to be nurtured, cared for and instructed until it was ready to burst forth upon a wider audience.

Mary Garden was not the first, nor was she the last, budding singing star to whom Florence and David Mayer gave encouragement. But she would turn out to be their greatest 'discovery'; she would become the most dazzling star in the American operatic firmament. It was a win-win situation; the young starlet was given an opportunity to shine while her patrons could bask in the reflected glory of having 'spotted' her. Mary certainly justified the leap of faith taken by the Mayers. They were always able to say they had kick-started Mary Garden's glittering career.

For better or worse, the connection between the wealthy Chicago socialites and the operatic diva was never severed; they were linked for the rest of their lives. Even when their obituaries were written, David and Florence Mayer were remembered as the arts aficionados who had taken Mary Garden, then a struggling choir singer, into their mansion home and set her on the path to musical stardom.

There must have been many times, however, when the couple wished they had never set eyes on her, let alone taken her under their wing. Rumours abounded that she had frittered away the couple's money while on a trip to Paris to advance her musical career, and that she had given birth to a 'secret' baby following an affair with a Frenchman. Headlines like these were scandalous in 1890s Chicago and the Mayers went to great lengths to establish the truth, spending many thousands of dollars in the process. However badly she might have been behaving, she was still their star student.

Eventually, critics were calling Mary 'the Sarah Bernhardt of opera', and her personal bank accounts bulged. She had clearly hit the big time. However, the more famous she became the less she recognised the debt she owed to her benefactors; where they might have expected gratitude, they received none. Instead, she gave the impression that Florence and David Mayer were somehow beneath her. After leaving the comfort of the couple's grand Chicago home, and having received thousands of dollars' worth of 'encouragement', she treated the Mayers as though they scarcely existed. She snubbed Mrs. Mayer in public and waged an unseemly war of words against her in the columns of the newspapers. She looked upon them as a pair of meddling pests who had outlived their usefulness; hangers-on who were trying to cash in on her new-found fame and fortune.

Mary Garden had come to America as a young girl from her home in Aberdeen, a port city on the east coast of Scotland. She mixed with the musical and theatrical greats of the day including Claude Debussy and Samuel Goldwyn, and the career she forged made her without question one of the greatest opera stars – perhaps the greatest – to ever emerge from Scotland.

But the manner in which she turned on her generous American benefactress, a woman who had showered her with the gifts of money, material possessions and opportunity, reeked of ingratitude, ungraciousness, callousness and a distinct lack of class. However wonderful her career may have been, Mary Garden's shabby treatment of Florence Mayer will forever be a stain on her character.

Mary's early life could hardly have been more different from the one she would eventually inhabit. Her family was not living in poverty by any means but her beginnings were undoubtedly humble. She was born on 20 February 1874, at 35 Charlotte Street, in the Woolmanhill area of Aberdeen, close to the city centre. Her parents, Robert Garden and Mary Joss, who was 17, had married only the previous month.

Robert Garden, five years older than his new wife, had been brought up in the Aberdeenshire countryside. His father, also Robert, farmed 100 acres at Bridgend, outside the village of Auchterless. Aberdeenshire was at the centre of the traditional fishing and farming area of north-east Scotland. It was a deeply religious part of the country, and having got the teenage Mary Joss in the family way, there would most certainly have been pressure on Robert to do the honourable thing and marry her.

The couple wed in Aberdeen's St Nicholas Parish on 8 January 1874, exactly 43 days before Mary Garden was born. Two younger sisters, Amy and Agnes (known as Aggie) followed and the family moved to a larger house at 41 Dee Street. A plaque on the building bears the inscription 'Mary Garden opera singer (1874–1967) lived in this house'.

The Granite City, as Aberdeen is known, was a busy, bustling place when Mary Garden was young. It was – and still is – the north of Scotland's chief seaport. Francis H. Groome, in his *Gazetteer of Scotland* published in the 1890s, remembered some of the cobbled lanes and courts near the city's Gallowgate as 'the dingiest and most unwholesome to be found anywhere in a British town'.

Groome was, however, 'enchanted' by Aberdeen's main thoroughfares, Union Street and Castle Street. He wrote of the city centre, 'It possesses all the stability, cleanliness and architectural beauties of the London west end streets, with the gaiety and brilliancy of the Parisian atmosphere'.

Mary Garden had fond memories of her first exposure to operatic music in the city as a young girl. In her biography, *Mary Garden's Story*, she wrote: 'I was still a tiny child when I was taken to the Music Hall in Aberdeen to hear a singer named Marie Roze. The hall still stands there, and even today I never go into it without feeling the thrill of that first contact with a stage personality. Mme Roze was a very handsome and majestic woman, and I shall never forget the way she sang *Ocean, thou mighty monster*. It was as if a new world had suddenly been unlocked for me.'

But in June of 1878, when Mary was just four, her father, a clerk in an Aberdeenshire ironworks, left Scotland for a new life in America with the intention of paving the way for his family to join him at a later date. He travelled to Liverpool and set sail for New York. Even though the separation was relatively short-lived, it must have been a heartbreaking time for the little girl. It would be almost four years before Robert Garden saw his family again.

The move also necessitated another change of address for Mary Garden, her mother and two sisters. They left Dee Street and moved in with her mother's parents, Patrick and Susan Joss, in a cramped house in the city's Guestrow. Mr. Joss, who hailed from Oldmeldrum in Aberdeenshire, worked as an agent for a local stone merchant.

Then in 1882, when Mary was eight, word came from across the Atlantic that Robert Garden had secured employment and accommodation and was making arrangements for his family to join him. In April the three girls and their mother made the trip from Glasgow to New York on the three-funnelled Anchor Line steamship *Anchoria*.

The family first settled in the Brooklyn district of New York then moved to the city of Chicopee, Massachusetts. After going back to Scotland for a holiday, where she learned to play the piano, Mary returned to the U.S. in 1888 when she was 14. Once again the family was on the move, this time to Chicago, where Mary was destined to find fame and fortune.

Chicago was still in the throes of massive post-fire redevelopment when she arrived – and two of the city's grandest buildings would have a profound impact on her life. The first was the massive Auditorium Building, now a National Historic Landmark. It was under construction when Mary arrived, opened in 1889 and contained a 4,200-seat theatre that would be the scene of many of her finest performances.

When Mary walked near the corner of Madison Street and State Street, she would have been impressed by the splendour and grandiosity of the massive Schlesinger and Mayer department store that stood there. David Mayer, her soon-to-be benefactor, was vice president of the company and one of the two men who had commissioned the great architect Louis Sullivan to design the building.

Mary Garden's musical education, when she got to Chicago, consisted of having learned to play the violin and the piano. Her mother had sent her to violin lessons at the age of six and dreamed that young Mary might one day become a soloist. But by 12 she had fallen in love with piano playing, and in particular the works of the Polish composer Frederic Chopin.

It was only when she turned 16 that she started taking singing lessons under the tutelage of Sarah Robinson-Duff. The theatre manager Will J. Davis, who was so entranced by her singing at the Union League Club dinner, remembered her as a 'timid, red-haired girl then scarcely out of short dresses'. However, by the time Florence Mayer came to listen to her, she was a mature choir member.

When the two women first met in Mrs. Robinson-Duff's studio in Chicago in 1894, Florence was 22 and married to a millionaire businessman, Mary was 20, single and struggling to make her way in the world. There was little to separate them by age but the worlds they lived in were poles apart.

Mrs. Mayer wrote that she was 'at once attracted and impressed with her charming personality and lovely voice'. She added, 'We became, as I thought, good friends'.

Two years later Mary's parents moved to Hartford, Connecticut, where her father embarked on a high-flying career of his own, leaving Mary behind to continue her musical studies in the Windy City. Mrs. Mayer then offered her a room in her large house so she could carry on with her lessons with Mrs. Robinson-Duff, whose reputation as a music tutor was growing.

Robert Garden had moved up the corporate ladder and found himself an executive job in the world of luxury cars. By the early part of the 20th century he had become president of the Harrolds Motor Car Company, the main agents for the famous Pierce-Arrow car range. In 1909, while Mr. Garden was at the helm of the company, President

William Taft ordered two Pierce-Arrows to be used for state occasions. These were the first ever official White House cars.

Back in 1890s Chicago young Mary was making the most of life amid the sumptuous surroundings of David and Florence Mayer's mansion home. She was flourishing as an operatic soprano; her tutor was enthusing over her progress. So too was Florence Mayer, and she felt her protégé's chance of making a breakthrough would be greatly enhanced if she spent some time in Paris, then the arts capital of the world.

Years later Mrs. Mayer wrote, 'I concluded to give her the advantage of two years' study in Paris. An additional year was added through the pleadings of Miss Garden. After that my responsibility and remittances ceased as this was one year longer than had been agreed to'.

Clearly Mrs. Mayer was treating Mary Garden partly as a young woman with star potential, and partly as a business proposition in which she could invest only a finite amount. She claimed it was made plain to Miss Garden that if her career took off as a result of Mrs. Mayer's largess, the money would have to be paid back.

The outlay was considerable, even for a couple with as much wealth as the Mayers. Not only was Miss Garden sent to Paris, so too was Mrs. Robinson-Duff, with the expectation that the musical lessons would continue in surroundings where art, music and culture were enjoying a massive renaissance. All travel, accommodation, food and necessary expenses were taken care of by the Mayers, who sent regular financial support from America to France.

Paris in the 1890s was at the epicentre of a cultural period in Europe that later became known as La Belle Époque, or the Beautiful Era. The Eiffel Tower had been built for the World's Fair in 1889; the Paris Metro was under construction; theatres and opera houses were packed for performances and the city was home to some of the greatest musical composers of all time including Camille Saint-Saens, Claude Debussy, Maurice Ravel, Jules Massenet, Erik Satie and Gabriel Faure.

It was exciting, romantic, scandalous, optimistic, elegant, fashionable, anarchic, decadent and liberating. Garden was a handsome and vivacious young woman with the world at her feet. She looked around her new city – and fell in love with everything.

Thanks to the generosity of the couple she would later refer to as 'those dreadful Mayers', the young budding songstress from Aberdeen was given the opportunity of a lifetime, one that others in the same situation could only dream of.

Garden embraced Parisian life as might be expected of a pretty 22-year old woman with no strings and a ready supply of money. Her singing lessons continued, she enjoyed nights at the opera, and her voice developed as Florence Mayer had predicted it would. There was no doubt she was a great singer, everyone who came into contact her agreed, but finding a 'gig' in a city where theatrical and musical greats from around the world had gathered was proving elusive.

She met many figures from the operatic world and became particularly friendly with fellow American diva Sybil Sanderson. By the 1890s Ms. Sanderson's life was in turmoil, her career was on the slide and she was battling depression and alcoholism. She would die of pneumonia a few years later at the age of 38. But for the few years they were acquainted the older woman greatly admired Garden and helped promote her cause.

Sybil Sanderson

There was of course a lot more for Garden to do in 19th century Paris than take operatic lessons. Reports reached Chicago that she had been seen frequenting restaurants with men and spending afternoons attending horse racing meetings, also in male company. Her lifestyle, according to the accounts that reached the ears of the Mayers and others in Chicago society, left a lot to be desired.

Scandal did not go down well in the snootier sections of Chicago – or any other American city for that matter. The word from Paris was disturbing but not salacious enough to warrant intervention, and Garden's excesses were tolerated – but only until the rumours grew too scandalous to be ignored. In 1899, three years after she left Chicago, came news that shocked everyone who knew her.

According to the Parisian grapevine, Garden had not been spending all her nights at the pension on rue Chaldrin that the Mayers were paying for. Instead, she had been shacking up with a man described as a Gascon drummer (possibly a slang term for a travelling salesman). To make matters one hundred times worse she had become pregnant and had given birth to an illegitimate baby boy.

The rumour mill was in full swing. Garden had not wanted the child, it was not in her game plan as an ambitious woman with a career ahead of her, the father was a ne'er-do-well, and the child had been given away, signed into the care of a French Catholic orphanage.

By all accounts the story was common currency in the American colony in Paris. Whether it was nailed-down truth or ill-informed scuttlebutt produced by Garden's rather decadent lifestyle has never been established. But when it reached the ears of those who mattered in upper-class Chicago society, it was scandal of the highest order.

A young lady bearing an illegitimate child was severely frowned upon in the late 1800s; giving away the baby was equally regarded as callous and unfeeling. If the back-fence talk from the French capital was true then Mary Garden would be seen not so much as a budding operatic superstar, but more as a 'fallen woman'.

The Mayers had to do something; at the very least they had to verify the truth or otherwise of the story. David Mayer was a cool-headed businessman who had built up a vast personal fortune, and his wife was a generous woman and very protective of her 'wards'. They were not the sort of couple to make a knee-jerk reaction based on gossip, no matter how prurient that gossip was.

But for Florence Mayer and Mary Garden, the fall-out from the episode would mark the end of their amicable relationship. Miss Garden always denied she had had a child; Mrs. Mayer always maintained in public that she thought the rumours were groundless. Nevertheless, the friendship between the two women evaporated; the affair drove a stake through the harmony and rapport that had grown up between them.

What happened next remains a matter for dispute. Two versions of events emerged; one favoured the diva, the other preferred the account of the benefactress. For those on the outside looking in, with a penchant for tasty gossip, it was all good knockabout stuff.

Florence Mayer's story was that the revelations about Garden's alleged baby surfaced in 1899, three years after she had sent Mary to Paris, and when her financial commitment to the singer's European musical education was due to end. She stopped the money at the agreed time which, she said, just happened to coincide with the scandal that engulfed her star student.

In a letter to the *Chicago Tribune* in 1909 Mrs. Mayer said certain reports had reached her while Miss Garden was in Paris, that she had them investigated and found them to be baseless. The first time she knew of reports that Miss Garden had given birth to a child was when she read them in a newspaper several years later, she claimed.

Miss Garden's account was quite different. She maintained that when Florence and David Mayer heard the stories of how she had been behaving, they stopped her money and had her thrown out of her Paris apartment and on to the street.

Jack Winsor Hansen, in his book *The Sibyl Sanderson Story: Requiem for a Diva*, states, 'Mr and Mrs David Mayer, Garden's wealthy sponsors in Chicago, had received some anonymous letters from Paris informing them that the girl had given birth to an illegitimate child. After the necessary inquiries they cut her off without a penny. Mary now owed more than a month's rent on the rue Chaldrin and the concierge was on the point of throwing her into the gutter'.

The truth was most likely somewhere in between. What is not in dispute is that Miss Garden's money from the Mayers ceased. One report suggested that the couple offered to buy the singer a ticket back to America on a steamship but that the offer was refused. Another account said Miss Garden's life was 'a desperate struggle for survival' for six months, that she had to sell her jewellery to survive and that she was living in a cheap upper-floor boardinghouse and down to her last few centimes.

The woman who came to her aid was her old operatic crony Sybil Sanderson. Although only in her mid-30s, Sybil's husband, Cuban sugar heir Antonio Terry had just died and she was drinking herself to distraction. She had, however, always liked

Garden, and once again the up-and-coming singer was offered the kindness of a room in a wealthy household, this time a grand townhouse in Paris.

As well as Ms. Sanderson, the only other person living in the house was her step-daughter, Natividad, known as Natica. She later married Guy de Faucigny-Lucinge, a high-ranking member of the Parisian peerage and later became the Princess de Lucinge.

For all the excellent tutoring work that had been done by Sarah Robinson-Duff, the person who gave Mary Garden her big break in Paris was Sybil Sanderson. She introduced the young Scots girl to the movers and shakers of the city's theatrical world and Garden's opportunity finally arrived in 1900 during a performance of the opera *Louise* by Gustave Charpentier in the city's Opera-Comique theatre.

The part of Louise was being sung by the soprano Marthe Rioton but it was clear she was unwell and her voice was unable to carry the part. Miss Garden had been studying the role and was hurriedly sent for. She got there half-way through the second act and was thrust into her debut role. When the curtain fell the audience went wild. She had given a bravura performance and the papers reported that she had 'taken Paris by storm'.

It was a meteoric rise to fame for the young woman from Aberdeen. One day she had been struggling to find a niche for her undoubted talent, the next she was the operatic darling of the most artistic city in the world. Mary Garden never looked back. She became known as 'La Petite Garden' and was recognised as much for the acting ability she brought to great operatic roles as for her actual singing.

However, she could never shake off the events of the three years she had spent there under the patronage of Florence and David Mayer, or the allegations that flowed from her behaviour during that time. Mrs. Mayer wrote that after her payment had ended in 1899 'a hostile feeling arose' towards her on the part of Miss Garden.

On the other hand, after the young soprano had made her breakthrough, Mrs. Mayer visited Paris several times and met Miss Garden on at least one occasion. There seemed to be no traces of any bitterness, she said. In fact, in an interview with the *Chicago Tribune*, she sang Miss Garden's praises.

Mrs. Mayer told the paper: 'She has grown to be more and more a Parisian, and she looks and dresses and talks and acts like one. Even her thought waves are Parisian, and she loves Paris so that she has not cared to return to America.' She even noted that 'money does not appeal to her'.

Garden returned to America at the invitation of theatrical producer Oscar Hammerstein I, the grandfather of the famous lyricist of the same name, to headline his newly-built Manhattan Opera House in New York. She became an instant success and within a year was a household name throughout America.

One night in December 1908 – a night when Miss Garden was not a member of the performing cast – Mrs. Mayer was in New York and took a box at the Manhattan to see a show. Minutes after sitting down, she heard the familiar voice of the young woman who she had taken under her wing more than a decade before and whose star was now soaring high.

The *Chicago Examiner* took up the story of what happened next: 'Suddenly, Mrs Mayer's face lit up with pleasure as she saw Miss Garden, with several friends, enter the box adjoining theirs…Mrs Mayer smiled at her and nodded…"she didn't see me", thought Mrs Mayer so she started up to greet and speak to Miss Garden.'

The newspaper report continued: 'Moving across to the partition between the two boxes, Mrs Mayer approached the place where Miss Garden had seated herself…Miss Garden turned around, stared full in the face of her benefactress, the Lady Bountiful of old Chicago days, then turned her back.'

It was an astonishing public snub. Mrs. Mayer was said to have returned to her seat and did not even glance in Garden's direction again for the rest of the evening. She later described the icy rebuff as 'so unwarranted, cruel and uncalled for'.

But when Florence Mayer regained her composure, she decided that the show of ingratitude – after the thousands of dollars she and her husband had showered on Mary – should not be allowed simply to pass. She consulted her lawyers and Miss Garden received a bill for $20,000 payable to the Mayers within one week. It was a full and final settlement of the debt she owed them for her three years in Paris.

Miss Garden, with help from her now wealthy father, paid up – she had little choice in the matter. The newspapers had an absolute field day and the affair was dubbed 'Mary Garden's $20,000 snub'. The *Chicago Examiner* headlined its story, 'Singer turned back on old friend at opera'.

Mrs. Mayer never got over the incident. After the lawsuit she said, 'I don't care to refer to the Paris trouble, much less publish it in the newspapers. Suffice it to say that Mary achieved the success I predicted for her but her head was turned and she became almost inhumanly ungrateful. I thought I could devote the money to a better cause and this I shall do'.

Miss Garden, interviewed at the same time, was less gracious. She said, 'It was only an unpleasant little episode and I have already forgotten about it'. She told a friend, 'It closed the book on my stupid indiscretion and got those dreadful Mayers off my back'.

It almost seemed as though the more famous she became, the more she wanted to expunge the couple and their generosity from her mind. The 'dreadful Mayers', as she so haughtily described them, had pointed her on the road to stardom. It is perfectly possible that, had Florence not taken such an interest in her, she might never have risen to the status of operatic superstar.

And the book never closed on her 'stupid indiscretion'. A few months later, on 25 March 1909, the arts critic of the *Chicago Daily News*, Amy Leslie, reported that while she was living in Paris, Mary Garden, by now a huge star of the Chicago opera scene, had had a baby out of wedlock. She added that Mr. and Mrs. Mayer's representative had visited the young singer and her child and – as a result of the meeting – had decided to cut off the regular allowance they had been sending her.

The article went on to say that the father of the child was a 'little, no-account Gascon drummer' or salesman. Miss Garden and the man had been living together and possibly married, she claimed.

Author Jack Winsor Hansen wrote, 'It is doubtful that Sybil (Sanderson) would have shared such confidential information about her protégée with any newspaper correspondent, but it would have been perfectly natural to tell her stepdaughter, which she did. Since the story was widely circulating throughout the American expatriate colony at the time, Leslie would have had no difficulty in picking up details of the twice-told gossip'.

Leslie later confirmed that her source had been Ms. Sanderson and that the account had been common knowledge in the American colony in Paris. She had never met Miss Garden, the father or the baby.

But the story set off a vicious response from Mary Garden. Without hesitation she turned her guns on her one-time benefactress and accused her in the pages of the newspapers of having been the source of Amy Leslie's story. She also flatly denied that she had ever given birth to a child.

Mrs. Mayer was forced to deny she was the source of the gossip and state that she did not believe Miss Garden had given birth to a child. She refused to make a public statement about the allegations but added, 'so many calumnies and perverted stories have been circulated' about it.

Garden never let these scandals disrupt her operatic career. She remained one of the greatest operatic divas in America until she retired from the stage in 1934, even spending a year as director of the Chicago Opera Association at a time when women rarely held such exalted positions.

Over the years she had long and bitter feuds with many musical colleagues, she was a notorious self-publicist, and she talked and wrote about her many affairs with men – some of which she later admitted were simply made up in order to provoke media attention.

She returned to her native Aberdeen and died in a nursing home in nearby Inverurie in January 1967. She had been suffering from dementia for several years. She is remembered in Scotland, especially her home city, as one of the country's greatest musical exports and someone whose life and achievements should be remembered with pride.

Even the poet Hugh MacDiarmid, in his epic work *A Drunk Man Looks at a Thistle*, mentions her with other artistic greats of the same time period. One of the verses reads:

> Heifetz in tartan, and Sir Harry Lauder!
> Whaur's Isadora Duncan dancin' noo?
> Is Mary Garden in Chicago still
> And Duncan Grant in Paris – and me fou?

She undoubtedly delighted theatre-goers in France and America. She forged an incredible musical career and the world of opera was certainly the better for her contribution. But no matter who was right or who was wrong in her ugly feud with the Mayers, the episode portrayed her in an extremely bad light; it was a black mark that made her appear unappreciative, self-centred and greedy.

Nowadays very few eyebrows would be raised at the revelation that an opera singer – or a singer in any genre – had become an unmarried mother. But in the 1890s it was a major scandal. In Mary Garden's case she was thick-skinned enough to be able to deny it, and refuse to allow the salacious press headlines to derail her career.

Mary Garden in 1954 - Library of Congress

Was the story true? Apparently it was common knowledge within the American community in Paris, although no-one is recorded as having ever clapped eyes on the child.

Leslie had no doubt it was true, but while she was a well-connected member of Chicago society herself, the fact she wrote for what might have been dubbed a 'scandal-rag' may have been enough to raise a question mark against her account.

There was, however, one person who had been with Mary Garden at the time the allegations first surfaced in Paris in the late 1890s. She had a clear recollection of the events and she had no apparent motive for lying or for twisting or embellishing the facts. In later years she was perfectly happy, without fear or favour, to give her version of the story.

Step forward Natividad Terry who, by the time she was interviewed by Jack Winsor Hansen, was the Princess de Lucinge. Natica, as she was known, had for several months shared a house in Paris with Mary Garden.

In the book *Requiem for a Diva*, the Princess said she was told by her stepmother to keep the story of Mary's illegitimate child confidential and that she never once mentioned it in Mary's presence.

She added, 'I'm sure she surmised that I knew…some years later, after she became such a big star, I occasionally wondered if that boy grew to manhood ever learning that Mary Garden was his real mother…Catholic orphanages in France keep very private records. When they are sealed, they're sealed for life.

'Years later I ran into her one night in Monte Carlo at the casino and reintroduced myself to her. When I recalled the delightful times the three of us had, she seemed so distant and aloof, as if she barely remembered me. I don't know if this act was prompted by not wanting to recall the painful circumstances under which Sibyl took her in, but if she hadn't Mary would have been forced to sell her body in order to survive.

'If Mary Garden ever owed her life to anyone, it was to Sibyl. Yet a few years later when Sibyl was desperate for money, I'm told she refused to lend her a sou.'

Believe who you will, but the Princess de Lucinge's few brief paragraphs perhaps reveal more about the character of Mary Garden than all the gushing theatre reviews and fawning newspaper articles ever did.

10

James Abercrombie

I really did not think that so great a share of stupidity and absurdity could be in the possession of any man

– Captain Charles Lee writing about the actions of
James Abercrombie at the Battle of Carillon

As humiliating British military defeats go, the chaotic retreat from Fort Ticonderoga was one of the worst. It takes its place among a long list of embarrassing military debacles stretching back centuries. In battles, skirmishes and sieges in far-off lands, the forces of the Crown have all too often conspired to turn potential victory into ill-starred and tragic defeat.

Britain's fascination with gaining an empirical foothold in every possible corner of the globe during the 17th, 18th and 19th centuries meant the nation was in an almost continuous state of war. Soldiering men from all over Britain – including the feared, kilted Highland regiments and the tartan-trewed Lowland Scots – were sent to fight in bloody theatres of war from mainland Europe to Africa, the Far East, North America and the battlefields of the Middle East.

They fought and died in countless military engagements in places far from their home towns and villages. In too many cases they paid with their lives due to the blundering incompetence of their superior officers. Time after time, these brave soldiers truly were 'lions led by donkeys', signing their own death warrants by unquestioningly

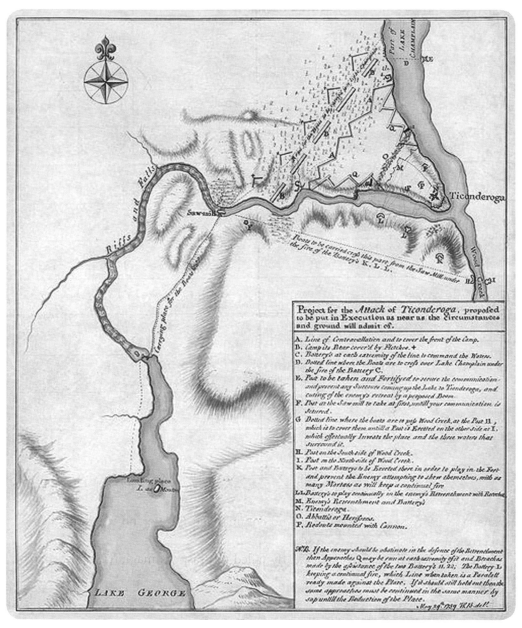

Map of Fort Ticonderoga and surrounding area in 1758

following cock-eyed battlefield orders given by men whose military credentials were often sadly lacking.

The list of inglorious defeat is lengthy: the Battle of Saratoga during the American War of Independence when 6,000 British troops were forced to surrender; the Battle of Isandlwana during the Zulu War when 1,200 British were killed; the massacre of Major

General Elphinstone's 16,000-strong command in the Afghan War in 1842; the botched Spion Kop offensive intended to relieve the Siege of Ladysmith during the Second Boer War; the disastrous Gallipoli Campaign of World War One.

In all cases they were characterised by the same failing: glaring leadership incompetence. Across the board, the majority of the men who paid the ultimate sacrifice were the ordinary army squaddies. The fiasco at Ticonderoga – or to give the conflict its proper name, the Battle of Carillon – was a classic case in point. Hundreds of battle-hardened soldiers, including men of the 42nd Highland Regiment, Black Watch, died needlessly as a direct result of preposterous leadership by a blustering arrogant commander who was hopelessly out of his depth.

Major General James Abercrombie made sure he remained a safe distance from the killing fields of Fort Carillon. He gave his foolish orders far from the front line as the bodies of his men piled higher. When the situation was beyond recall, the hapless leader known to his troops as Mrs. Nanny Crombie turned tail and fled the scene.

More than 2,000 men were killed or wounded before Abercrombie decided that retreat was the only option. It should have been a relatively straightforward victory, with the British and their American allies outnumbering the opposing French forces by five to one. Yet Abercrombie's plodding ineptitude and lack of military tact turned a winning situation into a devastating loss.

Abercrombie, born into a wealthy Scottish family, had not been appointed commander-in-chief of the British forces in North America for his outstanding military prowess and leadership skills. He had been given the job because of his many political connections in the United Kingdom. As a member of the country's ruling elite, he had been able to purchase an army commission, a practice that preserved the social exclusivity of the officer class.

Many of the men he commanded during the disaster at Fort Carillon, in northern New York, knew far better than he the dangers they faced, but could only look on in exasperated horror as Abercrombie, who commanded little or no respect, made one fatal error after another.

After the defeat, Abercrombie clearly failed to grasp its magnitude. In a letter to New York colonial governor James DeLancey, he wrote, 'We have not had the success we flattered ourselves with, and have lost a number of brave men, which I grieve and lament'. It was a message deliberately groaning with understatement to try to mask his deficiencies.

In his book, *The Epic Battles for Ticonderoga*, author and academic Dr. William R. Nester is blunt in his assessment of Abercrombie's performance in the field. He wrote, 'Being engulfed in the "fog of war" is inevitable for participants. Deliberately losing oneself in it, as Abercrombie did, is not'.

The Battle of Carillon took place in July 1758 at a crucial point in the French and Indian War, the name given to the North American theatre of the Seven Years' War.

France and Britain were locked in a fierce territorial battle in Britain's northern American colonies, with key campaigns being fought in Pennsylvania and New York. What is now eastern Canada, then part of a vast area known as New France, was a major strategic target for the empire-hungry British.

In 1757, the British had suffered a series of disastrous losses, notably the surrender of Fort William Henry. Native American allies of the French had broken surrender terms by attacking, killing and scalping hundreds of soldiers and civilians, including women and children.

William Pitt the Elder - Library of Congress

The British and American force that Abercrombie commanded was the largest British-led army ever deployed in North America at that time. He had at his disposal more than 15,000 troops made up of regular British army units and American provincials, mostly from New England. This was eight times higher than any British-led force that had reached the waters of Lake Champlain which straddled the border with Canada. The French could muster only 3,700, including Canadians and Indian allies, to defend their fort. Yet somehow Abercrombie still lost the battle.

William Pitt the Elder, known as The Great Commoner, had become Britain's prime minister in 1756, and the course of the French and Indian War was one of his major foreign policy concerns. It was Pitt, supposedly at the insistence of King George II, who installed Abercrombie as commander-in-chief in North America.

Pitt and Abercrombie had both spent 20 years as fellow members of the Whig Party in the House of Commons, Abercrombie as MP for Banffshire. Both had military backgrounds and Pitt reportedly admired the Scotsman's organisational abilities. Although the prime minister wanted to appoint Brigadier General Lord George Howe – 'the best officer in the British Army' – to the North American post, he was overruled. Abercrombie had more connections and seniority, so Howe became his number two.

Abercrombie may have been an organisational genius but he was inept when it came to understanding the art of warfare. His appointment to the elevated position of commander-in-chief of the British Army in North America was an unmitigated disaster. He simply was not up to the job; the defeat at Fort Carillon derailed the British offensive, demoralised the forces under his command, and cost the lives of hundreds of loyal soldiers.

The Scottish units, as was often the case, bore the brunt of the casualties. Of the 25-strong Black Watch officer contingent, eight were killed and all the other 17 wounded.

A total of 308 enlisted men were killed and a further 316 injured. It was a terrible toll for the Highland regiment, renowned for their brave battlefield exploits.

One of the most scathing accounts of Abercrombie's character and lack of military leadership was provided in a series of letters written by one of the officers under his command, Captain Charles Lee of the 44th Regiment of Foot. Lee described his commanding officer as a 'damn'd beastly poltroon', and referred to him as our 'Booby in Chief'.

He related that Indians refused to fight for him because they thought of him as an 'old Squah' (slang for Indian woman). The Native Americans, he wrote, told Abercrombie that 'he should wear a petticoat, go home and make sugar…and not blunder so many braver men than himself into destruction'. Lee was one of many who attacked Abercrombie's obvious failings. He certainly did so in the most colourful terms. He went on to describe the Scotsman as 'a blockhead sunk in idiotism' and a coward who was 'the first to leave the field'.

Few British army leaders have been so roundly condemned for their behaviour for presiding over a calamitous and entirely avoidable military disgrace. Not surprisingly, he never again saw action on any battlefield.

James Abercrombie (his name is sometimes spelt Abercromby) was born in 1706 at Glassaugh or Glasshaugh House, just outside the village of Fordyce in Banffshire. His father, Alexander, became the MP for Banffshire the year James was born and served for 20 years. Alexander's wife was Helen Meldrum of Crombie, another well-known and powerful Banffshire family.

The Abercrombies may not have been titled aristocrats but they were wealthy landed gentry and highly respected in the north-east of Scotland. Glassaugh was a fabulous mansion house and James can truly be said to have been raised with a silver spoon in his mouth.

His father put a dent in the family fortune by unwisely investing in two major financial scandals of the early 1700s. One was the Mississippi Bubble, the result of crooked Scottish financier John Law wildly exaggerating the wealth of Louisiana; and the second was the calamitous South Sea Bubble, a share collapse that ruined thousands of investors in 1720.

James, like his father, was involved in Scottish military life from an early age. When he was only 11, he was appointed an ensign in the 25th Regiment of Foot, later known as the King's Own Scottish Borderers. He went on to serve with the regiment in the War of the Austrian Succession, rising to the rank of colonel.

In 1728, when James was 22, his father died at the relatively young age of 51. William Duff, the 1st Earl of Fife, had succeeded Alexander as Banffshire MP in 1726. James then married the Earl's daughter Mary Duff.

The parliamentary succession in Banffshire began to resemble something of a dynasty. When the 1st Earl of Fife gave up the seat in 1734 he was succeeded by James

Abercrombie, his son-in-law, who held it for 20 years. Then in 1754 it was won by James Duff, 2nd Earl of Fife, Abercrombie's brother-in-law and William's son. He held the seat for 30 years until 1784, when he was succeeded by his illegitimate son, also James Duff, who held the seat until 1789.

So for 83 years the Banffshire seat at Westminster was in the hands of two prominent local families who were related through marriage. Such were the privileges enjoyed at that time by the wealthy ruling classes.

James Abercrombie's military career followed a similarly advantageous path, as his wealth and position in society presented him with opportunities that did not exist for the less fortunate. In the early 18th century, too much respect was granted towards the local landowner throughout most of rural Scotland. The qualities of wealth and status were hugely important, and those who enjoyed them took full advantage.

Abercrombie had been promoted to captain in the 25th Regiment of Foot, but in 1742 he wanted to ascend to a higher rank; rather than rising through the officer classes by merit or seniority, he put his hand in his pocket and bought a major's commission. As the 25th Regiment of Foot was an infantry regiment, it would have cost him £3,200. It was a dreadfully class-influenced practice that existed in the British Army at the time and one that meant the most high-ranking officers were inevitably the ones with most money and political clout. Quite simply, anyone with enough money could buy an officer's commission, and the costs were kept high enough to keep them out of reach of the common man. It seems ridiculous today that such a practice could ever have happened, but it persisted for almost 200 years until it was abolished in 1871. Preserving upper class exclusivity among its officer classes was clearly an important factor for the British Army of the time.

Crucially, when it came to characters such as Abercrombie, the practice also ensured that many of the military leaders of the day were not especially good. The result was often a military disaster like Fort Carillon and the needless death of hundreds of soldiers.

Whatever can be said about Abercrombie, there seems no doubt that he was anxious to serve king and country. He did not hesitate to go abroad and fight. When the War of the Austrian Succession broke out, he served as quartermaster general under General James St Clair – a noted Scottish soldier and the owner of Rosslyn Castle – at the unsuccessful Raid on Lorient in France in 1746.

He was also wounded during that conflict, at a relatively minor battle near Hulst in the Netherlands, although his injuries did not keep him inactive for long. Both militarily and politically he was going up in the world, and when the Seven Years' War broke out in 1756, he was sent to North America and promoted to major-general. His appointment saw him as second-in-command to the commander-in chief, Lord Loudoun, another Scotsman.

John Campbell, the 4th Earl of Loudoun, was not a popular figure in America. He had been posted there after having raised an infantry regiment to fight against the forces of Bonnie Prince Charlie during the 1745 Jacobite Rebellion. In America he also served as governor general of Virginia, but after the defeat at Fort William Henry in New York state in 1757, he was recalled to Britain and replaced by Abercrombie.

Everyone involved in the campaign, from the most junior soldier to the most grizzled and battle-hardened veteran, was utterly scornful of the appointment of Abercrombie. He was by now in his 50s, overweight, arrogant, unpopular, and with no leadership experience to speak of. To make matters worse he had never set foot in America before, his military participation having been limited entirely to Europe. America was a massively different and extremely challenging theatre of warfare, as Abercrombie was about to discover.

If one thing did keep up the spirits of the troops, it was the presence of Lord George Howe as Abercrombie's second-in-command. The 3rd Viscount Howe, whose family seat was in Nottinghamshire, was arguably the most distinguished and highly-regarded British Army officer of the period. He was innovative, a stickler for detail and, unlike Abercrombie, he displayed not the slightest snobbery, and mixed freely with the men under his command.

Howe was, in effect, the real leader in North America. Abercrombie may have been given the appointment but in all respects, he was second best to Howe. The other great advantage of Howe's involvement was that he knew the terrain in New York, Massachusetts and the other northern colonies like the back of his hand. He had embarked on a scouting mission with the notorious American frontiersman, Major Robert Rogers, leader of the famous Rogers' Rangers, to ensure he was acquainted with every detail of the North American wilderness and the dangers posed by unfriendly Indian tribesmen.

While the Battle of Carillon may not be one that springs readily to mind, its strategic importance should never be underestimated. The French and Indian War went a long way to settling the make-up of North America as we know it today; what is nowadays a footnote in history was truly at the heart of the struggle for North America in the mid-18th century.

The British recognised its importance, of that there is no doubt. The fort was the ultimate strategic prize; it had been built by the French in 1755 as a means of controlling Lake Champlain and the St Lawrence River. From the British point of view, the capture of the fort would be the first step towards an all-conquering march on the city of Montreal.

In North American military terms, 1758 was destined to become a successful year for the British. General John Forbes, a native of Dunfermline in Fife, defeated the French at Fort Duquesne and renamed the settlement Pittsburgh; Major General Jeffrey Amherst laid siege to the fortress of Louisburg in present-day Nova Scotia, causing a French capitulation; and Lieutenant Colonel John Bradstreet destroyed Fort Frontenac, a French trading post near present-day Kingston, Ontario.

By comparison the drubbing suffered by Abercrombie's inflated army at Carillon was both a damaging strategic blow for Britain's march northwards and a king-sized embarrassment. It had been a gilt-edged opportunity for a famous victory; Carillon was there for the taking. Of all the top army officers in America, it is difficult to imagine that any other would have blown the chance like the man from Banffshire.

British scouting intelligence indicated that Carillon was not easy to defend. It was on a low-lying piece of land, surrounded by water on three sides, and backing on to Lake Champlain. Two hills, Mount Independence and Mount Defiance, known as Rattlesnake Mountain, overlooked the fort. Easy pickings, thought Abercrombie.

The French had dug long deep trenches on the low plateau directly in front of the fort. In front of that again, trees had been cut down and were lying with spiked and pointed ends pointing skywards, creating an effective and formidable defence. Though cleverly thought out, it was rudimentary, and any half-decent British commander would have found a way round it.

But Abercrombie was not a half-decent commander. He was devoid of leadership skills, lacking in personality, unpopular with the officers and men in his charge and affected by a terrific upper-crust arrogance.

The moniker 'Mrs. Nanny Crombie' seemed appropriate and well-earned to those men who found him an indecisive, hesitant and wishy-washy individual to be leading such a force. He was constantly changing his mind, turning to Howe for guidance and then taking forever to formulate a battle plan.

When the stratagem was finally worked out, it could hardly have been more tragically wrong. Abercrombie played right in to the hands of the waiting – and sorely depleted – French forces. The phrase 'lambs to the slaughter' perfectly described the fate of the soldiers that day. Their leader's battlefield plan seemed to amount to only one word – charge! And charge they did, over and over again, straight into the path of the enemy gunfire.

The leader of the French forces at the battle was Marquis Louis-Joseph de Montcalm, a French soldier and nobleman who died fighting against General Wolfe at the Plains of Abraham in Quebec in 1759. He had arrived at the fort only weeks before the battle and was alarmed by what he found. The garrison was not strong enough to protect the area around the fort; there was only enough food for nine days; and, according to his scouts, the British were marching north with as many as 20,000 troops. Montcalm knew the situation was grim.

Certainly by the middle of June 1758 the French knew a major British offensive on Fort Carillon was imminent. Abercrombie had marched his formidable force to the lower shores of Lake George, the site of the destroyed Fort William Henry. French scouts and their Indian allies had followed their progress, estimated their numbers and reported back to Montcalm.

Abercrombie had many formidable fighting units under his command. There was the 1st battalion of the Black Watch led by Lord John Murray; the 27th (Inniskilling)

Regiment of Foot; the 44th (Earl Essex) Regiment of Foot; the 46th (South Devonshire) Regiment of Foot; the 55th (Westmorland) Regiment of Foot; and two battalions of the 60th Regiment of Foot, which later became the King's Royal Rifle Corps.

Ten thousand provincial militiamen from Massachusetts, New Jersey, Connecticut, Rhode Island and New York supplemented the 6,000 regular army troops. Also in the party were the famed Rogers' Rangers and the equally daring Gage's Light Infantry, led by Colonel Thomas Gage. The British regular units were resplendent in red coats and were armed with muskets, bayonets, knives, and hatchets or tomahawks.

Most of the provincial troops were wearing blue uniforms, but thanks to the foresight of Howe, their heavy coats were cut back to make it easier for them to engage in forest-style warfare. Rogers' Rangers always wore a distinctive green uniform.

Abercrombie also had at his disposal some seriously heavy artillery, enough to pound the enemy to smithereens. According to the New York State Historical Society, the train of artillery consisted of: four iron 18-pounder cannons; six brass 12-pounders; six brass 6-pounders; four 8-inch brass howitzers; 13-inch iron mortar; and 2-inch iron mortar; with eight brass royals and about 200 rounds for each.

The troops brought with them 900 bateaux (shallow draft flat-bottomed boats), and 150 whale boats. One onlooker recalled that, when the British fleet was in the water, it almost 'covered the entire face' of Lake George.

By any calculations this was a fearsome gathering of fighting men and weaponry. Even if the French had been up to fighting strength, the British display of military might would have been daunting. As it was, they were outnumbered five to one and faced the prospect of having to defend a far from impregnable fortress. Some of their Indian guides and scouts were so awestruck by the sheer size of the British contingent that they abandoned their allies and scarpered.

5 July 1758 was a beautiful summer's morning. The gung-ho British troops gathered at Lake George and set off up the waterways in a massive flotilla of craft; 900 bateaux carried the soldiers and the 150 whaleboats carried the artillery. It was one of the most striking and colourful British Army spectacles, one that has rarely been surpassed.

The New York State Historical Society described it thus: 'The scarlet coats and trappings of the British regulars and the parti-coloured plaids of the Scotch Highlanders, flanked by the sober homespun of the Provincials, with flags and banners everywhere, gave abundance of brilliant colour, while music of bands and bagpipes and the blare of trumpets and bugles sounded over the placid lake and echoes among its hills and mountains.'

Lord Howe was at his energetic and courageous best. He cajoled and coaxed the men, displayed his battlefield tactical nous, exuded confidence yet cautioned his men about the potential dangers that lay ahead. He was, by degrees, dashing and dauntless – the true leader of the British.

Colonel Charles Lee wrote afterwards, 'What a glorious situation was this! In short everything had so charming an aspect, that without being much elated I shou'd have look'd upon any man as a desponding bastard who could entertain a doubt of our success'.

Historian William Leete Stone recorded in similar vein: 'All was activity and gayety [sp] from getting in motion, from the instant the reveille startled the armed host from their repose at the dawn, until the embarkation was complete. So sure were all of an easy victory, that they went forth as to a grand review, or the pageant of a national festival'.

Little did anyone know how quickly events would take a dramatic and disastrous turn. By noon the following day most of the British forces had landed on the north end of Lake George, four miles from Fort Carillon. Again Howe took the lead, dispatching Rogers' Rangers on a reconnaissance mission to Lake Champlain while he led an advance party, including Gage's Regiment, up the west side of the La Chute River.

The intention of Howe's march was to try to engage the French that day, but as the afternoon wore on, it became obvious that the terrain was impossible. Thick woods, swamps and morasses, and tangled underbrush confused Howe and the men with him until they became bewildered and lost.

Then came the incident that turned the battle plan on its head – the 'beginning of the end' as one historian put it. A body of French troops, who were also hopelessly lost, confronted Howe and his men. A small skirmish ensued and Howe, leading his men against the enemy, was shot by a musket ball at point blank range.

The gallant Howe never recovered, and with his passing the British lost the soul of the expedition. It was the worst possible scenario. Almost like a scene from Arthurian legend, a solitary barge carried the body of the swashbuckling young officer back down the lake. Gone was the heart, the vitality and the intellect of the campaign in the person of Howe. Its success now rested on the shoulders of the blundering, incompetent and charmless Abercrombie.

Stone wrote in gloomy tones, 'The fate of this officer, who was the life of the men, at once threw a damper and a gloom over the entire army; and from that moment an almost general consternation and languor took the place of its previous confidence and buoyancy'.

Every move Abercrombie made after this, every decision he took, was disastrous. His own officers questioned all his orders yet he still arrogantly disregarded their advice. Much of the spirit had gone from the men with Howe's death and one historian described everything that Abercrombie did from that point on as marked by 'indecision and folly'.

Abercrombie's first mistake came as a result of indecision and hesitancy following Howe's death. He really did not know how to proceed – so he went backwards, to the landing place at the head of Lake George, to consider his options. It played straight into the hands of the French who, more than anything, needed time to prepare their defences against the inevitable British onslaught.

If Abercrombie had pushed his troops towards Carillon without delay he would have reached the fort within two hours. His decision to draw back and deliberate meant that two vital days were lost. While Abercrombie was dallying, Montcalm was digging in, preparing effective defences, and giving his far smaller force a fighting chance.

Montcalm may have been outnumbered but he was not going to give up without a fight. He ordered his men to build a heavy breastwork in front of the fort. Tall entrenchments, flanked

Victory of French troops at Fort Carillon by Henry Ogden

by batteries, were hastily built, and there was only one line of attack for the British. Felled forest trees with their sharpened branches turned upwards formed a blockade in front of the French barricades.

It was desperate backs-to-the-wall stuff on the part of the French, although it was nothing to the desperation and despair that was sapping the spirits of the British thanks to Abercrombie's ineptitude. Bradstreet, the hero of Frontenac, pleaded with Abercrombie to let him attack before the French could call up reinforcements. The Scotsman refused, and more vital time was lost.

One disastrous error followed another. Abercrombie was urged to use cannon fire against the French from Mount Defiance, but he ignored the advice. Colonel Lee, who despised Abercrombie, wrote that 'two small cannon well planted must have drove the French in a very short time from their breast work…this was never thought of, which (one wou'd imagine) must have occur'd to any blockhead who was not absolutely so far sunk into Idiotism as to be oblig'd to wear a bib and bells'.

Abercrombie took the advice of his inexperienced engineer, Lieutenant Matthew Clerk, who said the French defences could easily be breached, ahead of that of the Rogers' Rangers veteran John Stark, who knew the terrain and warned him the fort was well-nigh impregnable. For the Americans, it was a decision that summed up the superior attitude of the British towards the American forces.

Stone wrote, 'His (Stark's) advice was rejected by that supercilious commander, as worthy only of an ignorant Provincial unacquainted with British prowess'.

Abercrombie's biggest mistake – again taken despite the overwhelming advice of his fellow officers, including Howe – was his failure to use artillery in his attempt to take the fort. He had so many cannons and so much ammunition available to him, which if strategically placed, could have blown the French out of Carillon.

Instead, in what must rank as one of the most clueless decisions in British Army history, Abercrombie decided not to utilise the available artillery but to launch a full-frontal assault. He clearly felt his numerical superiority was enough to win the day.

Not that Abercrombie ever saw the battlefield conditions for himself. He relied 100% on reports from scouts and messengers. While his French counterpart Montcalm rode along the lines of his men, galvanising them and spurring them on to greater feats, Abercrombie spent the entirety of the battle in a disused sawmill two miles from the action.

Mrs. Nanny Crombie never once clapped eyes on the killing fields of Carillon; he never got close enough to see the fighting men under his command 'cut down like grass' as one soldier described it. He sent the men to die while he remained at a safe distance with a roof over his head. No wonder he was lambasted as a 'coward', an 'old woman' and a 'beastly poltroon'.

At 1pm on 8 July, Abercrombie ordered the attack to begin. There was to be no artillery used; no cannon fire. He wanted the fort taken by regular soldiers at the point of bayonets. Four columns of men advanced towards the fort, Rogers' Rangers leading the way and the officers and men of the Black Watch taking up the rear. They learned to their cost that, during the two days since Howe's death, the French had turned Carillon into an almost impenetrable fortress.

The attacking British troops were thrown into confusion by the denseness of the spiky barrier erected by the French. The thick, sharp, spiky remains of tree trunks proved extremely difficult obstacles. In vain, the Highlanders hacked at the branches with their broadswords, making little progress.

Then, from the hastily-built breastworks, a signal from Montcalm brought a terrific and well-directed fire upon the floundering British ranks. Swivel guns, musket fire and small arms fire cut down the slowly advancing soldiers. It was a scene of carnage; the British were like sitting ducks.

David Perry, a 16-year old from Massachusetts, had his first taste of military action that day, and wrote a powerful account of what happened on the battlefield. He said he and his colleagues had to cower from the enemy fire and that 'the ground was strewed with the dead and dying'.

Perry, who rose to the rank of captain, added, 'It happened that I got behind a white-oak stump, which was so small that I had to lay on my side, and stretch myself; the balls striking the ground within a hand's breadth of me every moment, and I could hear the men screaming, and see them dying all around me. I lay there some time. A man could not stand erect, without being hit, any more than he could stand out in a shower, without having drops of rain fall upon him; for the balls came by hands-full'.

For four hours the slaughter continued. At one point the gallant men of the Black Watch stormed the French breastworks only to be bayoneted. It was as close as the British got on a day that lives on in British military infamy.

Abercrombie ordered in his provincial reserve troops but the French tactics had worked brilliantly. They had momentum on their side and the bit between their teeth. Montcalm had proved himself a charismatic and inspiring leader and had out-maneouvered his woefully inadequate counterpart. By the time Abercrombie realised the scope of the disaster, there were 551 British troops lying dead on the battlefield, a further 1,356 wounded, and 37 missing, never to be seen again.

As night fell, Abercrombie decided enough was enough. He ordered his troops to retreat to the landing site at Lake George. Many ignored his call and had to be ordered two or three times to fall back. Those of the Black Watch who had survived helped take as many of the wounded as they could from the battlefield. Some had suffered such dreadful injuries that they died in the hours and days that followed.

Abercrombie's retreat was, by all accounts, as shambolic as his battle plan. From his bolthole in the sawmill, the Scotsman turned tail and fled. The portly 52-year old ran as though his life depended on it back to Lake George where his fleet of vessels was moored. One eye-witness said a 'sudden panic' had seized Abercrombie and he did not regain composure until the following day when he was sure the French were not chasing him.

Perry described the retreat as 'melancholy and still', like a 'funeral'. According to William Leete Stone, the army was 'in wild affright' and it took the cool head of Bradstreet to convince them there was no further danger, otherwise the boats would have been swamped. Charles Lee wrote that Abercrombie 'threw himself into one of the first boats, row'd off, and was almost the earliest messenger of the public loss and his own infamy'.

The retreating forces sailed down the length of Lake George and then to nearby Fort Edward before heading south to Albany, a distance of more than 100 miles. Author Fran-

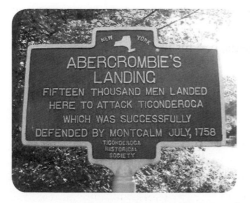

Left: The 'Abercrombie's Landing' marker erected by the Ticonderoga Historical Society close to the spot of the battle, right: Fort Ticonderoga as it looks today - courtesy of William Dolback

cis Jennings in his book, *Empire of Fortune*, wrote that 'Abercrombie marched back to Albany and his desk where he took up the really skilled occupation of his kind, writing excuses'.

Abercrombie could make all the excuses in the world – and he made plenty, constantly pointing the finger of blame at others – but his spell as commander-in-chief in North America was over. Pitt ordered him back to London and he never took part in a military offensive again. His successor was General Amherst, who in 1759 captured Carillon by besieging the fort. The British renamed the fortress Fort Ticonderoga, and nowadays it is a historic monument.

Charles Lee, who went on to serve as a general during the American War of Independence, made no attempt to disguise his withering contempt for Abercrombie. He wrote, 'I really did not think that so great a share of stupidity and absurdity could be in the possession of any man. Fortune and the pusillanimity of the French had cram'd victory into his mouth, but he contrived to spit it out again'.

Abercrombie had managed to turn a certain British success into a humiliating defeat. He had the blood of hundreds of troops on his hands, and he had returned to Britain in disgrace. Yet everything that was wrong with the British Army at that time became evident in his treatment thereafter.

First, he was promoted to the rank of lieutenant general only a year after his damning loss. In 1772, he was promoted again, this time to full general. He spent many years in parliament as an MP and was rewarded with the cushy post of deputy governor of Stirling Castle, where he passed away in April of 1781.

When he was not enjoying the privileges that come with being a high-ranking military man and seasoned Member of Parliament, Abercrombie relaxed at the splendour of his Glasshaugh mansion house in Banffshire. His blundering had left many wives without husbands and children without fathers but his suffering was limited to public scorn. He lived out the rest of his life in typical upper-class comfort.

John Dowie

*He has drained Zion City Bank of its deposits, until men and
women who have large deposits there, upon which they were depending
for their living, have been compelled to stand in line for hours, and
even days, waiting for a dollar or two out of thousands*

– LETTER OF INDICTMENT AGAINST JOHN DOWIE
WRITTEN BY OFFICERS OF ZION

The baby born in a small dingy flat in Leith Street, Edinburgh, on 25 May 1847 was
no ordinary child. His arrival on this earth had been foretold for centuries, since
Biblical days. This little boy, the son of a Scottish leather breeches maker and a wine
merchant's daughter, was in fact the third incarnation of the prophet Elijah, who would
be known to his followers as Elijah the Restorer.

That, at least, is what John Alexander Dowie would have had us believe – that after
Elijah himself, and John the Baptist, he was the third embodiment of the Prophet. As
the years went by, the boy who was born into poverty and squalor in Scotland's capital
proclaimed himself not just a prophet, but a priest and a ruler, destined to be king by
human lineage and divine authority.

Dowie did all the right things. He miraculously cured the sick; he made the crippled
and lame throw away their crutches; he preached fire and brimstone from his earthly

pulpit; he dressed in long biblical robes and grew a long white flowing beard (like the prophets from the Promised Land); and he built a city in which to found the one true church.

Not unlike his so-called previous incarnations, he attracted tens of thousands of followers who swore by his teachings and pledged themselves to his ministry. The authorities and the establishment derided and despised him and he was forced to defend himself and his church against allegations of rabble-rousing and heresy.

But there were crucial differences. The old prophets described in the Bible were humble and holy men, who lived frugal, abstemious and god-fearing lives. Elijah was so poor that God had to send ravens to carry him food.

By contrast Dowie was a bombastic, bullying demagogue. He ruled over his 'holy city' with an iron fist, making a fortune in the process – in fact he became a multi-millionaire. While he was commanding his flock to hand over their own wealth to him in the name of God, he was enjoying the life of Riley, building a string of fabulous mansion houses, and employing dozens of servants to wait on him hand and foot.

The Scotsman took advantage of Americans who were tired of their old religions and keen to throw in their lot with a new and exciting evangelical doctrine. He used his dramatic charisma to reel them in then fleece them for every dime he could. Zion, the city he built in northern Illinois, became the headquarters of his Christian Catholic Apostolic Church, and a byword for his personal corruption.

The would-be shaman was not a re-awakening of an Old Testament prophet. Instead, he was the forerunner of the crooked evangelists with their high-on-the-hog lifestyles who blighted America in the 20th and 21st centuries. Rather than giving to the poor, Dowie took from rich and poor alike to maintain a modus vivendi that became more lavish with every passing day.

He lived in palatial splendour. In Zion he and his family resided in Shiloh House, a magnificent 25-room mansion. He bought the sumptuous Ben MacDhui estate on the shores of White Lake, near Montague, Michigan, for $100,000 in 1905, and he purchased 7,000 acres of land in Mexico to fund an enterprise he called the Zion Paradise Plantation.

Dowie also embarked on expensive luxury trips to places such as New Zealand, Switzerland and Mexico, all of which were paid for by his thousands of devoted followers. He commanded all the 'ordinary' members of his church to work in Zion for comparatively low wages, and then drew a tithe from them as well. During times of austerity he ordered them to make cash deposits in the Zion Bank, of which he was head. It was the last they would see of their hard-earned money.

The Scotsman was fond of excessively quoting Bible verses to his congregation in Zion. If he had read from the apostle Paul's first letter to Timothy, 'For the love of money is a root of all kinds of evil. Some people, eager for money, have wandered from the faith and pierced themselves with many griefs', they would doubtless have recognised the irony.

An editorial in the magazine *American Medicine* in 1901 read: 'Who would have believed that the nimble-witted American, with his eye keen for financial frauds, would have been so gullible? While Dowie is contending that this is his third incarnation (Elijah and John the Baptist were the others) he duly orders as the first message of the Prophet the payment of tithes and offerings to himself, the first millionaire prophet.'

The magazine added, in caustic tones, 'An irreverent joker says Elijah depended upon the ravens, and Dowie upon the gulls'.

In 2013 a research fellow at the University of South Africa, Barry Morton, produced a paper scathing of Dowie. He wrote, 'Put quite simply the entire Zionist enterprise was founded by a professional con man – John Alexander Dowie – a man who perfected the dark art of "faith healing" to attract followers, after which he fleeced them for as much money as he could'.

Mr. Morton said investigators were looking into his activities in the early 20th century and that, even while he was still alive, many Americans regarded him as a 'mountebank and fraud'.

By hook or by crook, Dowie had come a long way since his poverty-stricken early days in Edinburgh. He must have been barely able to believe his good fortune. His sanity was often brought into question but the truth is he knew exactly what he was doing. He was using his personality to persuade people to part with their money – in the name of God – to fund a lifestyle he could once only have dreamed of.

He undoubtedly helped spawn the genre of preachers, alleged faith healers and televangelists who followed in his wake; men and women who claimed God spoke through them and that they could cure the ills of ordinary Americans – but only if they parted with vast amounts of dollars.

The most notorious, Jim Bakker, hosted a hugely popular television show with his then wife Tammy Faye. In 1988 he was jailed for 45 years in a federal prison after being found guilty of a number of frauds. He was said to have 'epitomised the excesses of the 1980s'; at one point the couple was receiving $1,000,000 a week in contributions for their so-called non-profit church.

Bakker and the others like him were almost certainly inspired to some degree by John Dowie. He was the pioneer for all the wily spivs and swindlers who followed in his wake; those who discovered there was enormous wealth to be made from exploiting the people who were searching for a creed in which they could believe and trust.

Yet his actions have been defended by many in the later Pentecostal movement who claimed that the attacks on his ministry and character were no more than religious intolerance, a common byproduct of religious diversity.

Those who claimed to have been cured by Dowie often wrote to him in reverential terms. His church's monthly journal *Leaves of Healing* contained countless testimonies. One woman, Jennie Paddock, said she was two hours from death suffering from a 12-inch fibroid tumour when Dowie prayed for her. She woke soon afterwards, rose the

"I AM IN FIRST-CLASS SHAPE, O N THE EVE OF MY TRIP ABROAD, TO TAKE A FALL OUT OF INIQUITY."
—DOWIE.

Bob Satterfield cartoon about
John Alexander Dowie (1904)

following day, and the tumour was gone within a week. She devoted the rest of her life to Dowie and Zion.

However, by his death in 1907, the city of Zion and the church he had founded were in dire financial straits. He had been overthrown, his followers had lost money, often thousands of dollars, and very few people regarded him with esteem or homage. He had once been deified but after his downfall that reverence could never be resurrected.

The luxurious lifestyle enjoyed by Dowie in the final years of his life was a far cry from his humble beginnings in the slums of 19th century Edinburgh. He was born into outright poverty in a tiny flat in Edinburgh's Leith Street, a thoroughfare that runs between the east end of Princes Street and the top of Leith Walk.

His father, John Murray Dowie, was a leather breeches-maker who had been born in Alloa, Clackmannanshire. His mother, Ann McFarlane, daughter of a wine merchant, had been born in Ireland. She was 12 years older than her husband and six months pregnant when the couple married in February 1847, at Edinburgh's Tron Parish Church. It was Ann's second marriage and baby John shared the house with his stepbrother, six-year-old James McHardie.

John senior was a part-time lay preacher, and by all accounts a respected man. He worked hard to improve his family's fortunes, and by 1849 the family had moved to another cramped flat in Edinburgh's Drummond Street, where their second child, Andrew, was born.

As a youngster, Dowie was said to have been 'amazingly precocious', and through the influence of his father, infatuated with the Bible. One acquaintance said he consistently asked searching questions on 'subjects generally regarded as beyond the range of a juvenile intelligence' and that there were few who could rival 'his knowledge of the sacred text'.

At the age of six he was said to have become captivated by a street preacher by the name of Henry Wright and to have taken a pledge of temperance. For the rest of his life he had an absolutely fanatical hatred, bordering on obsession, of alcohol and tobacco.

By 1860 John and Ann Dowie decided to leave Scotland with their two sons and join the growing wave of emigrants heading for a new life in Australia. Nine years earlier John senior's brother Alexander had departed Scotland for the South Australian city of Adelaide and established a prosperous footwear shop, the South Australian Boot Factory.

The family sailed from Leith to Plymouth where they boarded the 756-ton, three-masted wooden sailing ship *Schah Jehan*, which had been built 12 years earlier at the Denny and Rankin yard at Dumbarton on the Clyde. On 24 August the vessel set sail for Port Adelaide. The voyage took 102 days, passed through the Roaring Forties, and made no stops en route. It was an arduous journey (two infants died of illness on the vessel), but on 1 December the passengers and crew stepped safely onto Australian soil.

It was in the Southern Hemisphere country that Dowie's religious immersion became more pronounced. He never lost his fascination, some would say infatuation, with all aspects of the Bible, and there was no question about the direction his life would take. By his mid-teens he was described as a religious zealot, his boyish precociousness having given way to arrogance and 'Bible-thumping'.

Before embarking on his religious crusade, he took a job in his uncle's shoe shop, working his way through a variety of posts until he became a junior partner in a wholesale grocery firm. His father had become the president of the South Adelaide chapter of the Total Abstinence Society, which required members to abstain from drinking alcohol. Dowie was an active member.

While living in Adelaide he took Bible classes and in 1868, at the age of 21, he sailed back to Scotland to study Presbyterian theology at the University of Edinburgh. After two years he left university without attaining a degree and remained essentially self-taught. He preferred the literal word of the Bible to the teachings of theologians who he once ridiculed from the pulpit as 'a poor miserable lot'.

While at the university he studied Latin, Greek, moral philosophy and logic. He also served as an unofficial chaplain at Edinburgh Royal Infirmary, and while listening to diagnoses, watching surgical procedures, and hearing surgeons admit they were 'guessing', he developed a deep mistrust of the medical profession.

On his return to Adelaide three years later he was appointed a pastor at the rural parish of Hamley Bridge and Alma, north of the city. He gained a reputation as an extraordinarily-gifted preacher, although as time went by, behavioural eccentricities became evident. After nine months he resigned citing ill-health. In fact, he had fallen out so badly with his congregation that he had effectively been ousted.

His next calling in 1873 saw him installed as minister of the Congregational Church in Manly, New South Wales, a parish just north of Sydney. Six months later he moved to Newtown, an affluent Sydney suburb. The congregation there witnessed him becoming ever more eccentric and delusional. One Sunday he mounted the pulpit in full canonical dress, held up a glass of wine and cried, 'These be Thy Gods, O Israel'. He then gathered up his robes, marched from the church and never returned.

The young minister's abrupt and melodramatic departure from his flock in Newtown was the culmination of his growing disillusionment with the Congregational denomination, which he felt was too 'worldly'. Instead he moved towards urban revivalism and divine healing. He would later become known as the 'Father of healing revivalism in America'.

Dowie's bizarre lifestyle also showed in his choice of bride. In 1876 he married his first cousin Jane Dowie, daughter of his uncle Alexander. Both sets of parents were horrified and vehemently opposed the marriage, but the couple ignored their protests. They were married in North Adelaide Congregational Church on 26 May and went on to have three children. Marriage to a first cousin is still legal throughout Australia in the 21st century but is heavily stigmatised and rarely practised.

In Australia he became more and more eccentric and increasingly controversial. He preached from a theatre in Sydney and established a tabernacle in the Melbourne suburb of Fitzroy. He stood for the Australian Parliament but during his campaign he became a subject of ridicule.

He took to illegal street preaching in opposition to alcohol interests, was jailed for a month and blamed the drinks industry for every misfortune that came his way.

He was convinced liquor interests tried to assassinate him by planting an explosive device under a chair in his manse – and on this occasion he may well have been right. Five minutes before the crude bomb was detonated, Dowie stood up and walked away, a chance action that may have saved his life.

James Robinson, in his book *Divine Healing: The Holiness-Pentecostal Transition Years*, wrote of Dowie: 'His was to become a life suffused by inflated drama on which his reputation would thrive.'

For a whole host of reasons, Dowie was making headlines in Australia. His oratory powers and his incredible Bible knowledge were legendary. To his curriculum vitae he could now add 'miracle worker' or 'faith healer'. He had a growing and devoted following who hung on his every word. However, he had also experienced the inside of a prison cell, and there were many who viewed him as at best idiosyncratic, at worst unhinged.

His so-called faith healing was attracting nationwide attention. People with illnesses, often life-threatening, were attending his services and declaring themselves cured. They included tuberculosis sufferers, cancer victims and a woman who claimed she had been blind for three years but that Dowie enabled her to see again.

By the 1880s Dowie was in Melbourne. He and Jane suffered the heartbreaking loss of their seven-year old daughter Jeanie, who had been ill for several years. His authoritarian manner was becoming more pronounced and major arguments with his congregations were commonplace.

For Dowie, Australia was becoming a 'big village'. He was growing restless. A journey through New Zealand secured him many more followers, and in 1886 he founded the International Divine Healing Association (IDHA). Two years later he claimed to have experienced a vision telling him to carry on the work of God in the United States.

Few people believed that a 'vision' played any part in his decision to move to America. In his book, *An Apostle in Australia*, noted Congregational clergyman Edward Kiek wrote, 'Such a person could have but one ultimate earthly goal - the United States, then, as now, the paradise of the charlatan'.

There were other factors weighing heavily on Dowie's shoulders that no doubt helped prompt his departure from Australia. Despite his large following and growing reputation within the Evangelical movement, he was in dire financial circumstances. His failure to hold down a steady charge, his foray into politics, and his emergence as a charismatic divine healer had left him with little income. By 1887 he was all but destitute. One report said he had no home and had to borrow money for food.

His uncle and father-in-law Alexander – described as an extremely 'grounded' man – had absolutely no time for Dowie. The marriage between the two first cousins had caused an almighty family argument and Alexander had tried many times to persuade Jane to come back home. He regarded Dowie as a crackpot and rabble rouser and not a fit person to be wed to his daughter. While the financial situation was desperate, Jane and the children did return home for a few months, although it was only a temporary move.

On 7 July 1888, Dowie, Jane, and their two surviving children, Alexander, 11, and Esther, 7, sailed into San Francisco Bay. The Golden Gate Bridge had been completed the previous year and the city's cable cars had not long started operating. The city had expanded dramatically since the Gold Rush of the 1840s and 50s.

Back in Melbourne, Dowie's church had burned down in suspicious circumstances, allowing him to claim enough money to pay back some debts and book his family's passage on the voyage. It may have been God's 'vision' that took him to the United States but what he witnessed in San Francisco must have convinced him that he was truly in a land of opportunity. He had been penniless before leaving Australia, and reports said he had only 75 dollars in his pocket when he arrived in America. He would not make that mistake again.

At some point, it may have been during the voyage from Australia to San Francisco, or shortly after his arrival in the United States, Dowie came to the realisation that, if he was to carry on performing miracles and curing the sick in God's name, then he should make sure he profited personally from the enterprise. There were, after all, many vulnerable people in this new land just waiting for an apostle to lead them, and newspapermen gathered in their droves to report on the arrival of the faith healer to American shores.

He and his family took lodgings in the city. The press reports alerted the people to him and his reputation, and very soon he was inundated with people who wanted their ailments to be cured. His supporters claimed that, through God, he was performing miracles – and there was no shortage of witnesses prepared to stand up and tell the world that a long-standing complaint or condition had been completely healed.

One commentator said, 'There was a force in him whose tremors were felt at the ends of the earth. He had a wonderful faculty of persuasion … If he didn't impose on himself, he imposed himself on others…He had a singularly copious repertoire of abusive epithets and his self opinionativeness combined with his inordinate pugnacity made him a reckless and somewhat dangerous antagonist'.

Dowie and his family were still very poor, and they remained that way throughout the two years spent on the west coast, during which time Dowie relentlessly promoted his International Divine Healing Association. Just as he had done in Australia, he gained a significant following, as well as a degree of notoriety.

At this stage in his life it is safe to say Dowie had a massive ego and a thirst for drama which knew no bounds. But despite his big pulpit talk and histrionics, he still appeared to retain a semblance of sincerity for what he was trying to achieve. That was all to change within a few short years.

While his following was impressive, Dowie knew it could be better – that there were richer pickings elsewhere in the country. In the early 1890s he decided to move across the country and try his luck in the more conservative and religiously diverse Midwest.

He first established a church in Evanston, Illinois, and tried to build a network of chapters across the state and further east. Many people viewed him as a madman, others as a dangerous con artist, but there were a great number who listened to his loud, tub-thumping sermons and believed in him. That convinced him to continue on his journey to spiritual – and most importantly, financial – fulfilment.

In 1894 he moved to Chicago just as the World's Fair was being held in the city. If Dowie was looking for 'celebrity endorsement' for his teachings he had the good fortune to find it in the person of Sadie Cody, niece of William Frederick Cody, otherwise known as the great Wild West showman Buffalo Bill.

Sadie testified that in 1894 she had been suffering from an abscess in the base of her spine and a large swelling that was developing into a tumour. She was brought to Chicago where, she said, Dowie laid hands on her in the name of the Lord and that there then followed a 'great struggle' within her body.

She said she experienced a 'blessed awakening: with the abscess and tumour gone'. Sadie stated, 'I cannot find words to praise the Lord for what He has done for me. I will give Him my life's service, but that is small compared with what He has done. I consider Dr Dowie the greatest blessing God ever sent to Chicago, and I hope Chicago will appreciate it'.

Dowie was also said to have healed Amanda Hicks, cousin of Abraham Lincoln. Ms. Hicks, who was bedridden and expected to die, travelled by train to Chicago from her home in Clinton, Kentucky. Dowie and his wife laid hands on the woman and, according to Dowie, 'in a moment, the terrible agony of months departed'. He said that 'gallons of cancerous matter' passed from her body and she became well again.

While he was performing these 'latter-day miracles', Dowie railed with a passion against doctors, drugs, and the entire medical profession in general. His healing meetings outside the fairgrounds at the World's Fair were such an incredible spectacle that the crutches and braces of those who claimed to have been healed were stacked up against the wall of one of his meeting rooms.

If Sadie Cody and others expected Chicagoans to welcome Dowie with open arms, they were sadly mistaken. Within a year of arriving in the city he was facing 102 charges of practising medicine without a license. To be fair to him, the authorities laid jumped-up charges against him in the hope that one would stick, but ultimately he was cleared of them all. He later boasted in his sermons about how he had evaded the law.

Dowie also made great play of his Scottish heritage, gilding the lily to his advantage in his uproarious sermons. In the text of one speech, published in his weekly publication *Leaves of Healing*, he said, 'I am of the clan from which Ben MacDhui (sp) takes its name, the second highest mountain in Scotland; not Dowie, Dhui, as every Gaelic scholarly Scotchman knows. It was at the Ben that the last of the Israelitish kings found a refuge, as tradition says'.

It was hogwash of course, as was his claim that John Dowie senior was not his real father, but rather his mother had been impregnated by a royal duke who had died several months later. Her marriage to John Dowie went ahead to save disgrace. The assertion of an ancestry consisting of British royalty and kings of Israel was powerful and featured strongly in his sermons. His followers lapped it up.

Writing in the New York-based weekly magazine *The Independent* in 1906, William Barton, pastor of the First Congregational Church in Oak Pass, Illinois, wrote of Dowie, 'He has made rich vestments, and dropped his surname; for who calls a king by his surname? The world knows nothing of Mr Albert E Wettin of London, but calls him Edward VII, so he determined that the world should forget John A. Dowie and remember John Alexander, prophet, priest and king.'

Right back to his early days in Edinburgh – and certainly reading the statements attributed to him in Chicago – it is doubtful if Dowie ever inhabited what we would call the 'real world'. Although it is easy to dismiss him as some sort of delusional eccentric, that description would not settle well with the people who believed him and lost thousands as a result of his actions.

In 1895 Dowie abandoned the IDHA and established the Christian Catholic Church with its headquarters, which he named Zion, based in a former hotel on Michigan Avenue in central Chicago. Within a few years he had procured a number of buildings on one high visibility street. They housed a church, a bank, investment associations, a printing press, a school, an orphanage, a college, a home for 'erring women', and a four-storey healing home.

Dowie proclaimed himself general overseer of the new church. He was quite literally in charge of everything and everyone. He revelled in the attention he received in Chicago, a vast city in comparison with the relative backwaters he had left behind in Australia. Thousands of followers from across the USA swore he was the 'real deal' and believed in his healing powers; the press, the medical profession and the establishment in general reviled him. To them he was an agitator and an uncontrollable zealot.

The firebrand preacher who arrived in San Francisco with 75 dollars in his pocket claiming to be a miracle worker had come a long way. His 'Kingdom of Zion' in the centre of Chicago had not come cheaply. He insisted that he never charged money for the laying on of hands – he said so in a court of law when he was hauled up again for practising medicine without a licence. However, clearly the money had come from somewhere.

Part of the answer to his new-found wealth can be found in a November 1899 *Leaves of Healing* publication. In block capitals he wrote, 'I CALL FOR A NEW YEAR'S GIFT OF ONE MILLION DOLLARS'.

He told his followers, 'You can answer that call, each according to his several ability… if each one will do that fully, then Zion's storehouse will have meat for many workers… bring the whole tithe into the storehouse…bring your largest possible offering…God will pour you out a Blessing that there shall not be room enough to receive it'.

The rhetoric sounded remarkably similar to that used by some of the unscrupulous money-grabbing evangelists who followed him. It effectively said, 'Give me money and I shall lead you down the path of righteousness. Hand over your cash and I will cure your ills'.

The money for every one of Dowie's grandiose church plans was, of course, coming from the pockets and bank accounts of his devout followers. He started with scarcely a penny to his name and he never wasted an opportunity to hold out the begging bowl for more. It was a seriously 'hard sell' enterprise which pandered to people's belief in God.

For every person who worshipped the ground Dowie walked on, there were at least 10 who despised him. In1897, charges of practising without a licence resulted in a trial which provoked frenzied newspaper headlines and character assassinations. Again he escaped conviction but feelings against him had hardened, particularly among members of the medical profession.

He was dubbed a fraud and a swindler in the press, and in 1899 more than 2,000 medical students from Rush Medical College rioted during one of his lectures entitled 'Doctors, Drugs and Demons'. Men and women fled the hall as students threw stones and bottles of chemicals through windows and let off stink bombs in the aisle. Dowie had to be escorted to safety.

The episode convinced him that his future lay somewhere other than Chicago, where he made no bones about his belief that he was being 'persecuted'. Such was the level of opposition in Chicago that Dowie had organized a Zion Guard, who wore police-style uniforms and escorted their leader to protect him from mob threats.

The time had come for the Christian Catholic Apostolic Church, as it was now called, to move to its own purpose-built home. Not just a home, but a city, a new Eden, run by the church for the church – or should that read by John Dowie for John Dowie?

On the stroke of midnight on 1 January 1900, Dowie announced from the pulpit that the church was to relocate from Chicago to a city called Zion. It was to be built 50 miles north of Chicago, just south of the Wisconsin border. Dowie revealed detailed plans for its construction. A gift of land from a devoted follower in Indiana had made the move possible.

Dowie was ecstatic. In *Leaves of Healing* he wrote that the new city would enable church members to 'secure deliverance for themselves and their families from the rum-soaked, tobacco-reeking streets of Chicago'.

He spoke in glowing terms of the new city's potential: 'What a multitude of Saved, Healed, Cleansed, and Quickened Christians might go from such a center to preach Christ in every land beneath the sun! Lift your eyes, ye Sons of Light, Zion's city is in sight.'

Dowie knew every word of scripture. He told his followers that Zion, Illinois, was the Zion predicted in the Bible's book of Revelation. It would be a self-sufficient spiritual Utopia. There would be no tobacco, alcohol or gambling. The eating of pork and shellfish was forbidden, as was the use of swearing and the practice of dancing. Santa Claus was banned; so too were spitting, politicians and tan shoes. Whistling on a Sunday was punishable by jail.

He made sure there were no medical practitioners allowed to operate within the city boundaries. No doctors or hospitals or drugs were permitted in Zion. If people became sick then they had to rely on God or John Dowie to make them better.

The Chicago press was absolutely stunned by the size of the new city. Dowie's church, through the Zion Land and Investment Association, had secretly purchased 6,500 acres of prime farming land. Six days after his great announcement, Dowie and 90 of his followers boarded a special train from Chicago and went north to inspect the site of their new city.

Zion was largely complete by 1901. It included a lace-making factory and a range of other businesses, a large tabernacle and a number of what Dowie styled 'healing homes'. The Zion Bank was also established; it was an unincorporated entity wholly under the control of Dowie, and he exhorted all his followers to deposit money in it. It should have been obvious to all – even the blindest of adherents – that this was not going to end well.

The lace factory was crucial to attracting citizens to Zion. It had been set up by English lace manufacturer Samuel Stevenson from Nottinghamshire, who had become engaged to Dowie's sister-in-law Mary Anne. In 1900 Zion Lace Industries was established when Stevenson moved the operation to America. It promised work for thousands of people and was the economic basis on which the city was built.

Dowie being welcomed home to Zion City, Illinois – Library of Congress

In the summer of 1900 Dowie and his family visited Europe, where they converted a number of people from England, Scotland, France and Switzerland. Riots and disturbances marked the trip, with many regarding Dowie as a hoaxer. *The Financial News* ran an article which read that 'There is no more fruitful ground for the projector of new and bizarre faiths than the United States of America, with its wicked and teeming populations, largely leavened with neuresthenes'.

But those who were sceptical and critical of Dowie were now turning from his controversial teaching to another aspect of his life. It was becoming increasingly apparent that Dowie was a very rich man; he was living and travelling in a luxurious way. During the European trip he and his family stayed at the most sumptuous of hotels.

Philip Cook, in his book *Zion City, Illinois: Twentieth-Century Utopia*, recalls a speech Dowie made when he told followers, 'I am telling them in Chicago that if they desire to be rich, they must become Christians, and if they wish to become quite sure of becoming rich to get into Zion'.

Cook adds, 'Zion's belief in the sanctification of riches was in perfect harmony with American ideals'.

In other words, whether or not he was a divine healer or an apostle of God on earth, Dowie had focused his attentions firmly on capitalism. The prophet was living the American Dream. By the time he founded Zion City he was extremely wealthy. The money he had exhorted his (mainly middle and upper class) followers to hand over in order that God could continue to perform miracles through him had found its way into his personal coffers. He was the proud possessor of two large mansions in the United States and a plantation in Mexico.

Everything in Zion City belonged to him. The bank was his, all the profits from the lace factory and the other industries in town accrued to him personally. It was boom time for John Dowie and great while it lasted. However, cracks were beginning to show.

An editorial in *Life: A Monthly Magazine of Christian Metaphysics,* ridiculed the notion that Dowie had performed miracles. The writer stated: 'There is no doubt that people, many of them, get healed when they go to him or attend his meetings. But this is because they believe. If one believed that a donkey braying would heal him, believe it unfalteringly, he would be very likely to get well when he heard the donkey. But that is not true healing. There is no regeneration about this that lifts one above the plane of sickness.'

The magazine described Dowie's movement as 'Calvinism gone mad' and added, 'All such fanaticisms have their day and pass on. Let us not bother our brains about them'.

The truth was that many of those Dowie claimed to have healed were careful 'plants' in his extravagant theatrical healing ceremonies. They were vetted beforehand and only those pre-disposed to the belief of a placebo cure were allowed on stage. The healings, the pile of leg braces and crutches that littered his tabernacle, were all a massive money-making scam.

Zion City was an incredible feat. When it was launched there were 25 businesses, the largest being the lace factory and the Zion Department Store, which between them employed 3,000 people. It was built on the principles of community and theocracy, racial harmony, and freedom from crime and vice; a strict set of morals was envisioned.

Dowie had it all. At the height of his power and influence the man who had been born into poverty in Edinburgh had a fortune worth several million dollars in money and property. In the early part of the 20th century, he was making $250,000 a year from tithing.

Barry Morton, in his research paper, described Dowie's activities as 'systematic and large-scale fraud'. He added, 'The entire financial structure of the Christian Catholic Church and Zion City was carefully constructed to render all their assets under his complete, personal control. Dowie ran his church in very much the same way that Mobutu ran Zaire'.

By the early 1900s his 'miracle-making' had all but vanished, leading many to question his motives. While the city's economy was in decline, he was living a life of luxury. There were rumours that he was preaching polygamy and actively engaging in the practice. Reports emanated that the lifelong opponent of alcohol had turned to drink.

The money Dowie had extracted from his Zionist followers – either through tithes, to pay for miracles or, in the case of Samuel Stevenson, to establish a factory – was used by him as his own personal wealth. He squandered it and frittered it away and allowed his devotees to suffer huge financial losses.

One of his favourite money-making schemes was to exhort his congregation to buy up stocks and shares in the companies he had set up in Zion. Only after Dowie was gone from the city did his flock discover that the businesses were unincorporated and that the securities they had bought were worthless. He netted millions of dollars in this way.

Morton wrote, 'One can only conclude that he was a ruthless and predatory cult leader who used his charisma to exploit his followers. Rather than being a symbol of anti-capitalist values, in fact his role as a religious robber baron seems to have mirrored the Darwinian capitalist practices of his times'.

Then in June 1901 he stood on his pulpit and declared that he was in fact the second reincarnation of the prophet Elijah and that he was to be known forthwith as Elijah the Restorer. He took to wearing high-priestly robes and many of his followers deserted him – and more crucially, they took their money with them.

Zion City went into a massive spiral of debt. Its creator had effectively sucked the life out of it, and for the first time, the devoted followers who had uprooted themselves from their communities to follow him began to question his authority. There was no question that Dowie, now in his mid-50s, was showing signs of either believing his own publicity or a descent into senility – perhaps both.

His daughter Esther died in 1902, aged 21, after suffering severe burns when her curling iron overheated. The accident happened, said Dowie, because Esther had disobeyed the rule of Zion by using an iron powered by alcohol, and he thanked God for what had happened.

In 1905, after a pulpit sermon, he collapsed on the altar having suffered a severe paralytic stroke. He went to Jamaica, then his Paradise Plantation in Mexico to try to recover in a warmer climate. The city he left behind was in complete financial ruin thanks to his extravagances.

The residents of Zion had had enough. Dowie was now viewed as tyrannical and autocratic, and revolution was in the air. His most trusted lieutenant, Wilbur Voliva, led a movement in 1906 that deposed Dowie and took from him all his Zion City properties. Voliva calculated that Dowie had embezzled around $2.5million from the church. Government auditors put the figure at around $1million higher.

He was suspended from the church he had founded on account of 'polygamous teachings and other grave charges'. Dowie returned to Chicago and fought the suspension through the courts but there was no way back. His race was run and opinion had turned against him.

The strange, delusional John Dowie, often labelled a lunatic during his time in America and elsewhere, passed away in March 1907 in Woodford County, Illinois, near the town of Metamora, after a series of strokes had immobilised him.

After his death Dowie was given a mention in one of the 20th century's greatest modernist novels, *Ulysses* by the Irish writer James Joyce. At one point the main protagonist Leopold Bloom is walking in Dublin when he is handed a flyer that read, '…Elijah is coming. Dr John Alexander Dowie restorer of the church in Zion is coming'.

He was buried in Zion's Lake Mound Cemetery. His coffin was lowered into the ground, then his grave was filled with concrete. One explanation stated that it was Dowie's wish to prevent anyone taking his body and suggesting he had miraculously arisen.

A second school of thought – and perhaps a more likely one – is that the disillusioned Zionist followers he left behind poured in the concrete to make sure the Scotsman remained in the ground forever and 'never returned to this earth'.

12

Jock Semple

Instinctively I jerked my head around quickly and looked square into the most vicious face I'd ever seen. A big man, a huge man, with bared teeth was set to pounce, and before I could react he grabbed my shoulder and flung me back, screaming, 'Get the hell out of my race...'

– Marathon runner Kathrine Switzer about Jock Semple

Since 1897 the streets of Boston, Massachusetts, have echoed to the pounding of thousands of pairs of feet. They belong to marathon runners straining every sinew as they try to book their place among the greatest endurance athletes on earth. Their lung-bursting efforts are cheered on at an event that has long been one of the most famous and prestigious race meetings of all time.

The Boston Marathon is the oldest modern marathon in the world. It is steeped in decades of sporting history, and has witnessed records being broken and feats of stamina and courage unfolding. Even two world wars have failed to prevent the event being run, and it has grown into one of the major fixtures in the American sporting calendar.

Held on Patriots' Day, the third Monday in April, it is by far the biggest sporting event in the New England area and one of the largest in America. In 1996 it attracted an incredible 38,708 entrants, more competitors than any marathon in the world at the time. Of that number, 36,748 started the race. The first 15 years of the 21st century have seen an average field of 30,000, a far cry from the 18 hardy souls who set out in 1897.

Over the years there have been dramas and controversies, triumphs and tragedies, inspirational performances and countless hard luck stories associated with the Boston Marathon. It is a race with a glorious yet colourful and often contentious history.

The greatest tragedy to befall the event occurred in 2013 when terrorists struck. Two pressure cooker bombs exploded near the finishing line, killing three people and injuring more than 260 others. Among the dead was an eight-year-old boy, Martin Richard, who lived in the city. The atrocity was perpetrated by two brothers, Dzhokhar and Tamerlan Tsarnaev from Chechnya in south-west Russia. The latter was killed by police gunfire; his brother sentenced to death.

2013 was a disaster for the race and everything it stood for. Bostonians take great pride in Marathon Monday; it is one of the biggest days in the city's calendar. Since the bombings the city has united to honour the dead, but it will take a long time for the scars of terrorism to heal.

There have been many other talking points surrounding the event. During the Korean War of the early 1950s, the race organiser forbade Koreans from entering the race on the basis that they should be 'fighting to protect their country instead of training for marathons'.

A cheating scandal hit the event in 1980 when a Cuban woman, Rosie Ruiz, finished ahead of all the other female runners. Organisers and fellow athletes did not recall her in the early stages of the race and noticed no signs of fatigue at the finishing line. It later transpired that she had jumped out of the crowd half a mile from the finish and crossed the line first. She was stripped of the title and became known as 'the woman who stole the Boston Marathon'.

The female winner in 2014, Rita Jeptoo from Kenya, failed a drugs test, and there have been two fatalities during the event: Cynthia Lucero, a 28-year old who died in 2002, and Humphry Siesage, a 61-year old Swede who suffered a heart attack during the 1996 race.

In a remarkable incident in 1936, John Kelley overtook the leading runner Ellison 'Tarzan' Brown, and patted him on the back as he did so. The gesture inspired Brown, a descendant of the royal family of the Narragansett Indian tribe, to stage a dramatic rally and win. The spot where the pat on the back took place has become known as Heartbreak Hill, because it was said to have broken Kelley's heart.

But there was one other 'incident', one that shook the Boston Marathon to its core. It happened during the 1967 race, and the event made headlines for all the wrong reasons – the day two seemingly immovable forces of nature came into direct confrontation in a way that sent shockwaves through the athletic world and propelled its protagonists on to newspaper front pages everywhere.

One was a young female student athlete determined to make her mark, to force change, to drag the event kicking and screaming away from its 19th century origins and more in keeping with the revolutionary 1960s. The other was an obstinate, middle-aged race organiser, a stickler for tradition, who saw it as his job to uphold the conventions that had served the race well for decades.

Kathrine Switzer was a 20-year old journalism student at the University of Syracuse in upstate New York. The daughter of a U.S. Army major, she had developed a passion for long-distance running. It was her dream to follow in the footsteps of her athletics coach, who had competed in the Boston Marathon 15 times. However, the race was the preserve of men; no woman had ever taken part as an official runner.

*Kathrine Switzer
in 2011*

Jock Semple was 64, a gruff, hard-nosed, irascible Scotsman who had become Mr. Boston Marathon. He was the man who decided who was and was not going to take part in 'his race'. No women had run before, there was nothing in the rules to say they could and that was the way it was going to stay. There would be no female competitors, not on Jock Semple's watch.

Semple had a temper like an exploding volcano. He stood no nonsense from anyone, least of all 'lassies'. He had no time for the less serious marathon runners, the ones who wore fancy dress costumes and raised money for charity. 'Weirdies' and 'screwballs', he memorably called them in a magazine

Switzer and Semple were both strong and determined individuals. There was something of an inevitability about their infamous altercation. At the time, Semple, and many other men like him, were convinced that it was beyond the capabilities of women to run 26 miles; that such a feat on the part of a female was humanly impossible. Unbelievable as it seems now, there was a genuine belief that the effort might cause a woman's uterus to fall out.

Semple is not in the same league as the killers, swindlers, crooks and other downright nasty characters dealt with in this book. He was part of a generation that has largely disappeared, an outrageous but flawed character, a man of his time who carried with him a strict set of convictions and a ruthless single-mindedness – neither of which are crimes or even undesirable qualities.

He was, however, a man in a position of enormous authority and responsibility in the American sporting world. The organisation of a highly prestigious event had been entrusted to his charge. To allow the red mist to come down, to lose his cool in the manner he did, and to drag the marathon's reputation into the mud was inexcusable.

In the space of a few minutes one fateful day in 1967, Semple disgraced himself utterly. His behaviour was that of a small-minded, intolerant, stick-in-the-mud club official, his actions those of a prejudiced and jumped-up bully. When his notorious 'action' picture was flashed round the world, he was dubbed the Boston Marathon's 'Mr. Angry'.

Even though, in later years, he apologised and became a passionate supporter of woman's athletics – to the extent of reconciling with his old adversary Switzer – Semple will be remembered forever for this one moment of madness.

John Duncan Semple was born in Glasgow's tough Gorbals area, and grew up in the harsh, mean streets of industrial Clydebank. He came into the world on 24 October 1903, in a tenement flat in the area's Kidston Street, a road long since demolished as part of the city's slum clearance programme. His father Frank was a locomotive engineer and iron turner, and their cramped house stood in the shadow of the massive Dixon's Blazes ironworks.

He was given the middle name Duncan, the maiden name of his mother Mary. He had an elder brother

Workers leaving Singer Sewing Machine Factory, Clydebank

James and a younger brother Frank. By the time Frank junior was born in 1907, the family had moved to a flat in Graham Avenue, Clydebank, close to the world-famous Singer sewing machine factory.

Along with the John Brown shipyard, the Singer plant was a massive employer in Clydebank. Just before the First World War, it employed more than 7,000 people and produced an average of 13,000 sewing machines a week. Johnny Semple, as he was called, was a small, slightly-built boy who suffered from asthma. He had to work a series of odd jobs from a very young age to help the family make ends meet, and when he was 14, he left school to become a sewing machine mechanic at the Singer factory.

He had one passion in life and that was running. As a teenager he joined the well-known athletics club Clydesdale Harriers. In later years he recalled five-mile cross country runs in all weathers, as well as sprinting to victory in the 100-yard dash in front of 2,000 spectators while wearing only his bathing suit.

In an article with *Sports Illustrated* magazine in 1968 he said, 'We used to start from the public baths and run through ploughed fields, over ditches and dykes, through streams that were swollen up to your knees. It was grand being out there in the fresh air every Saturday and sometimes the more prosperous harrier clubs had a clubhouse and they'd have a cup o' tea and a couple of cakes waiting when you came in'.

The running made for a refreshing escape from the gruelling nine-hour shifts he worked during the week in the Singer factory. The family had moved again to another flat in Clydebank, this time in Radnor Street. But with the war over and the threat of economic depression ever-present, there seemed little future on Clydeside. At his father's suggestion Johnny prepared to sail the Atlantic to begin a new life in America.

On 17 March 1923, the streetwise 19-year old bade his family farewell and boarded the ocean liner *Cameronia*, which had been launched in 1919 from the William Beardmore shipyard at Port Glasgow. He was heading for New York, and the ship's manifest revealed a mini-exodus of Scots heading to America. The list included a charwoman from Dundee; a joiner from Glengarnock; an engineer from Kilbarchan; a carpenter from Renton; a car conductor from Methil; and a 30-year old housewife from Dunbar.

There were hundreds more. Like Johnny Semple, they were departing their native land in droves and preparing to take a chance in the hope that better prospects lay in wait for them in the cities of America.

Semple's destination was the great historic city of Philadelphia, Pennsylvania. He took residence with his uncle William Brown in the city's South 55th Street and worked as a carpenter in the shipyards and building industry. At 5ft 8ins he was a typical short, aggressive Scotsman who soon became known as Jock, a name that was to stay with him for the rest of his life.

His working life in industrial Philadelphia was a step up from the Singer sewing machine plant he had left behind. However, the manual work was stultifying and repetitive, and the environment in the factories and yards was dirty and loud. The city may have been new and exciting for the young Scot but it seems he had swapped one tough lifestyle for another.

Semple kept himself fit, but there was little chance for him to escape the city streets of Philadelphia and indulge his passion of cross country running. He yearned for the open green fields in and around Clydebank, to breathe fresh air into his lungs, and to hear again the adulation of the crowd as he crossed the finishing line in first place.

It was his family who helped him make the break. His brother James had followed him across the Atlantic in 1922 and had set up home in the industrial city of Lynn, Massachusetts. On 1 April 1930, the boys' mother Mary sailed into the port of New York on board the *Cameronia* for a holiday and stayed with James and his Glasgow-born wife Agnes Caldwell.

In Philadelphia Jock Semple was thrilled at the chance to see his mother again. He could have caught the train to Massachusetts but, in typically non-conventional fashion, he hitch-hiked to Lynn for the family reunion. It was a journey that was to change his life.

Lynn is only 10 miles north of Boston, and when Jock arrived he discovered that the big day in the calendar was only days away. The Boston Marathon was always run on 19 April – Patriots' Day, and a state holiday in Massachusetts. He was still 26, fit as a fiddle, and with the successes of his Clydesdale Harrier days still fresh in his memory.

With the entry deadline date closing in, he decided to take a chance and enter the big race. It was an event he had read and heard so much about in the newspapers, in magazines and on the radio, and to be given the opportunity to take part was an incredible feeling. It would also make for a memorable family day out with his mother and brother there to watch and support him.

It turned out better than he could ever have imagined. Thousands of spectators lined the streets to watch fewer than 200 runners pound the city streets in their quest for marathon glory. Bostonians clapped and cheered at every corner of the track. College girls whooped and hollered as the leading pack passed by. It was a far more exciting and flamboyant audience than the crowds in rainy Clydebank with their cloth caps and flannel suits.

By the halfway mark Semple, to his astonishment, was among the leaders. He was rubbing shoulders with some of the biggest names in long-distance running, including the American Olympic athlete Clarence DeMar, who won seven Boston Marathons, and the English-born Canadian runner Johnny Miles, a two-time marathon winner. These were ultra-serious athletes, and the Scot was keeping pace with them.

As the race wore on, a number of big names dropped out. DeMar, at the age of 41, was well ahead and on his way to victory. Semple was locked in a titanic struggle with another Olympian, the great Massachusetts runner James 'Hinky' Henigan, and as the finishing line neared, the Scotsman forged ahead to clinch an incredible seventh place.

At the end he was wrapped in a blanket, given a cup of beef stew and taken to the shower room to cool off. He had never experienced a feeling of such triumph and exultation in his life. To finish seventh in the greatest race in the world among such illustrious company was an amazing feat for a young man whose decision to run had been something of a whim. Had his mother not come for a visit, he might never have left Philadelphia.

Semple made the decision there and then that his days in Philadelphia, where he had latterly been working as a cabinetmaker, were over. He had fallen in love with Boston, and in particular its marathon. He wanted to live there; to compete regularly in the race; to make sport the focus of his working life, not waste away in the drudgery of the factories.

Seventh place in the Boston Marathon had given him a certain recognition in the city's sporting world. People were asking questions about him. Who was this gruff upstart, this immigrant from industrial Scotland, who had come from nowhere to upset the odds in the biggest event in the city's calendar? Why had no-one ever heard of Jock Semple before the race? Could he do better, could he even win?

Semple, however, never regained such heights. The 1930 race was the pinnacle of his athletic achievement. He competed in the race until 1949 and stopped taking part not because his body was giving up, but because he wanted to concentrate on his duties as a marathon official. After 1930 Jock took the event to his heart; he called it 'my race', he handled all the entries, gave every runner a number, organised the water bottles and measured the course down to the last foot.

His passion for the marathon can only be described as a love affair. He took marathon running with a seriousness bordering on obsession and jealously guarded the quality of the entrants in the field. It became an absolute labour of love; he was a true amateur, never receiving a penny for the years of effort he put in on the race's behalf. The truth is, he would have paid for the privilege.

However, in Semple's case, that level of unstinting devotion brought with it a sense of narrow-mindedness and insularity. The marathon had rules and the tough-talking Scot was determined they would be followed to the nth degree. There would be no deviating from the regulations; they became Jock Semple's regulations, and God forbid you if you crossed his path.

As the years went by the marathon grew massively in popularity, attracting fun runners as well as serious athletes. Its amateur organiser cut an increasingly cantankerous and quarrelsome figure, hell-bent on trying to ensure that the race remained true to its athletic origins. He simply did not want things to change. Yet things were changing dramatically; life in the 1950s and 60s was a far cry from his youth, and the Boston Marathon was moving with the times.

Semple was like a grumpy old man with his finger stuck in a dyke wall trying to stem the flow of progress, cursing and swearing at every 'fatso', every 'potbelly', every 'smart aleck' that managed to sneak past his defences.

As for women, the American Amateur Athletic Union (AAU) rule book in 1967 said that women could only run a mile and a half – not even close to the 26 mile 385 yard Boston Marathon course. In Semple's world, rules were rules and had to be strictly adhered to. The rules were to be respected, end of story. No women in the men's race. Period. No further discussion.

When he arrived in Boston in 1930 race day was relatively simple. Between 100 and 200 runners took part, many were top-class athletes, and there was prestige in finishing among the top handful, as Semple had managed in his first attempt. At the time there were no 'MIT Boys' or 'Tufts Characters' – as he dubbed the runners from the Massachusetts Institute of Technology and Tufts University who tried to 'infiltrate' his race.

Then again, Semple would come to experience many changes, as his life altered dramatically in the years after leaving Philadelphia and settling in Massachusetts. He married, he enjoyed working and mixing with sports people, and he relished being away from the big smoky city.

He took a job as a locker room attendant in Lynn earning $11 a week. By 1941, he and his wife Elizabeth (Betty) Aitken, from Alva, Clackmannanshire, were living in the nearby city of Beverly, where he worked at the giant United Shoe Machinery Corporation factory. The plant, known as 'The Shoe', employed thousands of local people, and until 1937 was the largest reinforced concrete structure in the world.

Compared with Philadelphia, the smaller cities of Massachusetts were less urbanised, and Semple was able to indulge his love of running. He ran religiously on a daily basis, and on Patriots' Day every year he ran in the Marathon. The shoe factory was a necessary evil to keep body and soul together.

During the Second World War, Semple signed up for the U.S. Navy. However, in 1946 his world was rocked by a family tragedy in Glasgow. His parents, Frank and

Mary, both suffocated when they were overcome by gas leaking from a coal fire at their home in Dunchattan Street, in Glasgow's Dennistoun area. A fatal accident inquiry recorded they died as a result of asphyxia from coal gas and a verdict of misadventure, or accidental death, was passed. Semple was understandably shattered.

The following year Semple gained a diploma from the Massachusetts School of Physiotherapy, enabling him to treat sportsmen. It was his passport to the life he had long coveted. He became the full-time physical therapist for the Boston Bruins ice hockey team and the Boston Celtics basketball team, and he had his own office in Boston Garden, the giant arena that housed home games for both clubs.

For the next 40 years he was a noisy, boisterous and aggressive fixture at the stadium. He coached the U.S. ice hockey teams at the Winter Olympics in 1948 in St Moritz, Switzerland and 1952, in Oslo, Norway. All the players that passed through Boston Garden, including many from visiting teams, were given a taste of Semple's arduous training regime and his massage and physiotherapy skills. He was likened to a tyrant, although his tough exterior belied one of the most colourful 'characters' on the Boston sporting scene.

But as well as his full-time job, Semple had to deal with the constant ringing of the telephone in his Boston office, calls from would-be marathon runners. He dealt with them in his typical brusque manner, often yelling down the phone that they had no chance of competing and to 'go to hell…and no more of your crap'.

He didn't limit his energies to the event in Boston; he was the epitome of the official amateur sports organizer, and was instrumental in arranging the fine details of races throughout the north-east United States. A runner at the Yonkers Marathon, in New York, once said, 'If a President's funeral were coming from the opposite direction, Jock would make it back off'.

In the memorable 1968 *Sports Illustrated* interview, written by journalist and broadcaster Myron Cope, Semple said of the Boston Marathon, 'To me, it's sacred. I know what it is to train for it and suffer. I can't stand for them weirdies to make a joke out of it'.

In 1957 he spotted a runner wearing swimming fins, a pair of webbed snorkeling shoes and a hideous mask. The Scot was unable to contain his contempt and anger and hurled himself, missing him and landing face down in a puddle. Police were called, and it took the best efforts of official race organisers from the Boston Athletic Association (B.A.A.) to persuade officers not to press charges.

On another occasion he ran alongside a competitor who was dressed in an Uncle Sam suit, complete with high hat, and carrying a storm windows advertisement on his back. Semple threw cup after cup of water at the runner in an effort to force him off the track.

When a black dog strayed on to the course and tripped up one of the leading runners, an enraged Semple flew at the beast and aimed a kick at it. Fortunately, he missed, but he had to plead – unsuccessfully – with the press reporters not to mention the incident.

Old Jock had become notorious as the man who patrolled the course, steam coming out of his ears, chasing away all those he considered 'unsuitable'. One of his fellow organisers, Will Cloney, said Semple seemed unable to contain his rage at the increasing numbers of fun runners who were, in his eyes, demeaning the race.

Cloney added, 'He hurls not only his body at them, but also a rather choicer array of epithets, which fortunately are made indistinguishable by his burr'.

By 1966, the race was still a men-only event. The tentacles of the era's social revolution had not yet reached the world of male athletics. That year a 23-year old female student Roberta 'Bobbi' Gibb, a young woman who had been brought up in the suburbs of Boston, joined the male competitors and completed the course in an impressive time of three hours, twenty-one minutes and forty seconds.

Semple could only watch and grit his teeth in fury and frustration. Bobbi Gibb was not an official entrant; she had not been given an official bib with a number, so there was nothing Semple could do to stop her. Rules were rules. Afterwards, he referred to her disparagingly as 'the Gibb dame'.

While Gibb was making history in Boston, Switzer was training her socks off at the running track at the University of Syracuse. She and her coach Arnie Briggs, a veteran of 15 'Bostons', had been preparing her for participation in the great event.

Like Bobbi Gibb, she wanted to make a statement, to prove to the AAU that women were physically able to run marathons. Switzer however wanted to go further than Gibb, she wanted to run the marathon as an official competitor, with an official bib number. It would put her on a headlong collision course with Semple, the man who lived by the rules.

During long, lonely slogs in late 1966 and early 1967 Arnie and Kathrine ran mile after mile in the worst of the weather upstate New York could throw at them. By the time April came round they had run the marathon distance several times; they had even completed a course of 31 miles. Switzer was more than ready to run in Boston on Patriots' Day. There was only one problem: as a woman she was not eligible.

Like all rules, however, the ones drawn up by the AAU that governed the Boston Marathon could be bent. Switzer went through the rule book with a fine tooth comb. There was, she discovered, nothing that specifically stated the race was men only. The governing body still insisted that women were only fit to run distances of no more than one and a half miles, but the marathon rules did not say so explicitly.

It was the loophole she had been seeking. She registered for the race under the gender-neutral name K. W. Switzer, had a doctor's certificate sent in confirming fitness to participate, and arranged for a male friend to pick up her bib number – 261 – on the morning of the race. She was conniving in a conspiracy and she knew it. What she didn't know was that the Boston Marathon's 'attack dog' was lying in wait.

Switzer was joined in the race by Arnie Briggs; her boyfriend Tom Miller, a 235lb hammer thrower and former American footballer; and a colleague from Syracuse

University cross-country team, John Leonard. She made no attempt to disguise the fact she was a woman; she wore earrings and lipstick and, as the runners gathered at the starting line, said she felt like 'one of the anointed pilgrims'.

Semple's marathon routine had been unchanged for years. First, he checked and double-checked that everything was in order for his beloved race. Then, dressed smartly in a sports jacket, grey flannel trousers, shirt, tie, and with a B.A.A. official tag attached to his lapel, he climbed on to the press bus carrying the reporters and photographers accredited to cover the event.

The bus gave him an excellent vantage point. He could spot 'weirdies' a mile off, and was not averse to directing all manner of swear words and other abuse towards them. One official said it was a miracle someone had not killed Semple as a result of his marathon behaviour.

On 19 April 1967, thousands of Bostonians had braved the rain to line the streets of the city for the race; Kathrine Switzer and her history-making team were cheerfully swapping stories with dozens of male athletes at the starting line. Jock Semple was on board the press bus, jaw clenched, surveying his domain, ready to pounce at the slightest indiscretion.

At noon the starting pistol was fired. Switzer had got past the stewards undetected and she set off with the other 599 marathon runners. Bobbi Gibb was there too but, for the second year in a row, she had chosen not to wear an official numbered bib. Gibb wasn't breaking any AAU regulations, but Switzer certainly was.

For three laps the happy band from Syracuse University relaxed into the race and started to enjoy the big day. They ran four abreast, revelling in the attention from the male athletes, all of whom, Switzer said later, were very friendly and very welcoming.

As they were running the fourth mile, the atmosphere changed. Switzer remembered a large flatbed truck almost squeezing them off the track. It was followed by a city bus carrying press photographers. They were furiously taking pictures of her, checking her name against her bib number. She was suddenly becoming big news and she laughed and waved at them, enjoying the fun of the moment.

Then, in a prelude of what was to come, she was jostled by a B.A.A. official. The man muttered something at her and pulled off one of her gloves. What happened next is described in Kathrine Switzer's own words:

> I heard the scraping noise of leather shoes coming up fast behind me, an alien and alarming sound amid the muted thump-thumping of rubber-soled running shoes. When a runner hears that kind of noise, it's usually danger – like hearing a dog's paws on the pavement.
> Instinctively I jerked my head around quickly and looked square into the most vicious face I'd ever seen. A big man, a huge man, with bared teeth was set to pounce, and before I could react he grabbed my shoulder

and flung me back, screaming, 'Get the hell out of my race and give me those numbers'. Then he swiped down my front, trying to rip off my bib number, just as I leapt backward from him.

'He missed the numbers but I was so surprised and frightened that I slightly wet my pants and turned to run. But now the man had the back of my shirt and was swiping at the bib number on my back'.

She remembered hearing Briggs shouting, 'Leave her alone Jock, I've trained her, she's ok'.

Then she looked round and watched Semple swatting Arnie away like a gnat.

Switzer had started the race in buoyant mood, hoping to change the face of American athletics. Now the day that had promised such excitement and fulfilment was turning into a nightmare. She said, 'The bottom was dropping out of my stomach. I had never felt such embarrassment and fear. The physical power and swiftness of the attack stunned me'.

Then, just as suddenly as it had begun, the assault was brought to an end. Kathrine's boyfriend, the muscle-bound hammer thrower Miller, had seen enough. He charged at Semple and hit him with a terrifying thump, a shoulder charge that sent the Scots official through the air. He landed in a crumpled heap at the side of the track.

Switzer and her three friends took off along the road. Journalists and cameramen raced after her. The easy-going Briggs was promising to kill Jock Semple. Switzer said she felt 'sick at heart'.

A short while later the press bus drove past the Syracuse runners. There, standing on the floorboards and holding on to the outside rail was Semple. Switzer recalls, 'As the bus came by…Jock, teeth bared again and shaking his fist, screamed in a Scottish brogue 'You all are in beeeeggg trooouble'…all around us men gave him the finger and shouted obscenities'.

The race carried on, Switzer and all her fellow runners finished, and she wrote her name into the history books as the first official female entrant to finish the Boston Marathon. But the pictures that flashed round the world that day were not of the jubilant 20-year old student crossing the finishing line; they depicted the face of Jock Semple, twisted with rage, hurtling along the road towards the slight frame of the young female athlete.

Cope, in his 1968 *Sports Illustrated* article, described Semple thus: 'You can see him grinding his teeth as though he were a pint-sized King Kong on the rampage. He seems to want to hurl Kathy Switzer off the course and clear into Boston Bay'.

Semple told Cope, 'I'm not opposed to women's athletics. But we're taught to respect laws – to respect rules. The amateur rules here say a woman can't run more than a mile and a half. I'm in favor of making their races longer, but they don't belong with the men. They don't belong running with Jim Ryun' (an American Olympic silver medalist).

The interview was given a year after his notorious attack on Switzer. Typically, Semple remained unapologetic, still hidebound by his precious rule book. Sadly, he was not alone. The director of the B.A.A., Will Cloney, said 'Women can't run in the marathon because the rules forbid it. Unless we have rules, society will be in chaos. If that girl were my daughter, I would spank her'.

However, attitudes changed more quickly than any of them imagined. In 1972, five years after Kathrine Switzer had struck her blow for women, the B.A.A. relented and allowed women to run officially. The rules had changed and officialdom changed accordingly. Semple, the most vocal and vicious opponent of women, did an incredible U-turn. He became, by all accounts, a 'staunch supporter' of women, and a 'progressive' voice.

The photographers covering the 1973 Boston Marathon snapped a picture they never thought would present itself. All smiles, with their arms round each other, posing for the cameras, stood Kathrine Switzer and Jock Semple, surrounded by a group of grinning male athletes. Six years after the crazed assault, the pair publicly reconciled – at least for the benefit of the cameras.

Switzer went on to run marathons all over the world and became a noted author and television commentator. In 1974 she won the women's race in the New York City Marathon, and in 1977, she was named the Female Runner of the Decade by *Runner's World Magazine*.

As for Semple, his views may have mellowed with age but he never really changed. He remained the same gruff, cantankerous, irascible and fractious character. He never lost his broad Scottish accent nor his west of Scotland temper. He never left his poorly-paid physiotherapy job at Boston Garden or lost his passion for the city's marathon.

His 15 minutes of fame had shown him in an absolutely disgraceful light. Semple had appeared as a despotic, intimidating bully, an authority figure consumed with intolerance, rage and violence aimed towards a woman less than three times his age and half his size. It was shameful behaviour and it was the episode for which he was remembered for the rest of his life.

In March 1988 Semple died at the age of 84 of cancer of the liver and pancreas. His beloved wife Betty had passed away four years earlier.

His actions may have brought himself and the entire American athletics world into disrepute, although the sport's hierarchy were nothing if not forgiving. In 1985, the Scot who became the unacceptable face of a nation's sporting values, was inducted into the American Long Distance Running Hall of Fame.

It was quite an achievement for the boy who had grown up on the tough streets of Clydebank, but it may have been a bittersweet moment. One year earlier the Hall of Fame had welcomed his old adversary Switzer as a member. She had beaten him to it; Jock Semple had never liked finishing second.

13

Alexander Cuming

He answered with a Wild look, that . . . if any of the Indians had refused the King's health, to have taken a brand out of the fire that burns in the middle of the room and to have set fire to the house..that he would have guarded the door himself and put to death every one that endeavored to make their Escape that they might have all been consumed to ashes.

– LUDOVIC GRANT, COMPANION OF ALEXANDER CUMING

The early colonists who emigrated from their native countries to the new lands of America encountered a wide range of hazards. Nothing was ever easy about setting up home in what was then a wild, unexplored and hostile wilderness. As far back as the days of the Pilgrim Fathers, all manner of dangers lay in wait for the men and women who sailed from far off lands and into east coast harbours such as Boston, New York and Charleston.

Few Europeans, and certainly not those from Scotland and other parts of Great Britain, had ever come across alligators, mountain lions, wolves, black bears, poisonous serpents and other deadly reptiles commonplace in America.

Those who ventured north, into New England and upstate New York, endured freezing winter temperatures such as they had never experienced back home. Snow, ice and winter gales turned much of the territory into a numbing, glacial wasteland. Many settlers died of exposure to the cold. Those who survived must have longed for a return to the relative comfort of the European lands they had left behind.

But these incomers to what was arrogantly branded the 'New World' discovered another ever-present danger. An enemy that lay in wait at every turn. One that knew every inch of the 'alien' soil; that seemed to know every move they were making; that had been there for centuries and were less than enthusiastic about their arrival.

Nowadays, political correctness dictates that we call them Native Americans. When the Europeans were landing and settling, there were no such niceties. People who called the tribesmen 'Indians' were being polite; more often than not they were talked of in snide and derogatory terms. They were the uncivilised 'red men'. They were commonly referred to by one disparaging and pejorative term – 'savages'.

To the men, women and children who made up the hundreds of North American tribes, this land was no 'New World'. For hundreds of years they had lived and hunted on the great plains and deserts, in the woodland and on mountains. They belonged to tribes with names such as Sioux, Cherokee, Lakota, Apache, Blackfoot, Algonquin, Navajo, Shawnee and many more. They were hunters, warriors, farmers, tent-makers, husbands, wives, and tribal leaders. The Indians lived in harmony with nature, understood the environment that surrounded them, and saw themselves as custodians of the land.

In reality these people were anything but savages; they had a highly-developed social structure, a strong sense of culture, and a set of spiritual beliefs that was deeply entrenched. Trade was a vital part of Indian life and most groups had a sophisticated inter-tribal commerce system. Rivalries existed, just as they do in all cultures, and there were frequent battles; the Comanche was a feared and warlike tribe. Others, however, lived perfectly harmonious, tranquil and non-violent lives. The Hopi tribe of the south-west took its name from a word meaning peaceable or civilised.

The arrival of the white man – the Spanish, French, British and Dutch – was a well-documented and unmitigated disaster for the Indians. As the decades rolled by, their land was taken from them in the most brutal fashion; many of them were enslaved, their villages were burned to the ground, and they were massacred by settlers. In reply the tribesmen indulged in brutal attacks on the colonists, capturing, killing and scalping them. The land they had cultivated and inhabited for centuries became a blood-soaked battlefield.

While there were atrocities on both sides there was never any doubt who the winner would be. The Indians may have been great warriors but they were massively outnumbered, both in terms of manpower and weaponry. The Europeans also brought with them epidemics such as smallpox, tuberculosis, chickenpox, yellow fever and typhus. The natives had no resistance to these unseen enemies, and mortality rates in some villages were as high as 90%.

Yet the clash of cultures did not always result in inevitable confrontation. In the early days of the colonial 'invasion' there were instances of the Indians and the settlers working well together. Jamestown, Virginia, the first British settlement in America, was built with the help of the Powhatan Tribe, whose members included Pocahontas.

Further north in Massachusetts, the Pilgrim colony of Plymouth was established with the help of the Wampanoag Indians; they taught the white settlers how to hunt, cultivate the land, and survive the harsh New England winters. The 1621 Pilgrim-Wampanoag peace treaty was signed between the Indians and the colonists, acting on behalf of King James I, and was the first treaty between Native Americans and immigrants.

It was, as everyone knows, a short-lived peace. However, the European settlers took care not to alienate the Indians entirely. The reason? Their knowledge of the wild and forbidding territory, and their fighting qualities made them valuable allies in the constant series of wars that characterised the first three centuries of American settlement.

In the French and Indian War, the Revolutionary War, the civil war, and various other conflicts fought on American soil, Indian tribes sided with whichever side took the most trouble to curry favour with them. They acted as warriors, guides and messengers – in many cases they were treated as mere dogsbodies. The white man used the Indians and took advantage of their special skills only when they proved a necessary means to an end.

There was, however, one group of settlers whose relationship with the Indians was more cordial than the rest. The Scots, in particular the Scottish Highlanders, felt an empathy with the tribesmen that was unique among the Europeans. They were both indigenous groups that had suffered oppression by an English-speaking enemy, and there were many similarities between the Scottish clan system and the Indian tribal way of life.

Many Scottish male immigrants took Native American wives and achieved the respect of their new tribal family. John Ross, the son of a Scottish father and a Cherokee mother, rose to become the chief of the Cherokee Nation, a position he held for almost 40 years. William McIntosh, who was descended from Scottish incomers, was one of the principal chiefs of the Creek Nation during the 19th century.

Another Creek Nation chief was Alexander McGillivray, whose father Lachlan was a prosperous fur trader and planter from Dunmaglass, outside Inverness. McGillivray, whose Indian name *hoboi-hili-miko* meant Good Child King, commanded as many as 10,000 warriors and was one of the most powerful Creek leaders.

Ferenc Morton Szasz, in his book *Scots in the North American West 1790–1917*, described the clear parallels that existed between the Scottish Highlanders and the Indians: 'The physical conditions of life, governed by the change of seasons and often perched on the edge of hunger, proved similar. There could not have been much difference between an Isle of Lewis beehive shieling and a Great Plains tipi (teepee) or a Mandan earthen lodge.'

A new race of Scoto-Indians emerged, and the assimilation of many Caledonians into the Indian way of life was remarkable. In general terms though the Native Americans were regarded as a nuisance, an enemy to be used, exploited and crushed. The overwhelming majority of the settlers had no interest in befriending the Indians, let alone marrying into their tribes. They were far more intent on what was little more than a programme of ethnic cleansing.

In the early 1700s immigrants were spilling on to American shores, settlements were being established and the 'New World' was in its infancy. However, the many thousands who had sailed from Europe to the east coast ports of America were rapidly encroaching onto Indian land, and the situation was becoming fraught and dangerous.

South Carolina, a landing place for many Scottish emigrants, had attracted boatloads of settlers. It was an attractive and desirable location, as there were important seaports and fertile farmland. Towns such as Charleston, one of the major ports along the eastern seaboard, had been established and several well-populated settlements had sprung up inland.

English, Dutch, Germans and French joined with the Scots to make up the majority of the incoming population. They landed not just at Charleston but smaller Carolina harbours such as Beaufort and Georgetown, and the Georgia city of Savannah. Many came via Barbados and brought black slaves, who at one time in the 1800s outnumbered South Carolina's white population.

Such a melting pot of different nationalities, not forgetting the Native American population, led inevitably to what seemed like never-ending tensions. The British and French in particular were engaged in an almost continual state of territorial conflict. There were many competing interests, a massive drive for land ownership and political control, and all with an eye on eventual westward expansion. If there was one group of people the white settlers needed on their side, it was the Indians, with their knowledge of the country.

Yet as the whites pushed inland, they impinged on territory that had been under the control of the Indians for centuries. The thick forests and fast-flowing rivers were well-nigh impassable but the settlers discovered a network of old Indian hunting trails. They promptly 'improved' them until they were wide enough for wagon trains and stagecoaches, and they were soon turned into what became known as 'migration trails'.

The predominant tribe in South Carolina was the Cherokee. They were, for the most part, a peaceful people and in the 19th century became known as one of the 'five civilized tribes' of North America. They were also one of the earliest non-European groups to become U.S. citizens. However, in the 1700s they were none too happy at the intrusion on to their traditional lands. In fact, they were outraged.

The Europeans, in an ever-growing battle for supremacy, were at each other's throats. They all needed to ingratiate themselves with an increasingly hostile Indian population, not just the Cherokee but a host of other tribes, including the Santee, the Natchez and the Congaree. Add into the mix the Negro slave issue and the

Engraving of the Cherokee warriors posing in European clothes while in England

violence and human misery associated with it and the area that is now South Carolina was in the early 18th century; a turbulent and chaotic province.

It was the Native American population who, in many ways, held the key to colonial success – yet it seemed that few among the settlers, for all their so-called European civilisation and intellect, had a clue how to approach them and deal with them on an equal human footing.

Into this maelstrom sailed the most unlikely character, a man whose willingness to exploit and make fools of the Indian people knew no bounds. Alexander Cuming, the son of a baronet from Aberdeenshire, had, as the saying goes, been born with a silver spoon in his mouth. He had failed in every endeavour back in his native Scotland and his brief intervention in colonial life in South Carolina was to prove jaw-dropping in its audacity.

In many ways, his foray into the Indian territories reads like something from a Boy's Own adventure comic. His actions were so bizarre and outlandish that it is almost difficult to believe he actually behaved in such a manner – that he did what he did. There is no doubt he was an eccentric – one historian went so far as to label him 'demented' – although his motives have only ever been a matter for speculation.

Thanks to some unbelievable and almost freakish powers of persuasion, Cuming seduced the Cherokee into pledging allegiance to the British Crown at a time when the need for Indian allies was never greater. No-one knows for certain why he did it and on whose authority or orders – if anyone's – he acted. And his persuasiveness left a lot to be desired, including as it did threats, deprecation, and what appeared to be an upper-class mockery about a culture of which he knew little.

Despite only being in America for a few short weeks, Cuming left an indelible mark on South Carolina that found its way into the history books. Not only did he embark on an incredible journey through hostile Indian lands, he also swindled and defrauded the colonists. Many handed over large sums of money and property to him in return for promissory notes. They never saw Cuming or their money again.

The man brought up in a grand house in the village of Peterculter ripped off colonists, including fellow Scots, who had spent fortunes, saved, invested and in many cases turned their lives upside down to enable them to cross the Atlantic in search of a new life. For good measure he took advantage of the Cherokee people – although they may have known more than they let on about his intentions and his peculiar antics.

Somehow the confident Scottish trickster persuaded seven Cherokee warriors to return with him to Britain. There they were granted an audience with King George II, swore loyalty to him and the British cause, and signed a formal treaty. When they met the king at Windsor Castle, their faces were painted, they had horse tails hanging behind them, painted feathers on their heads and were naked except for an apron around their waists.

His Majesty, wearing a splendid scarlet ceremonial jacket, must have been dumbfounded. It was far and away the most bizarre delegation he had welcomed during his reign. Even more bizarrely, no-one had asked Cuming to bring them. The Scot was clearly hoping the move would bring him personal gain, possibly a degree of influence with the king. He was to be sadly mistaken and sorely disappointed.

Cuming (or Cumming as his family name was sometimes spelt) was born in Edinburgh in December 1691. His father, also Alexander, was an MP for Aberdeenshire and the 1st Baronet of Culter; his mother, Elizabeth Swinton, was the daughter of Sir Alexander Swinton, a colourful and boisterous Scottish judge with the courtesy title of Lord Mersington.

His father was a long-time Member of Parliament and a man who was not afraid to ruffle feathers; a lawyer and member of the Faculty of Advocates in Edinburgh; and a mover and shaker in the Scottish aristocracy. In his parliamentary biography he was described as a man with 'a clear eye for the main chance'.

The most remarkable story that attached to Alexander Cuming senior was that, while visiting Holland in the early 1700s he 'fell in with the retinue' of the Electoral Prince of Hanover, later King George II of Great Britain, and that he saved the future king from being drowned in an accident.

His son recorded later that 'being aboard the same ship as his highness, from Ostend to Zeeland, his highness was pleased to give the said Sir Alexander an invitation to Hanover and to assure him that…if his highness should happen to live to have power in England, the said Sir Alexander should be distinguished by the first honours of this kingdom'.

Whether there was any truth to the story is a matter of conjecture, but it became part of Cuming family folklore, and Sir Alexander's son never forgot to remind the king about it when he did eventually succeed to the throne.

Cuming spent his childhood in the family estate and mansion in Peterculter, eight miles west of Aberdeen city centre and close to the River Dee. The beginning of the 18th century was a turbulent political period; especially from a Scottish perspective. When Cuming was a teenager the 1707 Act of Union dissolved the Scottish parliament and led to a truly British Empire, with Scots such as Cuming being given the chance to participate in empire building.

He joined the British Army early, and in 1709 fought at the Battle of Malplaquet in France, an encounter in the War of the Spanish Succession. He also managed to gain the rank of captain in the Russian Army, but by 1714, he was back in his native land having been called to the Scottish bar.

Four years later he left the legal profession under more unusual circumstances. In 1718 he claimed he was induced to leave the bar when he was promised a pension of £300 a year, bestowed by the Westminster government. This money was supposedly either for services carried out by his family, or for tasks to be performed by him. In any event, the money was discontinued at Christmas 1721.

Cuming insisted the payment had been ended by Prime Minister Sir Robert Walpole, who was said have held a grudge against his father for opposing him in Parliament. Most historians agreed that Cuming was simply unable to complete the services he agreed to perform. The *Dictionary of National Biography* states, 'It is far more likely that he was found of a too flighty disposition to fulfil the services expected of him'.

There is no question that, by this stage in his life, Cuming was exhibiting peculiar character traits. He was a dreamer and a fantasist with quite obvious narcissistic tendencies that were to become more apparent as he got older. He was not a threat or a danger to anyone; he was more of an oddball – a Walter Mitty-like character.

In 1720 he was elected a fellow of the Royal Society but never paid the annual fee and was eventually expelled Around the same time his father lost most of the family fortune, having bought South Sea Company stock. The crash of the stock price in 1720 (known as the South Sea Bubble) took a serious toll on his health, and he died at Peterculter in 1725.

Cuming married Amy Whitehall, daughter of Lancelot Whitehall, who had moved from Shropshire to become a commissioner of customs in Scotland. Any hopes his family harboured that she would be a settling influence on the young man were quickly dispelled. If anything, his quixotic and fanciful nature became more pronounced.

To make matters worse he had very little money to his name after his father's disastrous investment in the South Sea Company. He needed ready cash to support himself and his young son, also Alexander. A group of friends nominated him for the post of governor of Bermuda but he lost the election. Thus, he was 'stuck' in Scotland, the eccentric son of a poverty-stricken aristocrat, with little or no income, and therefore forced to sell the family seat in Aberdeenshire.

By 1729 Cuming's impetuous and giddy nature seemed to have shifted into over-drive. His wife, he announced, had dreamed that he would accomplish 'great things' in the New World and that an incredible adventure lay in wait. She urged him to make the voyage to America. Whether Amy truly believed in any of this, whether she really had a dream in the first place, or whether she wanted to see the back of her increasingly whimsical husband is open to conjecture.

On 13 September 1729, Cuming set sail from England with a plan already hatching in his mind. He arrived at Charleston (then known as Charles Town) on 4 December. Only five months earlier, the Lords Proprietors of the Province of Carolina had sold their shares to the British Crown and it had been split into two provinces, North Carolina and South Carolina.

South Carolina in the early 1700s was a land that a lot of poor immigrants called home. Many were Cuming's fellow Scots, including those known as Ulster-Scots; Scots whose ancestors had colonised Northern Ireland and who saw a better life in America. The ones who had made a success of their lives no doubt trusted another Scotsman not to 'do the dirty' on them.

Rice was the cash crop that made South Carolina wealthy. It had been imported from Madagascar in the late 1600s, leading the state to be christened 'The Rice Kingdom'. It was also one of the first parts of the U.S. where the economy was built on the African slave trade; in 1720, records showed that 65% of the population were slaves.

There was wealth, and Cuming knew exactly where to find it. Of course, his clipped accent and aristocratic bearing opened many doors for him.

There was also a school of thought that King George II had contacted Cuming and asked him to act as a secret ambassador and to intervene with the Cherokee people on behalf of the British Crown. That is certainly what Cuming wanted the world to believe; that it was all linked to his father having saved the king from drowning, and that he was now in the exalted position of Crown agent – with orders directly from the monarch – to increase trade with and seek allegiance from a powerful Indian tribe.

The theory fell on its face when the revelation of Cuming as a fraud and a swindler came to light. South Carolina was one of Britain's most recently-established American colonies. There is no way the king would have sanctioned anyone whose motive was to extort and rip-off money from his Carolinian subjects.

The truth is that Cuming embarked on the American adventure for two reasons. The first was to get his hands on some much-needed cash, and if that meant fleecing the population by using a get-rich-quick scam then so be it. The second motive was to gain prominence for himself, to satisfy the Walter Mitty side of his character. Perhaps he figured that by achieving something of great benefit to king and country his indiscretions would be overlooked.

One historian suggested that, far from being some sort of secret ambassador, Cuming was 'a one-man firework display wildly emitting sparks and coloured lights and blazing rockets'.

When Cuming arrived in Charles Town he looked every inch the wealthy, young Scottish aristocrat. Calling himself Sir Alexander, he appeared very self-assured, and gave no indication whatsoever of being in any sort of financial difficulties. Quite the contrary; he told anyone who would listen that he was going to 'do wonderful things for the good of the country'. He convinced people that he was a well-off member of the Scottish nobility with capital to invest in the new province. He also exhorted those with any money to invest in him – with the promise that they would make a sizeable profit.

Within a few short weeks of arriving in South Carolina the financially-strapped Cuming had set himself up as a leading financier for the new colony and floated his own currency. He had effectively established the Bank of Alexander Cuming – with nothing to back it.

Leonard Sadosky, in his book *Revolutionary Negotiations*, wrote, 'Almost from the moment he arrived in Carolina, Cuming acted equal parts aristocratic, military adventurer, and confidence man. He set about on a course of action that disrupted life in the province of South Carolina and transformed the internal and external politics of the neighbouring Cherokee nation'.

Cuming issued a series of fictitious promissory notes (or bills of credit) and promptly paid back any notes that were redeemed. He developed a reputation as a man of integrity and the notes soon acquired a currency and credit that was 'equal with money'. Soon many merchants, traders and others with money to spare were investing their cash with Cuming in the hope of making a profit.

Soon he set up a loan office and issued, according to one record, 'great quantities of notes…upon loan of 10 per cent interest'. He bought a number of plantations, with great public ceremony, enabling him to pose even more assuredly as a man of influence and wealth. At one of his properties he built a stone house with three-feet thick walls and strong doors windows. He called the building his 'Treasury'.

The people of South Carolina must have thought a saviour had landed amongst them. Here was a man who had suddenly appeared in the chaotic monetary world of the colonies, where well-meaning people were merely scraping a living, offering them financial hope and stability.

Naturally, it was all too good to be true. Still, the South Carolinians clung to the belief that Cuming, as a principled and honourable member of the Aberdeenshire nobility, had their interests at heart; that he was the 'real deal'. In fact, he exchanged the handwritten notes for agricultural produce and specie, or coin money. He kept the money and shipped the produce back to Britain.

The unfortunate people of South Carolina who invested with the slippery Scotsman would find out the painful truth eventually. It came as a sickening blow to the men and women who had given up so much to travel to the colonies that they could have been swindled by 'one of their own'. Every penny they had invested with Cuming was gone.

Cuming achieved all of this within a remarkably short period, between December 1729 and May 1730. Sadly, it took far longer for the victims of his money scam to realise what he had done, and Hurricane Cuming had not finished with the province yet. He next headed into the wilds for his adventure with the Cherokee.

The fate of the Native Americans had been exercising Cuming's fanciful mind for some time, years before he left Scotland. One of the reasons for his bid to become governor of Bermuda was a plan he had hatched to build a college on the island to 'educate' American Indians. There was no Indian population on Bermuda; it seemed another hare-brained scheme on the part of Cuming.

The Indians of the south-east colonies were keen to trade with the 'white man', and the Carolinians faced stiff competition from the Spanish in Florida, the French in Louisiana, the English in Virginia, and the many other Indian tribes in Tennessee, Georgia and elsewhere.

Cuming wanted to ensure that the lion's share of that trade found its way to Britain – and he devised an audacious scheme to secure it. With the ill-gotten gains from the South Carolina colonists stashed away, Cuming embarked on stage two of his outrageous American adventure.

On 13 March he gathered with him a small band of traders, including Sir Ludovic Grant, who had been born at his family's ancestral home near Fyvie, Aberdeenshire, and told them that, as a member of the Royal Society, he had an 'errand to see the country' and wanted them to accompany him.

Ten days after setting off from Charles Town, the small group, led by an impeccably-dressed Cuming on horseback, arrived at the Cherokee town of Keowee. It was a community at the foot of the Blue Ridge Mountains; birthplace of another Scoto-Indian leader, John Norton, it is now submerged under a man-made lake.

The Cherokee towns and villages were divided into three distinct geographical regions – the Overhill Towns, the Lower Towns and the Middle Towns – situated in what is now South Carolina and Tennessee. Keowee was in the Lower Towns and it was there that Cuming's bizarre brand of diplomacy first showed itself.

A meeting was held in the village's Town House that evening. It was reported that 300 Cherokee were in attendance along with nine traders. Cuming is said to have marched in, waited his turn to speak, then proposed a toast to King George II during which he demanded that the traders, then the leaders of the Indian people, kneel and pledge allegiance to the British monarch.

Then, in a clear and extremely dangerous breach of Native American etiquette, Cuming threw open the cloak he was wearing to reveal four loaded firearms and a cutlass. Brandishing weapons at a Cherokee meeting was strictly forbidden, and the manner in which Cuming addressed the Indians – apparently he had a 'wild and crazy' look in his eyes – was alarming in the extreme.

Remarkably, he got away with it. The Indians dropped to their knees and did as he commanded. Perhaps they were too flabbergasted to refuse?

Trader and interpreter Joseph Cooper said afterwards that if he had known what Cuming was going to demand of him, 'I would not have ventured into the Town House to be interpreter, nor would the Indian traders ventured to have been spectators, believing none of them could have gone out of the Town House without being murdered, considering how jealous that People had always been of their Liberties'.

Ludovic Grant said he later asked Cuming what he would have done had the Indians refused to do his bidding. Grant added, 'He answered with a Wild look, that if any of the Indians had refused the King's health, to have taken a brand out of the fire that burns in the middle of the room and to have set fire to the house…that he would have guarded the door himself and put to death every one that endeavored to make their Escape that they might have all been consumed to ashes'.

The traders, many of whom had spent years cultivating the Cherokee and using their persuasive powers on behalf of the British Crown, were aghast and deeply troubled at Cuming's sudden lurch into what can only be described as the world of ersatz diplomacy. To suggest he was putting the lives of himself and the traders in danger is a gross understatement. The Indian villages were not a part of the British Empire; Cuming and his companions were in a place that many of their contemporaries felt was remote from the civilised norms, the 'home of the savages'.

Somehow, against all odds, Cuming seemed to have pulled off some sort of coup. He had, by all accounts, walked into the heart of an Indian village, barked orders at their tribal leaders, and persuaded them forcibly to support the British side. It all seemed too easy. Yet there was more to come.

He demanded another meeting at the Cherokee town of Nequassie and insisted that the head men from all the regions – Overhill, Middle and Lower Towns – be present. The Cherokee not only agreed, they escorted him in order to grant him safe passage. Having only met this man a few days earlier and been obviously impressed by his powers of oratory, it seemed for all the world that they were mesmerised by him.

Before the party could reach Nequassie however, another remarkable incident took place. They stopped at the village of Great Tellico and met two important Cherokee chiefs, Moytoy and Jacob the Conqueror. Moytoy told Cuming that he had been touted as the next 'emperor' of the Cherokee people but it now fell on the Scotsman to decide who it should be.

Cuming was basking in the attention and new-found glory. That night a great celebration was held during which the Indians stroked Cuming with eagles' tails. The following day he decided in favour of Moytoy as emperor in exchange for more promises to be true to the British Crown.

In his diary, Cuming wrote, 'It was a day of solemnity, the greatest that was ever seen in the Country. There was singing, dancing, feasting, making of speeches, the creation of Moytoy Emperor with the unanimous consent of the head men assembled from the different Towns of the Nation'.

Next, he revealed his narcissism to its fullest by adding that there was 'a declaration of their resigning their Crown, Eagles' Tails, Scalps of their enemies, as an emblem of their all owning His Majesty King George's Sovereignty over them, at the Desire of Sir Alexander Cuming, in whom an absolute unlimited power was placed, without which he could not be able to answer to His Majesty for their conduct'.

When Moytoy and the Cherokee leaders told Cuming that the 'emperor' decision was his, Cuming seems to have assumed a feeling of dominance over the people like an all-conquering hero. Several days later, when he reached Nequassie, Cuming claimed a solemn ceremony was held and that he was 'placed in a chair…while the warriors stroked him with 13 eagles' tails, and their singers sung from morning till night'.

This, according to Cuming, was his Cherokee coronation. After that he styled himself Sir Alexander Cuming, King of the Cherokee. A Cherokee crown, the Crown of Tannassy – a wig with possum's hair dyed red or yellow – was apparently placed on his head at some point. As far as he was concerned the Cherokee, thanks to him, were now subjects of Britain.

The truth of these encounters has been lost both in the mists of time and in mistranslations, deliberate or otherwise, by interpreters. Research has shown that there was no such position as 'emperor' among the Cherokee people. Nor had an outsider ever been elevated to the position of king – especially after only a matter of weeks. It is possible that the whole charade suited the purposes of Cuming and Moytoy.

Cuming's next step was, in his mind at least, a logical one. King George in London – the Great Man across the Water – should, he said, meet a delegation of these people who had been so happy and willing to swear allegiance to him.

Again the Cherokee readily agreed; a young warrior called Oukounaco, the 'White Owl', from the settlement of Tennessee Town, was the first to volunteer for the journey. He was soon joined by six others. Oukounaco later became Attakullakulla, rose to a position of great prominence, and became Britain's greatest ally among the Cherokee for many years to come.

On 4 May the party boarded the man-of-war *Fox* in Charles Town harbour. Moytoy himself would have joined them but his wife was ill and he was unable to travel. A month later, on 5 June , the vessel arrived at Dover on the south coast of England. The last piece in Cuming's brazen and intrepid piece of diplomatic showmanship was about to fall into place. He would be feted by the highest power in the land, great rewards lay in store for him, of that he was sure.

Meanwhile, in South Carolina, the people who had given him money were coming to the shocking realisation that Cuming had left the country. His investors discovered, when it was all too late, that he was in fact a fraudster. They broke open his so-called 'Treasury' building to find it filled with 'empty boxes, old iron, and rubbish'.

One merchant, who was duped by Cuming and lost a considerable sum of money, wrote, 'He carried off fifteen hundred pounds sterling of good Carolina money, and few people were entitled to laugh at the victims because Sir Alexander had played no favourites – he had taken in everybody who had money to invest'.

Over and above the £1,500 was the money that Cuming had spent on acquiring agriculture produce to ship back to Britain. He had swindled the Carolina settlers out of something approaching £3,000, a vast sum in 1730. No matter what else he might have achieved during his short stay in America, his calculated decision to rob and deceive his fellow countrymen was a scandal – and he deserves a place in a Hall of Shame.

In Scotland, Cuming would be described as a chancer and a confidence trickster; in America he would be called a shyster. He brought nothing but misery to the people of the fledgling British colony of South Carolina and fled before they could discover the extent of his double-dealing.

His so-called achievements with the Cherokee were undoubtedly designed to advance his own reputation back in Britain. Furthermore, his desire to ship warriors across to London was no more than an almighty publicity stunt for his own ends – to inveigle himself into the good books of the King and what he hoped would be a grateful government.

The arrival of the Indians in England was not unheralded. Cuming wrote to the Duke of Newcastle, Thomas Pelham-Holles, the secretary of state of the Southern Department, advising him what was happening and why. Newcastle, in turn, advised the Board of Trade and its members ordered that all negotiations with the Indians be taken over by the King and Newcastle. Cuming, who had acted without official sanction, was effectively cut out of the process.

On 22 June 1730 the warriors were presented to King George II at Windsor Castle. The *British Gazetteer* recorded that they 'were naked, except an apron about their middles, and a horse's tail hung down behind; their faces, shoulders etc. were painted and spotted with red, blue and green and they had bows in their hands and painted feathers on their heads'.

The Cherokee stayed in rather spartan quarters at an undertaker's premises in Covent Garden. They were often seen out on the streets of London dressed in Indian attire, and caused a sensation among Londoners. The warriors, by all accounts, had a busy and thoroughly enjoyable time in London, although they were upset that Cuming played no part in the negotiations. An excerpt from the *London Magazine* or *Gentleman's Intelligencer* reveals there was still some support for him among the media of the day.

The magazine reported: 'Far from throwing any regard to him for this piece of public service, they seemed resolved to shew those savages, that the man whom they had chosen as their chief governor under his majesty, was a man of no consequence in this kingdom. They even did not so much as desire him to be present when they were to conclude what they called a treaty with the Indians he had brought over.'

One reason for the cold-shouldering of Cuming was the news reaching England about the plight of the Carolinians the Scotsman had double-crossed so blatantly. There was no doubt the treaty the Indians eventually signed in Britain was of enormous benefit to the nation, but there was little love for the man who had engineered it, a man now viewed as a crook and an unstable lone wolf. Cuming was now soiled goods with nothing to show for his efforts.

In October the Indians bade a sad farewell to England and sailed back to Carolina on the *Fox*. Cuming stayed behind; he was a wanted man in America. He became increasingly eccentric, turned his hand to alchemy at one point, then suggested an outlandish scheme for paying off £80 million of Britain's national debt by settling three million Jewish families in the Cherokee mountains to cultivate the land. He also put forward the idea of establishing banks and local currency in America.

The government dismissed all his notions. His constant reminders to King George that his father had saved the life of His Majesty fell on deaf ears. By 1737, the penniless aristocrat was incarcerated in London's notorious Fleet Prison as a debtor. He spent the next 28 years there until 1765 when he was nominated as a poor brother of the Charterhouse, a complex of buildings in London's Smithfield.

Cuming's wife Amy, who allegedly had the dream that prompted him to make his memorable journey, died in 1743. His only son, Alexander, had a short army career but went mad and died in London's Whitechapel in 1796, after which the baronetcy died out.

As for the self-proclaimed king of the Cherokees, he spent the last 10 years of his life behind the grim walls of the Charterhouse hospital, locked away from society and forgotten by the outside world. His crimes had well and truly caught up with him. He died on 28 August 1775, and was buried in East Barnet Cemetery.

However, the Cherokee Nation never forgot the old rogue. In fact, they remembered him with great fondness. He had taken them to England and made public spectacles of the warriors for personal gain, yet when Oukounaco left to return to America, he is said to have wept when he said goodbye to Cuming. In Cherokee history, the man who became a scoundrel, a pest and an affront to his own country, is remembered as a Native American hero.

14

James Duff

I know that J. W. Duff and his company of murderers killed many of my neighbors and friends. My uncle and cousins, Schram Henderson, my wife's father and brother, Turknette, were murdered; Duff and his gang butchered all my neighbors, Hiram Nelson, Frank Scott and his father, Parson Johnson and old man Scott. Rocks were tied to their feet and they were thrown into Spring Creek.

– HOWARD HENDERSON, RESIDENT OF THE TEXAS HILL COUNTRY

The American Civil War is arguably the blackest period in the nation's relatively short history. It was a horrible and brutal conflict; it claimed the lives of more than 600,000 of the country's finest young men in battlefield conditions that were as hellish as the trench warfare in France and Belgium.

It also revealed the national character of the so-called United States at its ugliest. Life was cheap; soldiers were cut down in the prime of their lives in the name of racial supremacy. The men who died at battles such as Gettysburg and Shiloh did so because half of America wanted to end the practice of Negro slavery, while the other half was determined it must continue.

The war pitted north against south – the Union against the Confederacy. Families were torn apart, with husbands, wives, brothers and sisters often supporting a different cause. Former president Franklin Pierce and his wife Jane disagreed vehemently – she was a passionate anti-slavery advocate, whilst he felt the union should be protected at all costs. The issue had a seriously adverse effect on their marriage.

In one remarkable case, two immigrant brothers from Scotland, Alexander and James Campbell, not only fought on different sides, but opposed each other in battle. Alexander, who lived in New York, signed up for the Union side while James, who was in Charleston, South Carolina, was a staunch Confederate. At the Battle of Secessionville, not far from Charleston, they lined up against each other.

Both survived the battle and the war but the *Charleston Courier* newspaper branded the brother against brother incident 'another illustration of the deplorable consequences of this fratricidal war'.

The *Courier* summed it all perfectly. It had been only 78 years since America had become united by gaining independence from Britain, but now American was killing American over the right to own black slaves. It seemed, on the face of it, a senseless slaughter, as though the flower of the nation's youth was being needlessly sacrificed. Yet more than 150 years later the issue still gnaws at the country, and the Confederate flag still flies in many parts of the south.

The civil war's death toll has recently been upgraded to more than 750,000, more than all the other American wars combined. In addition, more than half a million were horribly wounded, suffered amputation, psychological trauma and disease. Some argue the killing was necessary to end slavery and as a precursor to the civil rights movement, others that it was a tragic breakdown in diplomacy and demonstrated a deep-rooted bloodthirstiness.

An unknown Confederate soldier, after a discussion he had with a Union man between enemy lines on the battlefield, made the memorable remark, 'We talked the matter over and could have settled the war in 30 minutes had it been left to us'.

The key battles of the war are ingrained on the American consciousness: Antietam, Gettysburg, Bull Run, Fredericksburg, Shiloh, Chancellorsville, Vicksburg, The Wilderness and Spotsylvania. The city of Atlanta, Georgia, was burned to the ground in General William Tecumseh Sherman's March to the Sea,

Much of the fighting was done in the Confederate states of Virginia, North and South Carolina, Alabama, Georgia, Mississippi and Louisiana. The other states that broke away – or seceded – from the U.S. were Arkansas, Florida, Tennessee and Texas. Jefferson Davis, a former secretary of state for war in Franklin Pierce's administration and the son-in-law of former president Zachary Taylor, was the Confederate leader. He was a slave owner, originally from Mississippi.

Texas was not exactly the epicentre of the civil war. There were only a handful of major battles and a few skirmishes fought, the Blockade of Galveston Harbour being the most pivotal. Texas, which gained statehood in 1845, was a mere 'teenage' state when the war began in 1861.

At the time more than 30% of people living in Texas were enslaved, and the state voted to become the seventh Confederate State. It was a contentious vote with delegates to a special convention declaring solidarity with their 'sister slave-holding states'. A month later a special referendum was held. More than 453,000 Texans voted for secession while only 13,000 wanted to stay with the Union.

The reasons for leaving the Union were spelled out in a special document. The language was unequivocal and exemplified the widely-held belief, unshakeable in the states of the American south, that white people were in all respects superior to blacks and that the subservice of the Negro population was 'mutually beneficial'.

The document stated: 'We hold as undeniable truths that the governments of the various States, and of the Confederacy itself, were established exclusively by the white race, for themselves and their posterity; that the African race had no agency in their establishment; that they were rightfully held and regarded as an inferior and dependent race, and in that condition only could their existence in this country be rendered beneficial or tolerable.'

It added that the end of slavery would bring 'inevitable calamities' upon both races and 'desolation upon the fifteen slave-holding states'.

Compared with the other states involved in the war – north or south – Texas was massive. It stretched from the Mexican border along the coast to the borders of Louisiana and Arkansas to the east, New Mexico to the west and what is now Oklahoma to the north. It covered almost 270,000 square miles, much of it forest, hills and prairie land.

The so-called Texas Hill Country is a huge area of rugged terrain stretching north and west of San Antonio. In the 1860s much of the land was populated by German settlers. They were among thousands of Germans who fled to America in 1848 to escape persecution in their native land. Many were highly intelligent people, doctors, philosophers, teachers and inventors and were collectively known as Freethinkers or 'Forty-Eighters'. Others included peasant farmers; there was a wide diversity of religions among them; some drank heavily; others were strictly teetotal.

Not surprisingly, as enlightened and morally scrupulous intellectuals, they were vehemently opposed to slavery and abhorred the notion of white supremacy. When Texas voted overwhelmingly to join the Confederacy, the Germans formed the Union Loyal League; they armed themselves to the teeth to protect themselves against attack, organised a sophisticated underground communication system, and urged Union forces to invade Texas.

To the Confederates in Texas, the behavior of the Germans smacked of insurrection. There was little tolerance for dissenting voices once the state had voted to secede from the Union. Worse was to come in 1862 when the controversial Conscription Act was passed. The Germans, who made up five per cent of the Texas population, suddenly found themselves facing the prospect of being press-ganged into fighting for a cause with which they profoundly disagreed.

The only exceptions in the Conscription Act were wealthy white slave owners who were exempted from marching off to war with their fellow 'Johnny Rebs' as Confederate soldiers were nicknamed. The law was later amended to provide exemption to men who served the national and state governments and in heavy industry, teaching, medicine or other professions deemed to serving the public. But those between the ages of 18 and 35 who farmed the land were expected to fight – and that meant the Germans of the Hill Country.

There was quite simply no way that was going to happen. The German settlers did not share the views of their fellow Texans, they did not own plantations, few owned slaves, and they had a strong bond of loyalty to the government of their newly-adopted country. In small settlements like Comfort and Fredericksburg, Cherry Spring and New Braunfels, the people were defiantly opposed to the Confederacy. They were also justifiably fearful.

In April 1862 martial law was imposed in parts of Texas, including the Hill Country; all males aged 16 or over were ordered to swear an oath of allegiance to the Confederacy or leave the state. Militias were hastily organised to make sure that everyone complied. The militiamen were no more than rag-tag bands of murderous thugs who burned the homes of dissenters, lynched them from trees and drowned them in the fast-flowing rivers. These men went about their task with enthusiasm and became known as the *hangerbande* – or hanging band. War had effectively been declared on the peaceful Germans of the Hill Country.

The most notorious of the militia leaders was Captain James Duff, a Scotsman whose foul deeds and brutal behavior gained him the reputation of being the 'most hated man' in the counties to which he had been assigned. He embarked on a vicious reign of terror in the course of which he killed – or more likely ordered the killings of – anyone who disagreed with him and the Confederate cause.

His unit, Duff's Partisan Rangers, was given authority to use whatever means they chose to quell Union resistance in Kerr and Gillespie Counties. He indulged in torture, murder, hanging and the burning of property. His hard-hearted attitude towards those who refused to take the oath of allegiance is summed up in a comment he made: 'The God damn Dutchmen are Unionists to a man…I will hang all I suspect of being anti-Confederates'. (Germans in America were often mistakenly called Dutch – or Deutsch – men)

Duff's tactics in attempting to force people to sign an oath were despicable; they placed the Scotsman firmly in the category of 'war criminal'. There is one shocking episode for which Duff is remembered in Texas to this day – the ordering of the Nueces Massacre.

When a party of Germans left one of the hill villages in a bid to flee across the border to Mexico, Duff ordered a company of his men to follow and kill them. There are some who claim that Duff himself was present at the massacre site the following day and that he per-sonally killed – or ordered the killing of – some of the surviving wounded by shooting them in the back of the head in cold blood.

Duff, who had previously left the U.S. Army under a

Burial of German victims of Nueces Massacre

182

cloud, had a brutal and unforgettable impact upon the civil war as it unfolded in Texas. The campaign he waged on behalf of his Confederate masters was savage and went unchecked. His victims were left homeless; the houses it had taken them so long to build were destroyed. Whole families, including women and children, were rounded up and held in atrocious conditions; food and livestock were confiscated.

The killing that happened under his watch was senseless, barbarous and carried out without mercy or remorse. On many occasions Duff and his men taunted the relatives of those they had murdered. Other times they watched and mocked while women recovered the bloated bodies of their husbands and sons from rivers or tree branches. There can be no defence or justification for Duff's callous and brutal actions.

Reports credit Duff with the deaths of more than 50 men in the space of a year. A further 2,000 people fled to the hills to escape his terrifying mobocracy. He gained the moniker 'The Rebel Butcher of Western Texas'.

In his book, *Camp Verde: Texas Frontier Defense*, Joseph Luther writes: 'To obtain information, his (Duff's) soldiers sometimes resorted to bullwhips; other times they would hang a person by the neck and then release their victim just before strangulation, repeating the process until either the interrogation had been successful or the suspect was dead – not unlike modern-day "water boarding".

Journalist Helen Raley, writing in 1938, described the Nueces Massacre as 'The Blackest Crime in History'. She added, 'This slaughter of unarmed and wounded prisoners...was by command of a Scotchman named Duff and a Yankee renegade who was his lieutenant'. Duff, she said, had been 'drummed out of the United States regular army' in disgrace.

James Duff was born in 1828 in the Perthshire village of Logierait, a small farming community which nowadays sits just west of the A9 at the Balinluig junction on the road to Aberfeldy. It is located at picturesque spot at the confluence of the Rivers Tay and Tummel.

In the early 1800s, Logierait was a typical small Scottish village, with a church and an inn and in which locals indulged in traditional crafts. After leaving school at the age of 12 or 13, Duff became apprentice to a tailor named Alexander Robertson at Pitnacree House.

As a young man from Logierait, Duff had big footsteps in which to follow. The second prime minister of Canada, Alexander Mackenzie, had been born in the village six years before him. A century before, in 1723, so was one of the leading members of the Scottish Enlightenment, philosopher and historian Adam Ferguson.

Life in the Scottish countryside was clearly not for Duff. He worked as a farmer but the sleepy hollow of Logierait held little interest. He had his sights set on the opportunities and excitement that lay on the other side of the Atlantic. At some point during the 1840s Duff, while still a teenager, boarded a ship and set off for America.

By 1849 Duff had made his way to Boston, Massachusetts. In January of that year he signed up for the U.S. Army's 5th Infantry Regiment, known as the Bobcats. He was described as 21-years old, 5ft 10ins, with grey eyes, brown hair and a fair complexion.

The Scot did not last long in the regiment before he deserted, was quickly captured and then court-martialled. His sentence was remitted and he served until his discharge five years later in January 1854, at Fort McIntosh, near Laredo, Texas, by which time he had attained the rank of sergeant.

Desertion was not uncommon in the U.S. Army in the early 1850s. As many as 15% of all enlisted men deserted for a variety of reasons including low pay, boredom, lack of proper food and amenities. Many of the frontier outposts to which the men were sent at that time were extremely rough and ready places. Duff, by all accounts, ran off not long after he had signed up.

After his discharge, Duff became an army sutler at Fort Belknap, near Newcastle in Young County, Texas, before moving to San Antonio, where he established himself as a relatively successful businessman. He worked as a freighter, transporting goods to and from the city in his wagons. He helped carry a sacred Comanche standing rock known as the Wichita County Meteorite from the Indian lands to the old Capitol building in Austin, Texas. His wagons were also used to transport Comanches to Indian Territory, now Oklahoma, land used for the re-settlement of the tribes.

On 4 December 1856, he married Harriet Paul, a daughter of Major Gabriel Paul, in Young County. Ironically, his father-in-law went on to become a decorated civil war general who fought with the Union side and who suffered devastating injuries at the Battle of Gettysburg, as a result of which he lost his sight.

They lived for a short time in St. Louis, Missouri, where Harriet, who was 10 years younger than Duff, had been born. While there she gave birth to twin girls, only one of whom, Julie, survived beyond early childhood. A third daughter Margaret was born five years later. In 1860 the family was living in San Antonio where Duff was described in that year's census as a merchant.

There seems to have been nothing to suggest the brutality that was to taint his life in later years. He appeared a happily-married family man with a successful business and considerable personal wealth. The 1860 census lists the combined value of his real estate and personal estate as $35,000. His wealth had most likely been accumulated through his freight company with perhaps a contribution from Harriet, who was from a well-off family. He was in a very good financial position.

He was also a member of a secret society known as the Knights of the Golden Circle, whose objective was to annex territories in Mexico, Central America, South America and the Caribbean as 'slave states' in the USA.

When the civil war erupted and Texas was plunged into the secession crisis, Duff returned to army life, and from the outset played an active role in Confederate military affairs. In May 1861 he was part of a large Confederate force that seized the city of San Antonio and its army garrison on behalf of the State of Texas.

The formal unconditional surrender of the fort by Federal troops was achieved without bloodshed and Duff covered himself in glory. As well as the 10 officers and

337 men who surrendered at the garrison, Duff is said to have captured a further 30 in the city. He rose to the rank of brigadier general in the state militia but resigned and accepted a commission as captain in the Confederate Army.

In the weeks and months that followed the takeover of the city, Duff became a well-known military figure. He was already a conspicuous character by virtue of his successful business and big personality – and quite possibly his very recognisable Scottish accent. He had come a long way in a few short years, from his peaceful childhood in the Perthshire countryside to the bitter racial divisions that scarred Texas during the outbreak of the American Civil War.

Duff was not exactly on the war's front line. South-west Texas was a long way from the centre of the battlefield action that took place in states such as Virginia, Pennsylvania and the Carolinas. But he was determined to stamp his mark on whatever opportunities came his way. He did not have to wait long; by the summer of 1861 he was put in command of an irregular Confederate military unit known as Duff's Partisan Rangers. Thanks to him, that unit's name lives on in infamy to this day.

The Texas Hill Country is a beautiful part of the state. It is tranquil and rugged, peaceful and dramatic, with tree-lined rivers and great canyons. Nowadays it is a scenic tourist trap; back in the 1850s it was dotted with small towns, villages and farms. The people who settled here had to be hard-working and industrious.

President Lyndon Johnson grew up there, and he and his wife Lady Bird are buried near the banks of the Pedernales River. He once said, 'This is my country, the Hill Country of Texas. And through the years when time would permit, here is where I would always return, to the Pedernales River, the scenes of my childhood'.

In his book, *The Dogs of War Unleashed: The Devil Concealed in Men Unchained*, Joe Baluch writes, 'This pleasant place not always has been so inviting, so peaceful. In the 1860s, the "dogs of war" unleashed here a sanguinary paroxysm of terror and death, a calamity that fostered for decades thereafter bitterness and distrust'.

After the Napoleonic Wars, Germany was wracked by internal strife. Persecution forced scholars and intellectuals to flee their native land and find new roots in Texas. Schoolteachers, musicians, doctors, lawyers, and skilled craftsmen; it was a wave of highly educated men and women who arrived in the New World. They were Freethinkers who did not conform to the accepted Texas 'norm'.

Described as 'bookish and idealistic', their homes were filled with music and culture. There was no form of government, only volunteers. Pioneer settler Emma Altgelt wrote, 'Among the older inhabitants a sort of communism prevailed brought about by the conditions…One would give to others what could be spared, and take in return what was lacked'.

They were searching for something resembling a Utopian lifestyle, and apart from the occasional Indian raid, they came close to finding it. Then came the civil war, and for the Germans, everything changed. Not only were they principled people, they wanted no part in the war. They were hell-bent on avoiding conscription, and refused to swear an oath of allegiance to the Confederates under martial law to avoid repudiating their oath of loyalty to the United States of America. This was like a red rag to the bull – the 'dog of war unleashed' – that came among them in the shape of James Duff.

In April 1862 Duff and his Partisan Rangers – a hodge-podge of semi-professional soldiers, eager conscripts, and armed outlaws and thugs – were dispatched to ensure the terms of martial law were strictly obeyed in Gillespie and Kerr Counties, the heart of the Hill Country. All males aged 16 or over were to pledge allegiance to a regional provost marshal, a post to which Duff had been self-appointed. From the outset, Duff was uncompromising and merciless, ordering all men to report to him within six days.

Some Germans refused to take the oath, whilst others lived in such remote homes they did not even hear about the martial law imposition. Duff and his men marched into their villages, bullied them, threatened them, and arrested some under threat of being Unionists. They were sent for trial but Duff returned to San Antonio believing there was little to concern his Confederate masters. He had succeeded in rattling a few cages but that was all.

However, his brief appearance in the Hill Country had alarmed the German leaders, leading to the formation of the defence organisation Union Loyal League. By the summer of 1862 hundreds from the villages of Comfort, Fredericksburg, Kerrville and elsewhere had joined, pledging loyalty not to the loathed Confederacy, but to the Union.

In July a mass meeting of more than 500 men was held in secret at a spot known as Bear Creek for the oath to be sworn. Everyone present agreed never to reveal details of the organisation; confidential communication and recognition signs were identified; and it was made clear that any member who informed would be killed instantly.

Prussian-born judge, county treasurer and local farmer and mill owner Fritz Tegener was elected as the Loyal League's leader, with the rank of major. Tegener was a community activist; a charismatic individual who had immigrated to the village of Comfort in the 1850s.

However, no sooner had the meeting been held than word of the Union Loyal League leaked out. Someone had 'grassed' to the Confederate troops at San Antonio and suspicion soon fell on a Scottish ranch hand named Basil Stewart. True to their word the Germans showed no mercy. They selected a hitman who lay in wait for Stewart, then killed him and dumped his body in a remote part of the countryside.

It was time for the second coming of James Duff to the Hill Country – and this time he wanted blood both for the killing of Basil Stewart but more importantly to avenge the treacherous behavior of the 'God damn Dutchmen'.

As far as Duff and his men were concerned the Hill Country was in a state of rebellion. His task now was to persuade as many conscripts to sign up with the Confederacy, by force if necessary, and to demobilise and destroy the Union Loyal League by whatever means he saw fit. The ruthless Scot needed no second invitation.

Duff arrested dozens of men on suspicion of being Union sympathisers. They were sent to cramped prison cells to await trial; in many cases their homes and crops were burned and their families held captive in army stockades. One member of Duff's Rangers described how he helped take a suspect's wife and children prisoner, then destroyed the crops, overturned the beehives, and smashed every stick of furniture in the house, including a working loom.

Many families were forced to watch as the homes they had built with their bare hands – as well as all the possessions inside – were burned to the ground. They witnessed their menfolk being tortured and bullwhipped; some were strangled to within an inch of their lives before the process was repeated; others were hanged from the branches of trees. In some cases, men had rocks tied to their feet and were thrown into fast-flowing rivers.

In one notorious incident, Duff's men rounded up six men suspected of having ignored the oath of allegiance. They were being transported to Fort Mason while their families were being taken to a nearby stockade. The men were Gus Tegener, brother of Fritz; Howard Henderson and his brother Seabird; Frank Scott; and Allen and Hiram Nelson.

The group camped overnight beside the Pedernales River and in the middle of the night, Howard Henderson noticed that the two guards were asleep. He alerted Allen Nelson and the two made their escape. When Duff's men found out they were gone, they took immediate and brutal action against the remaining captives.

The prisoners were taken to a nearby tree. There, one by one, they were lynched. Their bodies were cut down and stripped of all clothing. Then the guards dragged their corpses to nearby Spring Creek and dumped them in the water. They then caught up with the women and children, bragged about what they had done to their husbands and fathers, and mocked them.

Duff arrived on the scene and acceded to the women's pleas that they be allowed to bury their dead. According to Joe Baluch, 'The women found their men floating in Spring Creek, unrecognizable, black and swollen. Selecting a burial site, they worked in shifts, digging a grave; then wading into the water up to their armpits, they rolled the bodies on to the bank in sheets and buried them'.

Henderson wrote a letter that was published in the book *A Hundred Years of Comfort in Texas*, by Guido Ranskleben. Part of the letter read, 'I know that J. W. Duff and his company of murderers killed many of my neighbors and friends. My uncle and cousins, Schram Henderson, my wife's father and brother, Turknette, were murdered; Duff and his gang butchered all my neighbors, Hiram Nelson, Frank Scott and his father, Parson Johnson and old man Scott. Rocks were tied to their feet and they were thrown into Spring Creek'.

The Hill Country was in a state of utter fear and dread. Duff and his bandit militia had embarked on a reign of terror. They had killed and tortured dozens of men, destroyed hundreds of homes and livelihoods, and left countless families without a roof over their heads. The Utopian lifestyle that the largely pacifist German immigrants thought they had discovered in the Texas Hill Country had been ruthlessly and comprehensively destroyed in the space of a few short weeks.

Duff cared not a jot for their welfare. He showed no remorse whatsoever for his actions. Instead, as the weeks passed, he seemed to believe more and more that he was doing the right thing. If innocent men died, if wives were left without husbands and children without fathers then – in his mind – it was all justifiable; the punishment somehow fitted the 'crime'.

In reality the resistance shown by the German settlers in Texas was nothing more than a sideshow in the larger civil war picture; the Hill Country's 'war within a war' was small fry compared with the battles raging elsewhere. Duff was a big fish in a small pond, a pocket dictator. Yet the brutality meted out by him and his men was symptomatic of the senseless slaughter witnessed throughout civil war in America.

The atrocities visited on the area by Duff very quickly achieved their objective. The settlers were unprepared for the cruelty and the sheer sadism displayed by the Partisan Rangers, one of several militia units who were supposedly under the control of state authorities. The Union Loyal League disbanded within a month. Tegener and the other leaders had never wanted to provoke such a fierce reaction; it had been formed as a means of self-protection.

By the end of July, a rumour had reached Fritz Tegener that the governor of Texas, Francis Lubbock, was allowing a 30-day period for those refusing to sign an oath of allegiance to the Confederacy to leave the state. Whether such a reprieve was given has been a matter of conjecture ever since – but it was music to the ears of Tegener and his followers.

On 1 August more than 61 men joined with him deep in wooded countryside at a spot called Turtle Creek, five miles south of Kerrville, and decided to flee Texas and head for the safety of the Mexican border. They took with them enough food, supplies and ammunition to last several weeks, and the 30-day timescale for the journey was well within their capabilities.

They were heading west towards the Rio Grande, and the plan was that they cross the river and report to the American consul in the city of Monterrey. The amnesty meant there was no need to rush; there was no danger of attack from enemy troops. Or so they thought. The Union supporting Germans had reckoned without their old foe James Duff.

News of the departure reached the ears of Duff thanks to spies in the German camp, of that there is little doubt. The Scotsman immediately dispatched a company of 94 men under the command of Colonel Colin McRae to go after them. If Governor Lubbock had really given his 30-day order, then there would have been no need to chase the immigrants. Duff clearly had other plans for them.

One of McRae's Confederates, English soldier Captain R. H. Williams, later wrote, 'Sinister rumors of Duff began to spread, and it was said among other things that he had given certain of his followers to understand that he wanted no prisoners brought into his camp'.

The message from Duff was clear. Not unlike the Massacre of Glencoe in 1692, the order had gone out to 'leave none alive'.

In truth this was not the most difficult task that had ever faced McRae and his men. The fleeing Unionists had been moving at a leisurely pace, not believing they were in the slightest danger. They had been joined along the way by a number of others, including Howard Henderson and Allen Nelson, and their numbers had swollen to 68.

The party made its way along the Pedernales, Guadalupe and Frio Rivers until, after eight days, they came to a clearing near the banks of the Nueces River, where they decided to camp for the night. They were within easy striking distance of Mexico although, had they travelled with any urgency, they could have been over the border in four or five days.

Some of the Germans reported seeing 'strangers' in the area, but the mood in the camp was light-hearted and positive. Tegener did not post any lookouts; there was never any fear of attack on the whole journey.

According to *Battle or Massacre? The Incident on the Nueces* by Stanley McGowen, one of the marchers named August Hoffman described the mood in the camp as 'gay and merry during the evening' and that people 'recited humorous pieces'.

Unknown to them, the 'strangers' that had been spotted in the surrounding countryside were the men of Colin McRae's pursuing Confederate unit. As the unsuspecting Germans were preparing to sleep for the night, the soldiers were preparing a surprise night attack with the orders of Duff to take no prisoners ringing in their ears.

Shortly after 1am on 10 August, two squads of men crept towards the sleeping Germans. They approached without a sound until they were disturbed by two of the Unionists who were out for a walk. One of the men was immediately shot dead by the Confederates, the other fled back to the camp and alerted the rest of his colleagues.

Captain Williams said that the German camp was immediately 'in a buzz, like a swarm of bees'. In the skirmish that followed the fleeing immigrants were said to have 'fought vigorously', although a number of their party left camp; whether they fled the fighting is unclear. By the time the battle was over, 30 of Tegener's men lay dead.

Another 17 escaped, but the greatest scandal arose over the fate of those – reports estimate between nine and 19 – who had survived the battle and lay wounded. Initially, the Confederates treated their injuries, brought them water and made breakfast for them. Captain Williams wrote, 'They had fought a good fight and bore themselves so pluckily that I felt sorry that I had taken any part against them'.

However, later in the day the injured men were taken to a wooded area. There, one by one, they were shot through the back of the head in cold blood. By any stretch of the imagination, and no matter how loosely defined the battlefield etiquette in remote Texas was, this was a massacre of the most despicable kind. Some said Duff was actually there, others that he had pulled the trigger. The more likely truth was that the troops were following his orders from a distance.

Captain Williams pointed the finger of blame squarely at a young lieutenant called Edwin Lilly, who he described as a 'remorseless treacherous villain'. He also said the men who had helped drag the wounded Germans to their execution site were 'cowardly wretches'. Lilly's motive, he wrote, was to 'make himself popular' with authorities in San Antonio, including Duff.

It was three years before the families of the dead men were allowed to remove their bodies and take them back to Comfort and the other little villages. McRae's unit simply left them lying there to be eaten by the buzzards, wolves and coyotes. Of the 17 who escaped, some drowned in the Rio Grande, some were captured and executed, and at least one was captured by Duff and hanged.

The incident has become known as the Nueces Massacre and has been labelled the 'Blackest Crime in Texas Warfare'. In 1866 a monument known as the Treue der Union (Loyal to the Union) was erected in the village of Comfort to commemorate those who died. It still stands to this day.

Duff's Partisan Rangers did not remain much longer in the Hill Country. By the end of the year the unit was expanded into the 33rd Texas Cavalry and served at a number of locations along the Texas coast. When the war ended in 1865 he was a wanted man and escaped to Mexico, where at one point he was said to be have been working as a housekeeper.

A few years later a Texas newspaper reported that he had made his way to Arkansas and had been keeping a store on the Arkansas River. The report added, 'He murdered a negro and is now in jail in Little Rock awaiting his trial. The murder was a cold-blooded one and the feeling against the murderer is intense, so much so that he is trying to obtain a change of venue (for trial) to Pine Bluff'.

Presumably Duff either escaped from prison or was found not guilty, a common verdict in the 1800s involving crimes against Negroes. By 1871 he and his family

Treue der Union monument in Comfort Texas. Picture courtesy of Ernest Mettenforf

had returned to Scotland and were staying in a farm at Kingoldrum, just west of Kirriemuir in Angus.

Duff, Harriet and their daughters Julie and Margaret were living on a 424-acre farm, of which 384 acres were arable land. The 1871 census records that there were 9 employees, four farm servants, a farm grieve, a cook and house maid, a domestic maid, and a governess. The family was clearly financially well-off.

But by 1880 he, Harriet and Julie were back in the United States, this time in Denver, Colorado, where Duff had again become a prosperous and respected businessman. He was the manager of the Colorado Mortgage and Investment Company, a business that handled British investment in the city. Duff persuaded British investors towards canals and helped in the building of the High Line Canal, which turned much of Denver into profitable agricultural land. He became something of a personality in the city and was held in great esteem.

In 1887 he and Harriet moved to London and lived in the suburb of Barnes, in Richmond. He passed away on 16 April 1900, at a hospital in Guildford. In his will, he left his widow Harriet a total of £7,064.16s.3d, a considerable sum in those days.

The couple's daughter Julie married a wealthy linen and jute manufacturer from Dundee called John B. Taylor. In the 1901 census Harriet was living with them at their home, Affleck Castle, near Monikie in Angus. She was said to have been living on her own means.

The tragedy of the killings that were encouraged and perpetrated by Duff in the Texas Hill Country was that, in the great scheme of things, events in that part of the country scarcely registered. The great generals, such as Lee or Sherman, Grant or Beauregard, paid little or no heed to what was essentially a civil war backwater. The German settlers effectively died for nothing.

In today's America, the issues that divided the country during the civil war live on. The Confederate flag flies from many buildings, private houses and cars. A powerful white supremacist movement still spreads the message that white people are genetically superior to other races, and Southern Rock musicians sing that the 'South will rise again'.

To many groups and individuals, Duff is remembered not as a villain, but as a hero. In 2014 the newsletter of a Confederate Veterans' group based in Bedford, Texas, reported with great excitement that the grave of the 'noted Confederate' James Duff had been 'discovered' in Scotland.

He lies buried under a gravestone in a cemetery near Dundee. The Veterans' group said that the stone had been found after a 15-year search and that he 'was probably the most well-known and historically important figure of the War whose gravesite remained undiscovered'.

15

John Murray

I do not think that forcing his lordship on shipboard is sufficient. Nothing less than depriving him of life or liberty will secure peace to Virginia

– George Washington about John Murray, Lord Dunmore

America has never been short of heroes since it broke free from the shackles of Great Britain in the 1780s and became the United States.

Some of the world's most illustrious men and women have been products of the so-called Land of the Free – from the founding fathers such as Benjamin Franklin, George Washington and Thomas Jefferson to the great political minds of 'Honest Abe' Lincoln and Theodore Roosevelt, the men of business including John D. Rockefeller and Henry Ford, and pioneering giants Thomas Edison, Samuel Morse and the Wright Brothers.

On the battlefield, Americans still talk of the exploits of Generals Ulysses Grant and Robert E. Lee, and war leader-cum-president Dwight 'Uncle Ike' Eisenhower; the literary works of Mark Twain, Harriet Beecher Stowe, Ernest Hemingway and John Steinbeck are still read avidly; the nation was captivated by the music of Elvis Presley and Louis Armstrong; sporting stars such as Babe Ruth and Muhammad Ali became national icons; and the glitter of Hollywood gave the world Walt Disney, Samuel Goldwyn and the greatest actors and actresses of the silver screen.

Throughout the nation's history there have been those who championed Jefferson's mantra that 'all men are created equal' – from abolitionist Frederick Douglass and educator Booker T. Washington, suffrage campaigner Susan B. Anthony and feminist leader Elizabeth Cady Stanton, through to the man who personified the civil rights movement, Martin Luther King, Jr.

They live on as legends, their names have shaped the young nation, they are memorialised and revered, the pages of history talk of their greatness.

Of course, there could not be good guys without their ne'er-do-well, reprobate counterparts. Every nation has them: rogues, charlatans, miscreants and blackguards. America, despite the nation's relative youth, can boast more than its fair share.

There was the traitor of the revolution, Benedict Arnold, who left Washington's Army and went over to the British side; the host of crooked politicians who brought shame on cities such as Chicago and New York, right up to President Richard Nixon, disgraced by his role in the Watergate scandal; leaders of the Ku Klux Klan whose actions symbolise America's struggle with racism; John Wilkes Booth who assassinated Abraham Lincoln.

The list goes on. Outlaws such as Billy the Kid and Jesse James terrorised the Wild West; there were serial killers Ted Bundy and Jeffrey Dahmer and the Oklahoma City Bomber Timothy McVeigh; ice skater Tonya Harding who launched a vicious attack on opponent Nancy Kerrigan; and stockbroker Bernie Madoff, whose Ponzi scheme swindle was the biggest financial fraud in U.S. history.

It is an impressively dishonourable Hall of Shame. But who was the original? Who was the man whose deeds were so dastardly that he was rewarded with the distinction of having been 'America's First Villain'?

The individual is by no means a household name. Yet when colonial rule was coming to an end with the American War of Independence, this character's catalogue of miscalculations, blundering foul-ups and downright stupidity was on the lips of people in every class of society, from the landed gentry of Virginia society to the slaves who worked in the plantations.

Step forward the man who can lay claim to having been America's original scoundrel, the nation's first ever bad guy – John Murray, the 4th Earl of Dunmore, a bumbling Scottish aristocrat appointed to the governorship of arguably the most valuable of the colonies at a time when skillful diplomacy was of the utmost necessity.

Murray's five-year tenure as royal governor of Virginia was, to put it bluntly, a disaster. When an administrator with a degree of savoir-faire was required, Murray was grievously lacking in finesse and the delicate art of negotiation. Instead, he succeeded in alienating everyone that mattered, including the people over whom he was ruling.

His incumbency of the governorship was one long series of clumsy errors. He was prone to drunken excesses that often resulted in embarrassing outbursts, and for all his devotion to 'king and country' in Great Britain he was remarkably insubordinate, even refusing direct orders to transfer from one governorship to another.

Murray's real problems stemmed from his ham-fisted reactions to the growing revolutionary fervour that was sweeping the colonies. He was in the eye of a storm, of that there was no doubt, although as a representative of the Crown he was still expected to display what might be described as 'conduct becoming' of a person in such a position. Diplomatic prudence should have told him not to burn too many bridges, as an independent America was potentially a valuable British ally.

Rather, his high-handed and confrontational manner ensured that he became a figure of hatred and disdain. George Washington, with whom he was friendly in his early days in America, questioned whether peace would ever come to Virginia while Murray was alive.

He tried to govern Virginia without consulting the House of Burgesses, Virginia's legislative body, and proclaimed martial law in the colony. At one point he threatened to burn to the ground the city of Williamsburg, then Virginia's colonial capital. He seized the city's store of gunpowder and weapons from the armoury and transferred them to a British warship to prevent the rebellious Americans getting their hands on it. He had a massive, long-lasting and very public feud with one of the most influential of America's founding fathers, Patrick Henry, who succeeded him as the first post-colonial governor of Virginia.

Lord Dunmore's War against the Shawnee Indians was named after him, and it is viewed as one of his few successes. Even so, there were suggestions that the war had been deliberately manipulated and that he was in collusion with the Indians to reduce the strength of the Virginia militia in the event of a colonial rebellion.

However, Murray's most controversial decision was his so-called Emancipation Proclamation, in which he offered freedom to slaves if they left their plantations and took up arms with the British against those fighting for independence. Those who joined were known as his Black Loyalists, and he formed them into what he called his Ethiopian Regiment. It was a bizarre and desperate move by a man who had himself kept slaves, and it caused convulsions of panic among Virginians.

Some of the slaves who abandoned their masters and signed up remained free – but not many. Initial excitement and hope among the black population soon dissipated when it became clear that Murray was motivated purely by self-interest. Many of the slaves died in a smallpox epidemic.

People rioted in the streets because of his behaviour and

Flight of Lord Dunmore. From Sotheby's History of Virginia, *published by American Book Company – Library of Congress*

decision-making. He suffered the ultimate indignity of being driven from his mansion and out of the colony he had been appointed to govern. He and his family had to flee their home and retreat to the safety of a British man-of-war anchored 12 miles off the coast, from which he ordered the bombardment and destruction of the port city of Norfolk.

Murray, who was in his early 40s and married when he arrived in America, even found time to become embroiled in a sex scandal, thanks to an affair with 19-year old Kitty Eustace.

Crisis management clearly was not the Earl of Dunmore's forte. He may not have been the worst royal governor to grace America's colonies, although his ineptitude, lack of reasoned judgment, and gross failings in strategy and discretion made him one of the most hapless.

Murray was an absolutely stereotypical toff. His family occupied a place among the highest echelons of the Scottish nobility, and as well as being prominent landowners, possessed enormous influence in aristocratic circles. He was born in 1730 in the magnificent Taymouth Castle, near Kenmore, Perthshire; the building was owned by the Earls of Breadalbane, one of many noble Scottish families to whom the Murrays were related.

His father, William Murray, was the 3rd Earl of Dunmore, who through marriage to Catherine Nairn had inherited the title of Lord Nairn. Marriage to close family relatives was common within the aristocracy, and Catherine was the daughter of William's uncle, also William Murray. The uncle's father, in turn, was the 1st Marquess of Atholl. It was a world of immense power and privilege.

Young John was sent to the exclusive Eton College for three years until the age of 14. Revolution was in the air in his native Scotland and his extended family was firmly behind the attempt by Bonnie Prince Charlie to overthrow the Hanoverians and restore the Stuart monarchy. At the age of 15, Murray was a page of honour to Prince Charles Edward Stuart at Holyrood Palace in Edinburgh.

In 1746 he accompanied his father at the ill-fated Battle of Culloden, near Inverness, where the Duke of Cumberland – known as 'Butcher' – routed the Jacobite forces. Although both escaped, English troops later placed the Murray family under house arrest. William was taken away, tried on charges of high treason and imprisoned in the Tower of London. He was released on a conditional pardon in 1750 after agreeing to pledge loyalty to the Crown.

While his father was under lock and key, 20-year old John Murray joined the British Army as an ensign in the Scots Guards and served in the Seven Years War. After William's release he succeeded to the peerage and became a representative Scottish peer in the House of Lords. However, only four years later he died in London in 1756 aged 60. His passing meant that John became the 4th Earl of Dunmore at the relatively young age of 26.

Described as a 'tall, athletic Scotsman with a shock of red hair', and with a title already under his belt, Murray was unquestionably an eligible young nobleman, a good catch for one of the many single daughters of the gentry. So it was no surprise that, on 18 February 1759, at a ceremony in Edinburgh, the 29-year old Murray married 17-year old society beauty Charlotte Stewart, daughter of Alexander Stewart, the 6th Earl of Galloway. As well as being related through William's uncle, Charlotte's grandmother Anne Murray was the daughter of none other than the 1st Earl of Dunmore – John Murray's grandfather.

Murray left the army to concentrate on politics, and the couple immediately started a family. When he was sent to America 11 years after they wed, Charlotte was expecting their eighth child. In 1761 he followed in his father's footsteps and became one of only 16 Scottish peers to sit in the British Parliament. That September the couple took part in the Coronation of King George III at Westminster Abbey.

The Earl and his charming wife made a handsome couple, popular in the highest circles of London life, counting royalty among their friends. It was a sumptuous life – a luxurious London apartment, a number of Scottish estates, a large and ever-growing family, and influential friends in high places. The couple had all the trappings enjoyed by the wealthy and entitled British aristocratic elite.

However, Murray was an ambitious man, and he had his eye on one of the plum overseas postings that, during the days of the British Empire, were routinely handed to men with his upbringing and position in society. Royal governors were appointed not for their talents or their ability to do the job but simply on account of their friends or family.

Governors were the representatives of the King and bore the title His Excellency, yet had little in the way of autonomy. They had to carry out the wishes of the Crown, which, not surprisingly, required the governor to advance British interests in the area – whatever the local people thought. A good governor was one who was able to achieve the delicate balancing act of carrying out royal instructions and serving local interests. Governor Christopher Codrington of the Leeward Islands said in 1701 that it was like 'walking between red-hot irons'.

There were some very able and respected British governors, but there were also some who had not the slightest clue how to conduct themselves. Edward Hyde, the 3rd Earl of Clarendon, served as governor of New York and New Jersey for seven years in the early 1700s. He accepted bribes, misappropriated public money, and then took to cross-dressing both in private and at public ceremonies. He once said that as he was representing Queen Anne, 'I ought to represent her as faithfully as I can'.

Hyde was corrupt, others were incompetent or feckless. Many were high-ranking military figures, others were leading politicians, and only a few were 'ordinary' men who had worked their way up to lofty positions. The majority of governors were the sons of the aristocracy, who in many cases had little experience of life beyond their exclusionary and sheltered horizons.

The man who preceded Murray in Virginia, Lord Botetourt, was one of the most popular and effective governors dispatched to the American colonies. Murray, by contrast, provided the ultimate proof, if any was needed, that an upper-class birth was no qualification for success in a position of such responsibility.

Murray had made no secret of his desire for an American governorship, and in 1770 he got his wish when he was named British governor of the Province of New York. He travelled to America alone, leaving his pregnant wife and seven children in England.

New York was a busy and prosperous city and he loved the place. He bought a large hunting estate almost 300 miles away near Lake Champlain and, no doubt relishing his new-found freedom away from family life, threw himself into the social life of the province. He also indulged himself in the arms of the beautiful young Kitty Eustace, daughter of a New York doctor John Eustace.

For a man of Murray's standing having an affair was not at all frowned upon. Among gentlemen of the upper classes it was positively encouraged; there was a certain cachet, a snob value, about taking a younger mistress. The trick, as high-ranking colonists such as Thomas Jefferson and Alexander Hamilton found out to their cost, was not to get caught or allow knowledge of the relationship to leak out. Public disapproval would never do.

Murray's choice of lover met with approval. Kitty was an exceedingly attractive young lady, oozing sensuality. The liaison between her and Murray might have stayed secret had it not been for a court case that found its way into the salacious tabloids.

In New York, where he cultivated and formed cordial friendships with local bigwigs, Murray's stay as governor was about to come to an abrupt end. Down in Virginia, the esteemed Lord Botetourt took ill and died rather suddenly. When word reached London, Britain's Secretary for Colonial Affairs, Lord Hillsborough, turned to Murray to fill the dead man's shoes.

His response was, to be blunt, childlike, and certainly not becoming of a grown man. Murray did not want to leave New York where life was good. He certainly did not fancy Virginia. So he went in the huff, pouted and generally threw a hissy fit.

He wrote back to Hillsborough stating he could not go...he would not go...it would not be beneficial to his health...or that of his family, all manner of excuses to stay in New York and avoid Virginia. He even suggested to Parliament that they send someone else, the governor of North Carolina, instead.

In his book, *A Cock and Bull for Kitty*, George Morrow writes, 'Wheedling – repeating his wishes until he got his way – was typical of Dunmore. It was the behaviour of a child, endearing to a mother, but probably not to the King of England'.

In the eyes of the people of Virginia, this was a very inauspicious beginning for a new governor. Even when his replacement, Lord Tryon, arrived in New York, Murray refused to leave, first taking himself off on a cruise then retreating to his country estate for a spot of hunting and shooting. He was determined to remain defiant for as long as possible.

He disgraced himself at Lord Tryon's swearing-in ceremony by getting drunk, complaining loudly at having New York 'stolen' from him, calling Tryon a 'coward' and allegedly assaulting one of his guests.

Meanwhile, the business of governing Virginia had been left in the hands of a wealthy planter called William Nelson, whose son Thomas went on to sign the Declaration of Independence. Months passed, and then one day, without warning, Murray rode into Williamsburg to be met by what George Morrow described as 'a very mixed group of local worthies'.

Murray no more wanted to be in Virginia than in a lion's den. He despised the fact that the colonists idolised the late Lord Botetourt and seemingly felt in awe of his predecessor's reputation. He appeared to make no attempt to succeed, to ingratiate himself in any way with the cream of Virginia society, which included some of the greatest minds of revolutionary America.

Virginia statesman Richard Henry Lee, a conscientious man of letters, wrote, 'Lord Dunmore's unparalleled conduct in Virginia has, a few Scotch excepted, united every man in that colony. If Administration had searched thro' the world for a person the best fetted to ruin their cause, and procure union and success for these Colonies, they could not have found a more complete Agent than Lord Dunmore'.

However, if Murray's early behaviour was, to say the least, obviously indifferent to his new surroundings, his new subjects were going to have to get used to it. Things deteriorated as the months and years went by. He was clearly and understandably devoted to the Crown, which was after all his paymaster, but with revolution in the air, a diplomatic balancing act was required. Murray appeared intent on applying his energies to royally shafting the colonists he had been sent to govern.

It is difficult to tell whether or not Murray was being intentionally obstinate in the hope that the government would move him. His brief spell in New York had not been a total disaster. A more likely scenario though is that he was the classic 'upper-class twit' who had found himself outside his aristocratic comfort zone and had absolutely no clue how to react.

Murray did enjoy a slight honeymoon period. In the years before the American War of Independence consumed the country, he gained a degree of respect for his administration. George Washington and Patrick Henry were friends and occasionally dined with him at the Governor's Mansion.

In 1772 a newly incorporated Virginia county was named in his honour. But Dunmore County lasted only six years until it was renamed Shenandoah County by American rebels who forced Murray from the colony during the war. Interestingly, Botetourt County, created in 1770 and named after his illustrious predecessor, still exists today.

Murray bought a plantation in York County which he called Porto Bello, meaning Beautiful Harbour, and named after the Battle of Portobello, fought in Panama in

1739 between the British and the Spanish as part of the War of Jenkins' Ear. He used it as a hunting lodge and purchased a number of slaves to work it. It may have been an attempt to blend in with his colonists, although the period of goodwill was short-lived.

He attempted to govern the colony single-handedly and dissolved the Virginia Assembly, incurring the hostility of the movers and shakers in society. It was a dreadful diplomatic move and raised all sorts of suspicions about Murray's true agenda. Naturally, the saintly Lord Botetourt would never have behaved in such a high-handed and undignified manner.

When he convened the Assembly again in March 1773, the uneasy peace lasted only two months. By May Murray and his legislative body were once more at loggerheads, this time over the temerity of the Assembly to join with the other colonies in writing a letter directly to Parliament protesting at so-called 'English aggression'.

Not surprisingly, Murray was furious and saw it as an attempt to usurp his powers. So yet again the Assembly was dissolved and yet again, despite his increasing unpopularity, he found himself attempting to run Virginia alone. He did have allies but they were few and far between, and his reputation as an administrator was plummeting.

In May 1774, following the Boston Tea Party, Britain charged the colonists with attempting to subvert the constitution and passed the Intolerable Acts law. The measure was used to close the port of Boston, preventing the loading and discharging of any goods or merchandise, including foodstuffs. British warships blockaded the port and relief supplies were sent to the city from all over the colonies.

It was one of the incidents that sparked the Revolutionary War and the Assemblymen in Virginia were wholly supportive of their rebellious Massachusetts brethren. The port was closed on 1 June and the Virginia Assembly resolved to keep the date as 'a day of fasting, humiliation and prayer'. Spluttering with fury, Murray demanded an explanation. When he got his answer he acted in his default manner and dissolved the Assembly for the third time in three years. The 89 Assemblymen continued to meet in Williamsburg's Raleigh Tavern, a meeting place that was more convivial than the formal Capitol Building.

The work of the Assembly continued in the tavern as if nothing had happened, and among the measures adopted there were appeals for a boycott on British imports and a Continental Congress, a body that united the 13 American colonies and called for independence by 1776.

Murray's diplomatic skills were proving inadequate. Of course, he was not blind to reality; he was well aware of the growing clamour for a break from British rule, yet he continued to behave in a way that antagonised and angered his Virginia subjects. The colony had provided some of the greatest minds of the revolution; they were less than impressed at having to kowtow to a man they regarded as little more than an aristocratic dullard.

Cabin and obelisk at the site of the Battle of Point Pleasant, the final battle in Lord Dunmore's War – Library of Congress

Perhaps the arrival in 1774 of his fragrant wife Charlotte helped his mood and concentrated his mind. She had been summoned by her philandering husband the year before but tragedy struck when one of the couple's sons, the Honorable William Murray, died at the age of nine. Early in 1774, after a 44-day voyage, she and the seven surviving children arrived in Williamsburg to massive fanfare.

Charlotte to some extent boosted her husband's flagging fortunes. She was described as 'a very elegant woman who looks, speaks and moves and is a lady'.

It came as a surprise to many people when, in the autumn of 1774, Murray partially appeared to redeem himself and his fading reputation. However, even in what was seemingly his hour of greatest success, his motives were questioned, his actions picked apart and found wanting. Murray went from hero to zero very rapidly.

He declared himself keen to promote the opening up of the lands to the west, still very much the territory of the Indian peoples. In an area south of the Ohio River, in what is now West Virginia, he entered a long-running and bitter territorial struggle between European settlers pushing west from Virginia, and Native Americans led by leaders of the Shawnee Nation and their allies, the Mingo tribe.

There had been a series of atrocities on both sides. In one incident, James Boone, the 16-year old son of pioneer Daniel Boone, was captured by Indian tribesmen and brutally tortured to death. In a notorious massacre, a group of Mingo Indians were slaughtered by frontiersmen at a trading post. Many of the Native Americans were mutilated, including the unborn son of a young woman, who was cut from his mother's womb and scalped.

Murray took it upon himself to march to the area at the head of a group of Virginia militiamen in a bid to break the deadlock. What became known as Lord Dunmore's War was a short, brutal conflict that ended in October 1774 at the battle of Point Pleasant. Murray and the Indian Chief Cornstalk negotiated an end to hostilities, although the peace treaty was short-lived.

He got his hero's welcome when he returned to Virginia, but doubts about his rationale for getting involved in the conflict, and whether he had a hidden agenda, began to emerge. Some suggested he was deliberately trying to reduce the strength of the Virginia Militia in preparation for the inevitable war of independence that was looming. Others questioned whether the peace treaty with the Indians was as beneficial to the settlers as Murray had claimed. The episode that was initially perceived as his greatest success was eventually regarded as a clumsy failure.

The *Dictionary of National Biography* states that Murray 'aggravated the disaffection of the colonists by concluding a disadvantageous peace with the Ohio Indians'.

Murray was unquestionably the author of his own misfortune. He had been such a diffident and confrontational governor from the start that few people were prepared to cut him any slack. His few achievements were treated with withering scepticism and the motivation behind them questioned.

It was obvious by the end of 1774 that revolutionary fervour was unstoppable. London knew a war with the colonists was inevitable, and while most were certain the might of the British Army would crush the upstart rebels, there were many prominent figures in the Westminster Parliament whispering that the end result could well be an independent America. If a war did not settle matters, America might well be 'lost' in the fullness of time, and talk of a diplomatic end game was very much on the table.

One way or another, America was going to be a force to be reckoned with, and the wise heads among the British establishment knew it would be advantageous to keep any new nation as an ally and a trade partner – certainly not an enemy. The last thing they needed was Murray misjudging what was required of him, rubbing the most influential colonists up the wrong way, damaging the future prospects of the Crown in the New World.

But Murray's blundering had only been a warm-up act. There was much worse to come. As the colonists became increasingly restive, Murray's behaviour became more erratic and unpredictable. He lurched from chaos to havoc and back again with consummate ease.

Patrick Henry was one of the most influential figures in America, let alone Virginia. Lawyer and planter, he was also a supreme orator and a member of the Virginia House of Burgesses. Henry was a passionate believer that force was needed to combat the British, and in March 1775, in Richmond, Virginia, he made one of the most famous speeches in American history.

His now immortalised words were, 'Is life so dear, or peace so sweet, as to be purchased at the price of chains or slavery? Forbid it, Almighty God! I know not what course others may take, but as for me, give me liberty, or give me death'.

His words rang through the colonies, like a shot from a starting pistol. Delegates to the Continental Congress in Philadelphia heeded Henry's battle cry and approved a resolution calling for armed resistance. There was no going back; the War of Independence was now only weeks away.

Murray's reaction to the outbreak of war was typically inflammatory. On the night of 20 April 1775, a day after British troops had entered Lexington, Massachusetts, the Scot plundered the public weapons magazine in Williamsburg, removed the entire stock of gunpowder, and had it transferred to a British man-of-war called the *Magdalen*, anchored in the James River.

The governor's reasoning for what became known as the Gunpowder Incident was that he 'thought it prudent' to remove it because of the level of unrest. The sailors who had been smuggled ashore were spotted by locals, the alarm was raised, armed militia rushed to the scene and a highly incendiary situation unfolded. The townspeople demanded the gunpowder be put back but Murray refused, claiming he had moved the powder as protection against a rumoured slave revolt.

That explanation did not wash with the Williamsburg public for long and a riot ensued in the streets. The angry crowd threatened to storm Murray's mansion and at one point he told them that if he was harmed he would 'declare freedom to the slaves and reduce the city of Williamsburg to ashes'. He also warned that 'I once fought for the Virginians but, by God, I would let them see that I would fight against them'.

Murray was forced to send his wife and children aboard the British navy vessel HMS *Fowey*, 12 miles off the coast, for their own safety. Henry then rode to the city at the head of the Hanover County militia to gain restitution from Murray for the missing gunpowder. The governor issued a proclamation against 'a certain Patrick Henry and his deluded followers' who had 'put themselves in a posture of war'. Henry got his money, a bill for £330, paid by a local plantation owner. Murray then took the ludicrous step of charging Henry with extortion.

It was an unholy mess and all the result of Murray's crass stupidity and complete lack of diplomatic skill. His time in Williamsburg was coming to an end; nobody wanted him there, not the politicians and certainly not the people. His hint that he might free the slave population had gone down like a lead balloon. It was a threat that had enraged the citizens. By early June his position had become untenable and he was effectively driven from the city and forced to take refuge on board the *Fowey*.

While on the vessel, the Assembly in Williamsburg continued to meet and forwarded him a number of bills for his assent. In typical petulant fashion, he refused to sign them. Eventually, the House of Burgesses resolved that their governor had 'abdicated' and took steps to run the colony in his absence.

Although Murray was still nominally recognised as royal governor of Virginia, his calamitous rule had ended, and he would never again hold any sway in the colony. He was a governor without a domain. That small matter, however, did not deter him from continuing to make his mark. The Virginians were not rid of the man yet. There was to be one final flourish from the aristocratic Scot before he sailed back across the Atlantic.

The slave population in Virginia at the time stood at 180,000. Negroes outnumbered whites in both Virginia and South Carolina and many plantation owners left the day-to-day running of their lands to either white overseers or African slave-drivers, or a combination of both. Murray's threat to issue a proclamation to free the slaves then let them take up arms against the American rebels was initially seen as scaremongering.

But Murray was deadly serious. From his place of 'exile' on board HMS *Fowey* he proclaimed martial law against Virginia, and offered freedom to all slaves of revolutionary supporters who managed to escape their masters. Thereafter they were to pledge loyalty to the Crown, and Murray in turn promised to form an all-black regiment in which they would serve.

The move sent shockwaves through the network of British colonies that were spread down the east coast of America. It was the white colonists' worst nightmare come true. A slave mutiny was something they had long dreaded, and the level of support for the British cause in the colonies dipped dramatically.

Future president James Madison had warned of the dangers before Murray issued what became known as Dunmore's Proclamation. Madison wrote, 'if America and Britain come to a hostile rupture, I am afraid an insurrection among the slaves may and will be prosecuted. To say the truth, that is the only part in which this Colony is vulnerable…we shall fall like Achilles by the hand of one that knows that secret'.

Murray was obviously well aware of the 'secret' to which Madison was referring. His proclamation labelled the patriots 'traitors' and declared, 'all indented servants, Negroes or others...free that are able and willing to bear arms, they joining His Majesty's troops, as soon as may be, for the more speedily reducing this colony to a proper sense of their duty, to His Majesty's Crown and dignity'.

George Washington, who led the American forces to independence and became the new country's first president, was forthright in his feelings towards the Scotsman. 'I do not think the forcing his Lordship on shipboard is sufficient. Nothing less than depriving him of life and liberty will secure peace to Virginia, as motives of resentment actuate his conduct to a degree equal to the total destruction of that colony,' he said.

The reaction was, not surprisingly, extremely different among the slave population. When the proclamation was published in the *Virginia Gazette* in November 1775, the colony's blacks celebrated, despite the warning that accompanied the newspaper announcement stating that any slave who defected would be put to death. One 15-year old girl who was captured after escaping was given 80 lashes of the whip then had hot embers poured on her sores.

Richard Henry Lee sarcastically styled Murray the 'African Hero'. But hundreds of slaves left the plantations to join Murray's so-called Ethiopian Regiment. Within weeks they had reached Murray's ship, some swimming for miles from Yorktown, and soon they were rigged out in the regiment's garb, complete with the words 'Liberty to Slaves' emblazoned on their chests.

It was the first time slaves in the colonies had gained any sort of freedom, and even though they were runaways, they were fulsome in their praise of Murray. Black women throughout the colonies started naming their newborn babies Dunmore in the former governor's honor. By the end of the year, more than 300 escapees had joined him, a figure that was to swell to 800 by the summer of 1776.

Any family life the slaves had on the plantations was torn asunder. The slaves, mostly men, who did escape knew full well it was unlikely they would see their families again. In their eyes, some freedom was better than none at all, and most saw the British side as the most likely ally.

If only they had known the truth. Firstly, Murray had been given no official sanction to make such a divisive proclamation. It was revealing, after all, that he granted no amnesty to the slaves on his Porto Bello hunting lodge. He did not act in the interests of the slaves; he was not the great emancipator. Everything he did was designed to strengthen his own weakened position and to avenge the colonial upstarts who had banished him from Williamsburg.

If he was trying to ingratiate himself with his British masters, he was failing miserably. Parliament was keeping tabs on his bizarre behavior with an increasing sense of disbelief and hopelessness. The slaves who had left their families to join his all-black regiment were blissfully unaware they had backed a very obvious loser. They would soon discover that Murray's promises were bogus.

On New Year's Day 1776, Murray was instrumental in the destruction of the great port city of Norfolk, Virginia. He ordered the troops on board his small fleet of three ships to shell the city constantly for eight hours. More than 800 buildings were destroyed by the shelling and soldiers within the city walls completed the carnage. By the end, what had been the most prosperous city in Virginia had been flattened.

The Ethiopian Regiment had been among Murray's forces that fought at the Battle of Great Bridge in December. But anger among the colonists at the attack on Norfolk forced him to flee with his troops to the small stronghold of Gwynn's Island, located in Chesapeake Bay, near the mouth of the Plankatank River.

In July 1776, more than 800 runaway slaves were quartered with him on Gwynn's Island. Within a month the smallpox outbreak and other illnesses had claimed the lives of 500 of them, although an unlikely rumour was spread that Murray himself had organised to have them inoculated with the virus. Murray accepted he was never going to get reinforcements and that the short-lived experiment of liberating slaves to fight for Britain had been a failure. In August he sailed north towards New York, leaving the surviving Negroes behind.

These poor people, who had ignored the prospect of death if found escaping, and who had left their friends and families behind in the hope that the British Army would offer them a better life than the plantations, were left high and dry. The aristocratic 'pied piper' they followed had fled, dissolved their regiment, and left them to fend for themselves in an island wilderness.

Some left in the British ships, some succumbed to illness and wounds, some were captured and sold in the Caribbean, others tried to find their way back to their families. Whether they made it or not, or whether their old masters carried out the threat to punish them by death, is unknown. Murray had no interest in their welfare or safety. They would have been better off staying on their plantations.

Murray's actions backfired spectacularly on Britain. His old adversary Patrick Henry told the Virginia Convention that the deposed governor's 'blatant recruitment' of slaves meant the colonists could no longer be expected to swear allegiance to the Crown.

Using dramatic oratory, Henry said that for a representative of the Crown 'to be encouraging insurrection among our slaves, many of whom are now actually in arms against us' revealed the king as 'a tyrant instead of the protector of his people'. He called on Britain to make the 'only honourable response' and declare a full Declaration of Independence. A resolution to that effect was later carried unanimously.

Murray, who had fled Virginia in disgrace and humiliation, suffered defeat after defeat until he eventually left America for good. He headed first for New York, where he served in a volunteer militia, then back across the Atlantic to London where he immediately took up a seat in the House of Lords. For all his blundering, his position in the upper strata of society was assured.

In one House of Lords speech in 1777 he defended his use of black slaves to fight the British corner. However, British military leaders in America and elsewhere were in no mood to follow his example, and preferred a force of all-white fighting men. He had given hope to the slaves of America, when, in fact, there was none.

Britain only recognised American independence in 1783 and Murray continued to draw his pay as colonial governor despite being at home. In 1787 he was 'rewarded' with another colony post, this time serving as governor of the Bahamas for nine years until 1796.

A bizarre series of events saw his daughter hold two separate wedding ceremonies with the same royal Prince, one of the sons of King George III, only for the marriages to be annulled. In 1793 Lady Augusta Murray and Prince Augustus Frederick, the Duke of Sussex, were married secretly in a Church of England ceremony in Rome. Later that year they married again in London, but yet again did not reveal their identities.

English Law decreed that both ceremonies were in contravention of the Royal Marriages Act and annulled them, meaning Lady Augusta could not use the titles of Princess or Her Royal Highness.

As for Murray, he returned from the Bahamas and retired to a mansion house in Ramsgate, Kent, where he died on 25 February 1809, and was buried at the town's Church of St Laurence.

In Scotland his deception of the slave population is little known. He was a man of great wealth and privilege who gave false hope to some of the most downtrodden and impoverished people in the western world. He abandoned them without giving a thought to their fate and he deserves to be remembered for his cruel and heartless behaviour.

However, he is known in his native land for almost comical reasons as the man who ordered the building of one of Scotland's strangest buildings – The Pineapple – near

The Pineapple

the village of Airth, Stirlingshire. Originally intended as a gift for his wife, it has been described as the 'most bizarre building in Scotland'.

Murray ordered it built to house a walled garden and two large hothouses to be used for the growing of pineapples. The roof was decorated with a massive stone pineapple. But Murray left for Virginia before the building was complete and it remained unfinished – a folly.

Murray's behaviour went beyond foolishness, although The Pineapple seems a fitting legacy. If every folly needs its fool, then The Pineapple and John Murray, 4th Earl of Dunmore, represent a match made in heaven.

16

John Mein

Mean is the man, M—n is his name,
Enough he's spread his hellish fame;
Infernal furies hurl his soul,
Nine million times from Pole to Pole.

– ACROSTIC ON AN EFFIGY PARADED IN THE STREETS OF BOSTON

Bookseller, librarian and publisher to the people of Boston, Massachusetts – it was the perfect description of a genteel, respectable and trouble-free occupation. Befitting a fine upstanding citizen and pillar of the community, it was ideal for someone who preferred a low key lifestyle; a quiet, studious individual, not given to confrontation or impetuosity.

In theory, even in the 18th century when Boston was America's 'Cradle of Liberty', that description should have held true. But firebrand Scot John Mein did not conform to the typical cosy image of bookseller or librarian. He was a malcontent and rabble-rouser, more at home venting his spleen in bars and political meetings than dusting off dog-eared old books on his shelves.

Had he put his mind to it, Mein could have enjoyed an easy and very prosperous life. In the years before the American Revolution, Boston was very much the place to be. It was the home of great patriots such as statesmen and philosopher Samuel Adams; another founding father John Hancock, whose exaggeratedly large signature adorns the Declaration of Independence; John Adams, the nation's second president; and silversmith Paul Revere, who made the famous ride to Lexington to alert the militia about the advance of British forces.

Mein arrived in the city 11 years before the War of Independence broke out, at a time when the prospect of revolution was the talk of the town. The Sons of Liberty was a radical and controversial organisation set up to change the way the colonies were treated by their British masters, and to help lay the groundwork for the armed struggle that was to come.

The city saw some of the most pivotal and violent events of pre-revolution America. The notorious Boston Massacre of 1770 saw British soldiers open fire on protesting colonists, killing five and wounding six others in an incident that added fuel to the fire of already red-hot patriotic fervour. Even more famous was the Boston Tea Party, when protesters dressed as American Indians emptied crates of tea into Boston Harbour in protest at a British tea tax.

If one American city can be said to have ushered in revolution, it was Boston. The mood was fervently anti-British and troops stationed there were engaged, often unsuccessfully, in a constant struggle to keep public order. Angry clashes, inflammatory public meetings and provocative speechifying were commonplace. There were hotheads a-plenty in the bustling Massachusetts port.

If Mein could have hand-picked the least suitable place to immigrate to when he left Scotland in 1764, it would unquestionably have been the city into which he sailed – Boston. Not only was he a fiercely patriotic British Tory and resolutely opposed to the American patriot cause, he was also in possession of a fiendishly hairstreak temper and given to forcefully speaking his mind.

They were character traits that were, to put it mildly, unfortunate, in the midst of the anti-British hubbub and rowdydow that defined late 18th century Boston. They did not serve Mein at all well; in fact, they proved his undoing. He was just one of many loud and boisterous political agitators scrapping it out in the city, but he lacked the adroitness needed to rise above the throng.

The small, pugnacious Scot certainly did not fit the image of the stereotypical librarian or bookseller, yet he was very much at home in Boston's publishing world. Those who scribbled their opinions in newspapers, periodicals, almanacs and scandal-sheets attacked their political opponents with incredible ferocity.

Mein entered into the verbal sparring match with a clenched-teeth enthusiasm. He despised the patriots and let it be known in no uncertain terms in the columns of any and all of his publications. He gave the revered leaders of the revolution crude and unflattering nicknames; he poked fun at them in print; he continually accused them of flouting British trade laws and of illegal profiteering. His attacks had their desired effect: they rattled his political enemies. It was all good knockabout stuff – but then Mein took it all too far.

It was one thing to try to beat up those of a different persuasion using the power of speech, it was quite another to beat them up using brute force. Marching into a rival newspaper office and challenging the proprietor to an old-fashioned Scottish 'square go' (fight) was never going to convince the other side of his argument.

The Scotsman could not hold himself together in the intense atmosphere of pre-war Massachusetts. His volatile temper got the better of him on several occasions, and his obnoxious character made him many enemies. He was free with his fists and casual with his pistols, and it was only a matter of time before he was run out of town, narrowly escaping with his life.

While the Boston Massacre and the Boston Tea Party are writ large in the American history books, the little-known John Mein Affair or Mein Wars is scarcely even a footnote. However, there was a time, just before America took up arms against the British and fought for its independence, that the Scottish publisher was one of the most hated figures in colonial Boston.

Every year on 5 November the gangs of Boston used to hold a Pope Night celebration, burning effigies of the Devil, the Pope and a chosen political scapegoat. After parading the effigies, the gangs would brawl in the centre of the city, and the winners would drag away the effigies and burn them. It was a violent ceremony, in tune with the turbulent times.

In 1769, the Pope Night gangs made Mein the target of their political wrath. His larger-than-life effigy was carried through the streets to the city's Copp's Hill, where it was solemnly and ceremoniously burned. The gang members were nothing if not poetic. They carried the following acrostic message alongside the Scotsman's effigy:

> Insulting wretch, we'll him expose,
> O'er the whole world his deeds disclose;
> Hell now gapes wide to take him in,
> Now he is ripe, O lump of sin!
> Mean is the man, M—n is his name,
> Enough he's spread his hellish fame,
> Infernal furies hurl his soul
> Nine million times from Pole to Pole.

It was the ultimate entry on Boston's unofficial 'roll of dishonour' for the Scottish man of letters whose stay in the city was relatively brief but whose impact was memorable. The choice of effigy figure was reserved for the most despised members of colonial society, including customs official Charles Paxton, and Admiral John Byng of the British Navy.

Mein was born in the Scottish capital, Edinburgh, around 1734. His father, also John, was a slater to trade and the family was described as 'comfortably off'. As a professional tradesman in the city, John senior was a burgess and guild brother of Edinburgh, positions his son would also hold.

The Mein family appear to have been a well-known and well-connected Edinburgh family for many generations. It is not clear exactly who John Mein's direct ancestors were, but in 1659, the city's Craigcrook Castle was bought by a family member – also John Mein – and sold 10 years later.

The man who bought Craigcrook was described as an Edinburgh merchant and may well have been the same person whose wife was involved in one of the most famous incidents in Scottish religious history 22 years earlier. Jenny Geddes was the given name

Boston Chronicle front page, June 1768. Note John Mein's name at top left - publc domain of the woman who threw her stool at the Dean of Edinburgh in St Giles' Cathedral as he tried to introduce the Anglican Book of Common Prayer into Scottish churches. Her real identity is generally accepted to have been Barbara Hamilton, the wife of Edinburgh merchant John Mein.

She may well have been an ancestor of the John Mein who sailed to Boston; perhaps it was from her that he inherited his fiery temper and willingness to indulge in public protests.

Mein was well-educated and grew into a well-read young man. He was an avid reader and set his sights on a future in the literary world; Edinburgh was the perfect location for him. The city was at the heart of the Scottish Enlightenment, it was a major publishing centre for newspapers and periodicals and some of the greatest literary figures of the century – Tobias Smollett, Robert Burns, Allan Ramsay and James Thompson – played dominant roles in the city's dynamic cultural life.

In 1754 Mein became apprenticed to one of the most prominent and best-known booksellers in Edinburgh, a man by the name of John Traill. He spent six years learning his trade in the city's Parliament Close, just off the Royal Mile and in the shadow of St Giles' Cathedral.

When he left the guiding hand of his mentor, it was to set up in a bookselling business of his own. By 1760 he had followed in his father's footsteps as a burgess and guild brother (an old term for a freeman) of the City of Edinburgh. His book shop was also located in Parliament Close, not far from Traill's premises.

In 1761 Mein advertised the sale of 'a great variety of pretty little entertaining books for children'. He was, by all accounts, succeeding in his chosen profession. There was certainly no suggestion that the young man selling books for little children would grow into a firebrand and one of the greatest public enemies in the city of Boston.

Yet like many young men of his generation, he had grown restless with some of the more stuffy aspects of Edinburgh life and society. He wanted to explore the world, and where better than the new lands of America? In the early 1760s he, along with a number of other well-to-do Scotsmen, sailed to Boston to assess the potential for a new life in the New England city.

One of the other men who travelled with him was Robert Sandeman, a nephew of the noted theologian of the same name from Perth. The two were highly impressed by life in Boston and vowed to return as soon as possible. The cost of a trans-Atlantic fare did not pose a difficulty for either man, and plans were laid for a return journey in 1764 with a view to setting up in business together in America.

In November 1763 Mein placed a notice in his shop announcing that he would be terminating his business on Whitsunday (the seventh Sunday after Easter) of the following year. In May 1764 the contents of his house, including many of his personal effects, were sold by public auction. In the second half of the year he and Sandeman again made the trip from Glasgow to Boston.

The two got to work quickly, setting up shop in an old wooden building in the city's Marlborough Street, not far from the Charles River. The firm was known as Mein and Sandeman and sold books, Irish linens and 'excellent bottled Bristol beer near two years old' that Mein had brought from Edinburgh.

But within months the strong personalities of the two men had clashed. The partnership was dissolved and Mein took over the largest bookshop in Boston, The London Bookstore, in King Street, the major commercial thoroughfare in the city. One of the two gentlemen who ran the store had taken seriously ill and Mein was able to buy it at a bargain price.

Through his contacts in Britain, Mein had access to many thousands of the finest books in the world. In the autumn of 1765 he set about transforming The London Bookstore into a mecca for Bostonians who enjoyed reading. Every classical work of literature was there, so too children's books, adventure stories, history books, dictionaries and lexicons, and the works of the greatest poets the western world had produced.

By the end of the year he had opened the city's first lending library, a move that sparked a literary revolution in Boston. John Adams was one of the shop patrons who took advantage of the 1,200-strong book library that Mein had gathered. It was an impressive collection, and all books could be taken out for a fee. His routine payment schedule was £1.8shillings per year; 18shillings for 6 months; and 10shillings and 8pence per quarter.

The bibliophiles of Boston could choose from authors including Miguel de Cervantes; Henry Fielding; William Shakespeare; Tobias Smollett; Samuel Johnson; Aesop; John Milton; Jonathan Swift; Moliere; Daniel Defoe; Alexander Pope; Voltaire; and Scottish clergyman John Knox.

An advertisement from 1765 refers to a catalogue of 'Mein's Circulating Library' consisting of 'above Twelve Hundred Volumes in most branches of polite Literature, Arts and Sciences'. The store is described as being located at 'Second door above the British Coffee-House, north side of King Street, Boston'.

The advert goes on to state, 'This collection will be considerable enlarged from time to time and the number of volumes will be more than doubled in less than a twelvemonth, if the Publisher meets with due encouragement'.

A year later the collection stood at 2,000. Book lovers who patronised his premises were in literary heaven. There was enough reading material in Mein's store to satisfy the bookworms and scholars of the city. In the early days of his Boston stay, Mein's presence in the mercantile centre was a welcome addition to the retail landscape of this booming city.

In the Bostonian Society's publication, *Mapping Revolutionary Boston*, King Street was described as a thoroughfare where 'dockworkers, carpenters, ropemakers, coopers, shipbuilders, tavernkeepers, bakers, tallow chandlers, and printers all rubbed elbows with merchants and politicians, ministers and doctors, slaves and prostitutes'.

Paul Revere –
Library of Congress

John Hancock –
Library of Congress

Samuel Adams –
Library of Congress

The present-day State Street, it housed Boston's Old State House, now a history museum; the Custom House; the original Town House, the seat of colonial government; the famous Bunch-of-Grapes Tavern where revolutionary Whigs such as Paul Revere gathered; and the historic pier known as Long Wharf. Mein was in exalted company; King Street was the place every merchant aspired to be.

The street was also the scene, in 1770, of the Boston Massacre, an incident that soured already strained relations between the people of Boston and the British soldiers stationed in the city.

At one point in the 1750s, Boston was the most populous city in North America, with more than 16,000 people living there, but it was quickly overtaken by Philadelphia and New York. There was also a huge disparity between the haves and have-nots. While men like John Hancock and Samuel Adams lived in the lap of luxury, the families of the working classes existed in outright poverty.

Thanks to his bookshop Mein had become an established figure in Boston life. Tension was in the air, however, and Mein was never slow to let his extreme royalist views be known to whoever was listening. It is interesting to speculate on the political discussions he had with his valued customer John Adams, the cool-headed lawyer, soon to be independent America's first vice president.

Among those with whom Mein frequently associated in the taverns and coffee houses in and around King Street were fellow Scotsmen John Fleeming and his partner William McAlpine. The two ran a printing shop and bookstall in Marlborough Street, where they printed a number of books, including some for Mein.

At some point in 1776 the Fleeming and McAlpine partnership broke up and Fleeming went into business with Mein. The pair wasted no time getting themselves established. Fleeming sailed to Scotland, bought a press, other printing materials, and hired a number of journeyman printers to work in the new enterprise. It opened in October and was based first in Wing's Lane, then in larger offices at Newbury Street. When the business was at its height the two men employed 17 printers and other workers.

It did not take long for the business to be the foremost book printing firm in New England, although there was an early hint of chicanery on the part of the two Scotsmen. Boston bookworms believed books printed abroad were of superior quality than those printed locally. The two men printed books with a London imprint, claimed they had been imported, and passed them of as the genuine article, no doubt at inflated prices.

In 1767 Mein and Fleeming took their biggest step into the world of publishing, one that was to plunge them into the heart of Boston's revolutionary maelstrom. They decided to publish a newspaper, stating that certain 'gentlemen of taste' had urged them to do so. The publication was to thrust Mein into the limelight as one of the city's most controversial and reviled political figures.

The *Boston Chronicle* first appeared on the street on 21 December 1767. It was unashamedly supportive of the Tory cause and the continuation of unfettered British colonial rule over the American colonies. Boston historian E. J. Witek, who has written extensively on the period, said of the paper, 'It appeared that its content was exclusively the responsibility of Mein, and that Fleeming was responsible for the printing and technical matters…it became a thorn in the side of the Whigs due, I believe, to Mein's personality and personal beliefs'.

Also appearing in the bookshops and stalls of the city was the long established *Boston Gazette* that had first appeared in 1719. By contrast it supported the Whigs, freedom from British rule, and it regularly published articles by the likes of Paul Revere, John Hancock, and Samuel Adams.

The two publications were soon at loggerheads. The political language used by both sides in the lead up to revolution was increasingly intemperate, and amounted to mud-slinging and character assassination. Mein, editor of the *Chronicle*, embarked on what can only be described as a campaign of abuse against everyone and anyone who opposed the measures imposed upon America by the British administration. Many of those he attacked were among the most respected men in the city.

Mein became a swaggering presence in Boston. He was a man of considerable influence, a newspaper editor, a bookseller, and a bookbinder, with the only public library business operating from one of his premises. His behaviour was becoming increasingly erratic and volatile, and a major confrontation was inevitable.

In his book, *The Founding of a Nation: A History of the American Revolution*, Merrill Jensen wrote, 'The Boston Chronicle was…the handsomest newspaper in America. It was also one of the most aggressive, and it met the Boston Gazette on its own ground and slugged it out'.

It did not take long before Mein was 'slugging it out' with the men behind the *Gazette* a bit too literally. In the *Chronicle*'s first edition, Mein had written a savage article critical of former prime minister William Pitt the Elder, who had supported American colonists in their fight against the hated British Stamp Act.

In mid-January of 1768, the *Gazette* hit back at Mein with a perfectly-delivered sarcastic blow that enraged the Scot. In an article penned by a columnist calling himself 'Americus', the paper sprang to the defence of Pitt, whom it described as a 'defender of American Freedom' and a 'man who should not be disparaged'.

In a twist of the literary knife, the author then described the Scotsmen behind the publication of the *Chronicle* as 'Jacobites'. Mein was a very loud and rabid royalist, and the 1745 Jacobite Rebellion which sought to restore the Stuart monarchy was still fresh in the minds of all Scots. Mein was most certainly no Jacobite and he was grievously insulted at being branded one. When he read the offending *Gazette* article he was incandescent and immediately went on the warpath.

Mein marched to the *Gazette* office on King Street, stormed inside and confronted the paper's principal publisher Benjamin Edes, a fervent patriot and revolutionist and an extreme political agitator. Mein, however, was not in any way intimidated by the reputation of Edes. He demanded to know the identity of the anonymous author 'Americus' who had written such a damning article.

Edes, quite possibly relishing the confrontation more than the frenzied and incoherent Mein, replied that journalistic ethics forbade him from revealing the author's name and told Mein that he, as a printer and newspaper man, should know better than to ask such an 'unpertinent, improper question'.

The calculated response on the part of Edes simply riled Mien even more. He told the American that, if he did not reveal the identity of Americus, then he would assume that he (Edes) was the person responsible. He then added that 'the affair shall be decided in three minutes'.

It was, in effect, a challenge to Edes to fight. Mein was taking it further and suggesting that Edes would not last long in a fist fight with him. Edes, perhaps shying away from the highly-strung Mein, decided that discretion was the better part of valour and told his opponent to come back the following morning. He would decide overnight whether to reveal the name, he said.

Not surprisingly, when Edes arrived at his office the next day, Mein was already waiting for him. Edes took the high ground and said that 'Americus' was going to remain anonymous as the paper must protect its sources, at which point Mein again challenged him to 'take a walk'. Edes declined for the second time in two days and eventually the trigger-tempered Mein left the *Gazette* office.

It was deplorable behaviour on the part of Mein but the affair did not end there. In fact, it took a far more serious turn. The following day the *Gazette* printed a trenchant and acerbic account of Mein's confrontation. That evening Mein encountered Benjamin

Edes' partner, John Gill, in the street. He attacked Gill with his cane and clubbed him several times, knocking him to the ground and causing him physical injury.

Gill, who along with Edes was one of the central characters behind the Boston Tea Party, issued a lawsuit against his attacker. His counsel in court was noted lawyer and patriot James Otis, the man who Mein believed had in fact been the author behind the 'Americus' nom de plume. Otis was reportedly the man who coined the catchphrase, 'Taxation without representation is tyranny', later modified into the 'No Taxation without Representation' battle cry of the American rebels.

The court proceedings did not go well for Mein. There was no doubt about his guilt and it was something of an open and shut case. He was fined £130, a substantial sum in those days. It was later reduced on appeal to £75 but Mein also had to pay all court costs. It was a stiff penalty for a moment of madness.

It is stating the blatantly obvious to say that for a man with such a fiery temperament to have appointed himself as editor of a newspaper at a time when the political temperature was at fever pitch was not the best of ideas. It was always going to go badly. He simply did not have the mentality to stay in control of his emotions.

That said, Mein was producing some highly entertaining, well-written and well-informed articles on a regular basis. There is nothing the citizenry of any city or country enjoys better than to see the high and mighty being taken down a peg or two in public. The *Boston Chronicle* may have been thoroughly one-sided and biased in favour of the royalist cause, but the quality of journalism was high.

There were, however, constant and well-founded accusations that Mein was not his own man and that he was in fact in the pay of the British government. Many of the reports he was printing contained information that could only have come from government sources, most notably the officials at the Custom House.

If a journalist is judged by the quality of his contacts, then Mein was doing an impressive job. However, rather than him having to seek out friends in high places, it is more likely that he was spoon-fed the information so the British could embarrass the prosperous and influential patriotic leaders. Whatever the motive, the *Boston Chronicle* demonised these men and made their lives extremely uncomfortable.

In 1767 British Chancellor of the Exchequer Charles Townshend introduced a series of measures known as the Townshend Acts, designed to raise revenue in the colonies by imposing taxes on imports such as tea, paint, paper, glass, lead and oil. The British Empire was heavily in debt but the Americans argued the measures were 'unconstitutional' and should be resisted.

The outraged colonists organised a boycott they called the 'Boston Non-Importation Agreement'. The city was at the epicentre of the protest as most of the British vessels carrying goods arrived there, so the merchants and traders agreed to boycott goods that were subject to the Townshend Acts until the taxes were repealed. Some goods such as salt and hemp were exempt, but the boycott encouraged the Americans

This Day is published,
(Price one Shilling)
A CATALOGUE OF
MEIN's Circulating LIBRARY;
Confisting of above Twelve Hundred Volumes, in most Branches of polite Literature, Arts & Sciences,
VIZ.
Hiftory, Plays, Arts, Gardening,
Voyages, Novels, Sciences, Navigation,
Travels, Divinity, Poetry, Mathematics,
Lives, Phyfic, Hufbandry, Law,&c.&c.
Memoirs, Surgery,
Which will be LENT to read,
At One Pound Eight Shillings Lawful Money per Year, Eighteen Shillings per half Year, or Ten Shillings and Eight Pence per Quarter,
By JOHN MEIN, Bookfeller,
At the LONDON BOOK-STORE,
Second Door above the BRITISH COFFEE-HOUSE, North Side of King-Street, BOSTON,
Where the Books are ready to be delivered out to Subfcribers.
CONDITIONS to be obferved by every Subfcriber.
I. Every yearly Subfcriber to pay One Pound Eight Shillings, lawful Money,
II. Subfcribers for half a Year to pay Eighteen Shillings,
III. Quarterly Subfcribers to pay Ten Shillings and Eight Pence.
IV. That the Money is to be paid at the Time of fubfcribing ; and that Subfcribers are to pay one Shilling for their Catalogue,
VI. Subfcribers, to prevent being difappointed in the Books they want, are defired to fend a Lift of fix or eight different Numbers taken from the Catalogue, as thus, No. 1, 25, 75, 450.
IX. Thofe who refide in the Country, and who chufe to fubfcribe, may have two Books at a Time, on paying double SubfcriptionMoney, and defraying the Expence of Carriage.
☞Attendance is given at the Library,from X o'Clock to One in the Forenoon, and from Three to Six Afternoon.

Flyer for John Mein's circulating library

to be self-sufficient and decrease their reliance on the Mother Country.

Mein, of course, was having none of it. He claimed he needed print and paper for his business and the only place he could get it was Britain. If any of his enterprises were to go out of business, he said, men would be laid off.

The leaders of the boycott were the same men who were feeding Boston's revolutionary fervour. By August 1769, anger against those who breached the accord was at an all-time high. The merchants, many of whom were suffering by being part of the protest, decided to name and shame. The Sons of Liberty published a list of the few 'violators' who had refused to take part.

Under the headline, 'A list of names of those who AUDACIOUSLY continue to counteract the UNITED SENTIMENTS of the BODY of merchants throughout NORTH AMERICA; by importing British Goods contrary to the Agreement' were the identities of eleven merchants. One of them was John Mein.

The document added, '…they have preferred their own little private advantage to the welfare of America… it is therefore highly proper that the public should know who they are at this critical time, sordidly detached themselves from the public interest…they will be deemed enemies to their country…those who afford them their countenance or give them their custom must expect to be considered in the same disagreeable light'.

It was dynamite and it painted Mein as a greedy businessman acting in the worst interests of his adopted land. It was true, he was totally opposed to the boycott and was doing his bit to undermine it. However, he was deeply wounded and embarrassed at being 'outed' as a man prepared to do the dirty on his fellow traders.

Once again Mein's hairstreak temper got the better of him. He knew all the leading members of the Sons of Liberty, and through the columns of his newspaper, he went to war against them. His chums in the Boston Custom House were more than happy to help. They passed him the cargo manifests of every goods-laden vessel that came into the harbour, what was on board, and for whom it was destined.

The documents were like manna from heaven for Mein. If there had been any doubt that hypocrisy was alive and well in colonial Boston, then Mein was about to shatter the illusion. What the manifests showed clearly was that many of the revolutionary ringleaders – Hancock, Adams, Otis and others – were all importing British goods in breach of the agreement they had themselves drawn up.

Week after week, the pages of the *Boston Chronicle* carried the manifests of cargoes that had sailed into Boston. The list detailed all the merchants who were importing goods and proved a huge embarrassment to many of those who were either leaders or supporters of the Sons of Liberty.

Mein, with a flair for the dramatic, did not quite reveal their names 100% but instead gave them insulting and demeaning nicknames. John Hancock became 'Johnny Dupe, a young man with long ears and a silly grin'; James Otis was referred to as 'Muddlehead' due to his increasing signs of mental instability; and Samuel Adams became 'Sam the Publican' in reference to his activities as a tax-collector.

Others were known by a variety of disparaging names, all perfectly recognisable to the people of Boston. There was 'Deacon Clodpate, alias Tribulation Turnery, esq.'; and 'William the Knave'. They shouldn't have been surprised at the revelations, for Mein gave them ample warning of his plans.

In the *Chronicle* of 19 October 1769, Mein wrote that if the Committee of Merchants and Sons of Liberty leaders did not cease their 'abusive hints' against him, 'the Public shall be entertained with anecdotes of the lives and practices of many of these worthies as individuals; for all due pains shall be taken to unkennel them; and already a great store of materials has been collected'.

More than anyone else, Mein went after John Hancock. He was the richest man in Boston, and much of that fortune had been made through the smuggling of goods such as molasses, tea, tobacco, rum and wine. The two men despised each other. Mein carried a report that Hancock, one of those who had drawn up the Non-Importation Agreement, had imported five bales of British linen on board his vessel, the *Lydia*.

Hancock denied it but Mein had all the documents. The affair reached the editorial pages of the *Newport Mercury* in Rhode Island, in which it was written that Hancock 'would perhaps shine more conspicuously…if he did not keep a number of vessels running to London and back, full freighted, getting rich, by receiving freight on goods made contraband by the Colonies'.

Nowadays Mein might have expected an award for campaigning journalism; in 18th century Boston he was running in fear from the mob – and of course his temper was never far from boiling over.

One pro-revolutionary report stated that Mein had 'treated the whole body of merchants and traders in the most haughty, imperious and insulting manner'. The report added, 'Mr Mein at present is so obnoxious to the people on account of his publishing the manifests that he's obliged to go armed and 'tis but a few nights since that two persons who resembled him pretty much were attacked in a narrow alley with clubs, and would in all probability have lost their lives if the mistakes had not been timely discovered'.

Mein was indeed carrying a pistol with him for safety reasons. His swaggering bravado and confident demeanour betrayed a fear that his life could be in danger at any time. Anti-British fever was rising and there was little public appetite for the rantings of an apologist for America's colonial masters.

The Scotsman had been denounced as an 'enemy of the country' by the merchants and traders of his adopted city. He was receiving death threats on a regular basis. The net was closing in on Mein and his stormy career in Boston would soon be at an end.

Near the end of 1769 Hancock received a letter from a bookseller in London called Thomas Longman. Mein, he claimed, owed him in the region of £1,600 for books he had supplied to his Boston bookstore. Would Hancock help him recover the debt? It was the breakthrough the revolutionary leader had been hoping for.

Hancock's reply to Longman no longer survives but it may well have included the phrase 'hold me back'. In October 1769 he responded in the affirmative and was given power of attorney – then proceeded to prosecute the case with zeal.

But the mob got to Mein before the law did. On 28 October, Mein was walking along King Street when he was surrounded by a threatening crowd baying for his blood. One of the men, Thomas Marshall, a captain in the Boston Militia, had laid the sharp edge of a shovel to Mein's neck and the crowd was chanting for him to use it.

Mein was in danger of being killed and he knew it. The Boston mob was well-known for its ruthlessness and violence. He did the only thing he could think of that would enable his escape. He went for his pistol and began firing.

How many shots Mein fired is not known. What is certain is that his actions caused the crowd, including Marshall, to quickly disperse. However, as Mein turned to run towards the safety of a British vessel at Boston Harbour, a young soldier described as a grenadier lay wounded on the street, having been shot by one of Mein's bullets. It is uncertain whether the man was a British Grenadier or a member of the Boston Grenadier Corps, a militia unit.

Mein took refuge in the guardhouse at the end of King Street where, amazingly, he went undetected. Luckily for him the grenadier's wound was not life-threatening, otherwise he would have been facing a charge of murder. He then made it to the safety of the British schooner *Hope*, one of many vessels berthed at the harbour. Within days he was leaving America and sailing towards England as his effigy was being prepared for the Pope Day parade.

The publishers of the *Boston Evening-Post* rather sarcastically noted that 'Mr John Mein, our intrepid assertor of truth and falsehood, has kept himself out of the way (for reasons best known to himself) since Saturday last'. His old foes at the *Gazette* gleefully reported that Mein had 'eloped' and had been spotted at Halifax, Nova Scotia, where the *Hope* had called on her way across the Atlantic.

When Mein arrived in London he tried unsuccessfully to reason with the book supplier Thomas Longman. By that time a second firm of suppliers to whom Mien owed money had also approached Hancock. Mein was thrown into the King's Bench debtor's prison in Southwark, south London, where he languished for a year.

Without his writing, the *Chronicle* became a shadow of its former self. Many faithful readers withdrew their subscriptions, whilst Hancock was pursuing his court case against Mein with every fibre of his being. In the summer of 1770, Mein's partner John Fleeming decided to bring down the curtain on the newspaper.

In the final edition he wrote, 'The printers of the Boston Chronicle return thanks to the gentlemen who have so long favoured them with their subscriptions, and now inform them that, as the Chronicle, in the present state of affairs, cannot be carried on, either for their entertainment or the emolument of the printers, it will be discontinued for some time'.

Mein left prison and returned briefly to Boston to defend himself against Hancock – strangely enough the shooting of the grenadier was never brought against him by the authorities. However, there was no money left in the pot and Mein had to face the grim reality that Hancock had beaten him. In November 1770 the Suffolk Inferior Court in Boston ruled against Mein, and Hancock was allowed to dispose of all the Scotsman's assets.

He returned to Britain a beaten and broken man. The man who had clubbed one of his newspaper rivals with a cane in the street, agitated against the might of the Boston political establishment, fired a gun at a mob and shot a grenadier sailed away from Boston again, this time for good. Within years America would have its independence from Britain and all the unrest and turbulence he had stirred up would have been in vain.

He worked for a while with the British government as a propaganda officer – there were some who suggested he had been doing that all along in Boston – but he faded into obscurity, and died in London sometime in the late 1700s.

Meanwhile, as Mein's career died on the vine, his nemesis John Hancock saw his star rising higher than he could ever have imagined. He was elected as president of America's Second Continental Congress, the body that ushered in the Declaration of Independence.

The man who made his fortune by smuggling alcohol and other contraband goods into the country became the first signer of one of the most famous documents in the world – and he made sure the world would never forget him, leaving a famously large and elaborate signature on the paper. To this day Americans refer to an ornate signature simply as a John Hancock.

17

Dishonourable Mentions

T he roll-call of Scots who found their way to the 'new lands' of America only to disgrace themselves is not quite endless, but it is certainly lengthy. This final chapter gathers together the 'crimes' of a handful of the scoundrels - from a leading fur trader who illegally distilled corn whisky for his Indian customers to a disgraced army man who tutored one of America's most notorious Wild West outlaws. It even took a Scotsman to kill a signatory to the American Declaration of Independence.

Kenneth Mckenzie

At his remote trading post deep in the wilds of North Dakota, Kenneth McKenzie was called 'The King'. He took the title seriously. McKenzie lived like a king, welcomed important visitors to his 'palace', wined and dined them in sumptuous surroundings, and treated his 'subjects' with an air of regality.

His table groaned with fresh buffalo meat, the best dairy products and vegetables grown in the grounds. At mealtimes he dressed in a fine uniform, and everyone in his employ wore formal attire and was seated according to rank. It was as though the British Empire had set up camp in the middle of the most hostile territory of America's Wild West.

McKenzie was what we know today as a mountain man, portrayed on TV and the movies as a kindly, grizzled old character complete with coonskin hat. The reality was very different – McKenzie and his kind were young, fit, daring, intrepid adventurers. They earned their living as fur trappers deep in the heart of Indian country. There was a fortune to be made supplying fur to the markets of the east coast and Europe, and these men were engaged in the first major commercial enterprise of the American West.

To reach an exalted position in such a cut-throat world, McKenzie must have possessed two indisputable qualities – he must have been a shrewd and economically savvy young businessman, and he must have been as tough as hell.

By the age of 30 he was known as the 'King of the Missouri'. The truth is that from his Fort Union trading post near the North Dakota/Montana border, McKenzie directed operations across an area the size of a small empire.

But even kings and emperors fall from grace – and McKenzie fell from a great height. He may have thought himself untouchable, or that Fort Union was too remote to be subject to the laws of the 'outside world'.

McKenzie was no stranger to remoteness. He was born in 1797 in the wilds of the Scottish Highlands, in the Ross-shire hamlet of Bracklach, in the parish of Lochcarron. He was apparently of 'distinguished parentage' and it is possible his father was a tacksman for one of the McKenzie landowners in that part of the Highlands.

In 1816 he emigrated to Canada and found a job as a clerk with the North West Company, at that time run by Lt-Col William McGillivray, originally from Dunlichity, near Inverness. When the company merged, he lost his job and in 1822 he headed for St Louis, Missouri, the city at the centre of the fur trade, where many rival companies were competing for business.

He joined the Columbia Fur Company and quickly became the most dynamic figure in the trade. Within three years he was the company head, having proved himself adept at dealing with the many Native American tribes in the area. Hostile tribes such as the Piegan Blackfeet would deal only with McKenzie.

McKenzie sold out Columbia Fur to the American Fur Company but he remained in charge of the 'Upper Missouri Outfit' division. He dominated the beaver pelt and buffalo hide trade, and established himself as the ruler of his great American 'empire'. From his base at Fort Union, near the confluence of the Missouri and Yellowstone Rivers, he reigned supreme and achieved his 'King of the Missouri' title.

Historian Hiram Chittenden wrote, 'From every direction tribes of roving Indians came to his post to trade. Altogether it was a remarkable business that he followed, and one which only a man of great ability could have handled so successfully'.

Equally remarkable, however, was McKenzie's downfall. His dominance was challenged by a company organised by two young men, William Sublette and Robert Campbell, who unlike McKenzie had a ready supply of cheap alcohol with which to tempt the Indians.

It was forbidden by federal law to use liquor in Indian trade but somehow McKenzie had to get on terms with his competitors. Undeterred by the niceties of the law, he built a fully-functioning still at Fort Union, and began making whiskey from the corn he was receiving from the Mandan Indians.

He kept within the law by giving it to the Indians rather than selling it, although the actual distillation was strictly illegal. In 1834 he gave his usual gracious welcome to a young New England businessman called Nathaniel Wyeth and showed him round the working still which he proudly called the 'Cincinnati Project'.

Wyeth, however, was a nasty piece of work; a troublemaker and pot-stirrer. He passed through Fort Leavenworth in Kansas, reported McKenzie's illicit whiskey-making venture to the authorities and the game was up. Public reaction was hostile to McKenzie, his bosses could not save him, and he was fired from his position with the company.

The 'King of the Missouri' was now a king without a throne. He had come crashing to earth with a thud, his crime almost certainly a belief that he was above the law.

McKenzie married twice, first to an Indian woman with whom he had a son, Owen. He married his second wife Mary Marshall in 1842 in Davidson County, Tennessee, and they had four children together. The couple lived in the Carondelet neighbourhood of St. Louis until his death in May 1861.

John Mackie

Of all the outlaws who brought terror and death to the lawless Wild West, perhaps the most fascinating and charismatic individual was Billy the Kid. He really was a kid; he was only 15 when his criminal career in the desert lands of New Mexico and Arizona began. At the age of 21, he met his well-documented death.

Billy the Kid

In a few short years The Kid embarked on a spree of killing that put him in the top tier of America's frontier desperados. He was a ruthless, gun-slinging drifter whose famous image shows him wearing a cowboy hat and bandana, holding a Winchester rifle, and with a Colt revolver in the holster of his gun belt.

The Kid – real name Henry McCarty – was born in New York City and arrived in Santa Fe, New Mexico, via Indianapolis and Kansas. His mother, who had just married a man named Henry Antrim, died of tuberculosis in the New Mexican town of Silver City when he was 15 and his life of crime started immediately.

Within a year he had been jailed for robbing a Chinese laundry. He staged the first of his many jail breakouts and his life as a fugitive from the law was under way. In the course of his short career The Kid – who changed his name to William Bonney – would meet many contemptible characters who would influence his life of crime. One of his earliest and most profound mentors was a violent Scottish ex-soldier and horse thief by the name of John R. Mackie.

Mackie had been born in Glasgow – nothing else is known about his early life. He was in America during the civil war and served as a drummer boy with the Union Army's 6th Cavalry. The regiment was stationed in Fort Grant in the Arizona Territory in 1875 and Mackie found himself in trouble after he shot a civilian in the neck in a dispute over a game of cards.

He was locked up on the military reservation but a court in Tucson accepted a plea of self-defence, Mackie walked free but he was dishonourably discharged from the U.S. Army. After that he frequented the village of Bonita, not far from the camp, and his life degenerated into one of horse thievery.

When The Kid escaped from New Mexico, he found himself in Bonita – and Mackie, 10 years his senior, briefly became his best mate. Horse rustling was a great skill to have in the American West and the Scotsman was an expert. He was to become the apprentice outlaw's horse-stealing master.

The owner of the town's Hotel de Luna, Miles Wood, recalled how soldiers from Fort Grant would visit the saloons and dance-halls, leaving their horses tethered outside. Mackie and 'young Henry' as The Kid was then known, would steal the saddles, saddle blankets and often the horses too. Then they would hide out in the wilderness until they got the chance to sell them to passing strangers.

On one occasion a lieutenant and a doctor from the fort came to the bar saying no-one would steal their horses. They attached long picket ropes to the horses and carried one end into the bar. Wood recalled, 'Mackie followed the officers into the saloon and talked to them, while Billy cut the ropes from the horses and run off, leaving the officers holding the pieces of rope'.

It was good, easy money for the two men; however, the officers in charge at Camp Grant soon tightened their security. The Kid became a wanted man again and went on the run. He and Mackie did not meet up again until 1877 in the Arizona town of Globe, then known as Globe City.

Mackie stole three horses in an area known as Cottonwood Spring, not knowing that his and The Kid's capture were imminent. Unaware that they were even wanted, the two made their way back to Fort Grant – but hotelier Miles Wood had become the town's justice of the peace, and when the two men breakfasted at the Hotel de Luna, he decided to wait on them himself.

He recalled, 'I had the breakfast for the two placed on a large platter and I carried it into them. I shoved the platter on the table in front of them and pulled a six-gun from under it and told them to put their hands up and go straight out the door'.

Wood and the hotel chef marched the thieves more than two miles to Camp Grant where they were locked up. But The Kid had no plans to hang around in custody. That night, as the camp's officers were at a regimental dance, his Scottish friend Mackie helped him escape again and he disappeared into the Arizona night. It was the last time Mackie would see his young friend – The Kid had learned many valuable Wild West survival lessons from the roguish Scotsman.

The Kid was killed when he was 21 by Sheriff Pat Garrett. There is no record of Mackie's fate. Outlaws in the American West did not have a long shelf life. The Scotsman was 27 when he first met The Kid – if the Glaswegian gunslinger made it into his mid-30s he would have achieved Wild West longevity.

John Murphy

On 29 December 1874 Scotsman John Murphy climbed up the rickety wooden steps to the gallows in Carson City, Nevada, to hang for shooting and killing his fellow countryman John McCallum. The following day's *New York Times* reported that, in the course of a lengthy, rambling public address from the scaffold, Murphy 'made some remarks professing his belief in spiritualism and at the same time uttering horrible blasphemy'.

A public execution was a great event in frontier America and hundreds had gathered at the foot of the city's Lone Mountain to see Murphy dispatched. He didn't disappoint his audience. One newspaper report stated that he 'ran up the steps to the scaffold with as much nonchalance as though he was going to deliver a Fourth of July oration'.

In the course of a 90-minute speech to the on-looking crowd, Murphy railed against capital punishment, his own conviction, and the teachings of the Bible. He regaled the crowd with his belief in spiritualism and even pled for the life of another condemned prisoner. He didn't shy away from the fact that he had gunned down his fellow Scotsman in cold blood.

Questions about Murphy's sanity had persisted since his conviction. His thick brogue left everyone in no doubt he was Scottish. However, he could never remember where in Scotland he was from, only that he had run away home to go to sea, come to California at the height of the gold rush, worked as a miner and entertained crowds as a boxing-booth fighter.

He had become a cook in the tough lumber camps that dotted the hills of Nevada during the silver rush known as the Comstock Lode, and first came across John McCallum when the two were employed by a logging and fluming company at Spooner's Station, near Lake Tahoe. Any love the two men had for each other evaporated when McCallum was given Murphy's job in the kitchen.

According to Jim Hewitson's book, *Tam Blake & Co.*, a fight broke out between the two men over the best way to make Irish stew. Whatever caused the bust-up, McCallum struck Murphy several times on the head with a broken mustard bottle, leaving him with an ugly scar on his face. Murphy went to Carson City to get the wound treated and swore to kill McCallum.

He was as good as his word. McCallum was made aware of Murphy's murderous threats and was forced to skulk around the countryside to avoid him. A few months after the altercation however, when McCallum was walking past the city's St. Charles Hotel, Murphy sprang out of hiding and brandished a pistol.

When McCallum turned to run diagonally across the street, Murphy shot him then chased him into nearby livery stables where he fired three more shots into McCallum's body, one in the back at close range. McCallum died a few days later and Murphy was convicted of first degree murder.

Murphy was not the only Scotsman who fell foul of the law in the old West, although the brutal and premeditated nature of McCallum's death, the lack of remorse shown by the killer, the length of his trial (which dragged on for months and attracted massive public attention), and Murphy's final appearance on the gallows, gave the case a certain sensationalism.

The convicted man had his execution delayed on three occasions because of fears he might be insane. However, he always insisted he should die and was said to be 'the most happy occupant of the carriage' that bore him to the gallows in 1874.

The columns of the *Daily Alta California* newspaper reported, 'Murphy looked far more calm than his conductors, and exhibited such wonderful control over his nerves as would make some men heroes on battlefields or on the stormy deep'.

The details of Murphy's delusional speech to the crowd included the prisoner freely admitting he had shot McCallum. He said that, as he drew his pistol on him, he told his fellow Scot, 'Johnny Murphy never misses his aim'.

It was all great theatre, and once his speechifying was done, Murphy had a final glass of wine and a quid of tobacco. He kneeled on the trap door, read from a spiritualistic prayer then stood up to be pinioned and have the noose placed round his neck. The trap was then sprung and the 45-year old Murphy was left hanging on the gallows for 20 minutes.

The Scotsman may have lived and died in a typically violent Wild West manner – but at least he gave the townsfolk of Carson City a memorable show before leaving this world.

Lachlan McIntosh

Lachlan McIntosh

Along with the nation's presidents, the signers of the Declaration of Independence are the most revered men in the history of the United States. Men such as Benjamin Franklin, John Adams, and Thomas Jefferson were the founding fathers, the great and the good.

Not all were household names; many passed into obscurity, but their moment in the spotlight has lived forever in American history. There were even two Scottish-born signers, the Rev. John Witherspoon and lawyer James Wilson.

For most of these men, signing the Declaration was the pinnacle of their lives. They had signed into history a hugely important document that is still referenced every day in the United States. Rightly or wrongly, they were put on a collective pedestal. Killing one of these men, for whatever reason and in whatever circumstances, was about as dastardly a deed as you could imagine in the newly-formed nation. Yet that was exactly what Scottish Highlander Lachlan McIntosh did.

Of all the little-known signatories, Button Gwinnett, who was born the son of a clergyman in Gloucestershire, England, was the most obscure. He signed the famous piece of parchment in August 1776. In May the following year he was shot dead by his Scottish opponent in an early-morning pistol duel.

To be absolutely fair to McIntosh, he was not the aggressor in the case. The two men had been at loggerheads over political and military leadership in the state of Georgia and there was no love lost between them. The 'pistols at dawn' challenge was made by Gwinnett following a heated public argument. Nevertheless, McIntosh pulled the trigger and killed him.

McIntosh had been born in the hamlet of Raits, just east of Kingussie in Inverness-shire. He was only 11 when his father John moved the family to America along with a group of 100 Scottish settlers. A year after the family arrived, Lachlan's younger brother Lewis was killed by an alligator while swimming in Georgia's Altamaha River.

Then in 1740 his father was taken prisoner and died shortly afterwards. Young McIntosh spent some time in the Bethesda Orphanage in Savannah, Georgia, and then he and his brother William took up soldiering and rose through the ranks of the Georgia Militia.

As a bright young man he moved quickly through the ranks; he then took up a position as a clerk with the noted colonial merchant Henry Laurens, acquired some land himself, and became a prosperous rice planter. By 1770 he was a colonel in the militia and was one of those agitating for Georgian independence from Britain. In 1776 he was promoted to the rank of brigadier general.

Button Gwinnett was McIntosh's deadly enemy in Georgian politics. A cantankerous and fiery character, he had been a candidate for the brigadier general position and was outraged at losing to the Scotsman. He had considerable political power, and after signing the Declaration, became president of the Georgia Assembly and immediately set about effectively persecuting McIntosh and his family.

Gwinnett turned vindictive and accused McIntosh's soldier brother William of negligence for allegedly failing to protect plantations during an abortive invasion of Florida. He then accused a second McIntosh brother, George, of 'treasonable conduct' by 'secretly supporting…the designs of the British King and Parliament against us'.

It was all nonsense, but Gwinnett's conduct eventually prompted the normally level-headed McIntosh to brand him a 'scoundrel and a lying rascal' at an Assembly meeting.

Gwinnett's response was immediate. He challenged the Scot to a duel the following morning on pasture land outside Savannah. Duels were not uncommon ways of settling disputes in the 1770s, and both men were at the appointed spot early. The two men saluted each other, McIntosh showed Gwinnett his pistols loaded only with single balls and no more conversation passed between them.

The two men stood back to back, walked eight paces, turned and fired. Both were shot in the thigh; Gwinnett being hit with such ferocity just above the knee that his thigh broke. McIntosh asked if he wanted another shot but all those present all said no. The seconds said both shooters had behaved like 'men of honour' and marched McIntosh towards Gwinnett for a handshake.

Three days later Gwinnett died. The dead man's allies had McIntosh charged with murder but he was acquitted. George Washington, then leading the Continental Army, sensed the danger the Scotsman was facing and intervened on his behalf. He called McIntosh to Pennsylvania to serve with his troops for fear Gwinnett's friends would exact revenge on him.

McIntosh was put in charge of the Continental Army's Western Department, based at what is now Pittsburgh, Pennsylvania. He then returned to Georgia and commanded forces at the Siege of Savannah before being taken prisoner and held in captivity for almost two years.

After the war McIntosh's life went into a downward spiral. His plantation was wrecked by British forces and he lived in relative poverty until his death in Savannah in 1806. Button Gwinnett's signature is the rarest of all those that signed the Declaration of Independence and is much sought after to this day. The State of Georgia contains a McIntosh County and a Gwinnett County.

James Forbes

James Forbes is one of those Scotsmen who has earned the distinction of having founded a town in the United States. Nowadays known as Los Gatos (the cats) the settlement that lies just south of San Jose in California was built round Forbes Mill, a flour mill established by the Scotsman in the mid-1850s.

Since then it has attracted many bohemian and artistic types. John Steinbeck wrote *The Grapes of Wrath* in the town; acting sisters Olivia de Havilland and Joan Fontaine went to school there; violinist Yehudi Menuhin was a resident and so was Neal Cassady, one of the major figures in the Beat Generation. Netflix was established in Los Gatos in 1998.

But the man whose flour mill started the ball rolling in the 19th century was an altogether more shadowy and unpleasant figure. The historian for the area has described Forbes as a 'suede-shoe man' – a slippery, dodgy individual.

Forbes, born in 1805 in Inverness, was forever up to his neck in shifty financial dealings; he was brash and confident, with a high degree of self-importance. California at the time was in Mexican hands and fiercely Catholic. Despite this, Forbes was devious enough to 'squeeze' thousands of dollars out of a group of Jesuit priests and then sell property under false pretences to an order of nuns.

He was the son of a Scottish father and a Spanish mother and lived in Inverness until he was 12, when he emigrated to Argentina with a wealthy uncle. Jesuit priests schooled him in the Uruguayan capital Montevideo until his late teens, and when he was in his early 20s, he fought for Argentina against Brazil in the Cisplatine War. He was badly wounded by a sabre in battle and had to have a plate inserted in his head.

The rich uncle had part-owned a shipping line, but when he died, Forbes was left penniless, so he made his way to California. He arrived in Yerba Buena, now San Francisco, in 1831, and found employment as an accountant on a large ranch near the city of Richmond. He was described at this time as 'determined and headstrong'.

Forbes made his way to the Santa Clara valley where he married Ana Maria Galindo. She was the daughter of the man in charge – the majordomo – of a large Franciscan Mission. The coupling was ideal for Forbes. He had married into a family of considerable influence and the fact that his bride was a Mexican citizen enabled him to stay in California. Los Gatos historian William Wulf has suggested that expediency, rather than romance, was the reason for the union.

Ana Maria went on to bear him 12 children. However, he is said to have treated her as no more than a common 'servant'. If he had people round to the house for dinner, he would often not allow her to join them. Instead, she would have to spend her time in the kitchen or servants' quarters.

Forbes' marriage worked well for him. He had a short spell working for the Hudson's Bay Company, a highly successful fur trading business, and was appointed British vice-consul for Alta California, a massive region stretching north from San Diego.

In 1851, with California now under American control following the Mexican-American War, Forbes invited Jesuit missionaries to set up a university at the Mission to educate his nine sons. However, he refused to leave his quarters in the building until they had paid him $11,000. The priests had to plead for the money with the Jesuit headquarters in Rome.

Using the money from the Jesuits, he built a mansion next to the Mission, where he lived for several years. He sold that to an order of nuns but neglected to tell them there was a $20,000 lien on the house. It was all very underhanded and shady and directed against Catholic orders, some of whom had helped educate him.

When the California Gold Rush was in full swing, Forbes hit on the idea of producing bread for the miners. Flour was selling for $50 a barrel and he saw it as too good an opportunity to miss. In 1852 he built the mill at a spot called Los Gatos Creek, named after the cougars and bobcats that inhabited the area.

He had borrowed at least $130,000 to finance the operation, although almost from the outset, he was dogged by financial difficulties. By the time his mill was fully functional, a number of other businessmen had hit on the same idea. Then the gold rush began to wind down and the price of flour crashed. His business collapsed, and the flour mill and a 2,000-acre ranch he had bought were sold off at a sheriff's bankruptcy sale.

In an interview with the *Los Gatos Weekly Times* on March 27, 1996, according to William Wulf, Forbes was bright but 'a bad guy who ended up losing control of circumstances'. The town of Los Gatos was built around the Scotsman's mill, yet he is regarded as a disreputable and rather sordid individual rather than a man of whom the townspeople feel proud.

Dugald Crawford

The American election of 1896 was, as all presidential elections, fought on the grounds of the forceful personalities of the candidates, Republican William McKinley and Democrat William Jennings Bryan. But the main issue was an unusual financial argument – should the U.S. currency be supported with gold coinage only, or with gold and silver?

Wealthy businessmen and bankers wanted a gold standard, arguing it would keep the value of the dollar high. Others, mostly farmers, labourers and small businessmen, thought the value of the dollar was too high and wanted a silver standard imposed to lower it.

The struggle between the 'gold bugs' backed by McKinley and the 'silverites' supported by Bryan led to one of the most bitter election struggles for years. There had been a financial panic leading to an economic depression three years earlier that had cost millions of jobs. Many believed the depression would end if the government issued more paper money backed by silver.

Among the electorate, feelings ran high. It was a time for cool heads, common sense debating and rational behaviour. However, in the city of St. Louis, Missouri, one Scottish-born businessman lost all sense of reason and found himself – for a brief spell – one of the most reviled and notorious men in the nation.

Dugald Crawford was one of the leading businessmen in St. Louis. He owned a dry goods business – what we nowadays call a department store – at the corner of Fifth Street and Franklin Avenue. It had been established in 1866 and was one of the most popular stores in the city. Not surprisingly, given his wealth and position in society, Crawford was a staunch Republican and supporter of the gold standard.

Crawford was born in 1830 in Rothesay on the Isle of Bute. He emigrated to Canada, where he married Aberdeen girl Jane Forsyth in 1861, in the York district of Toronto. The couple crossed the border and made their home in the booming city of St. Louis, and within five years Crawford and partner Alexander Russell had opened up their store in the centre of the city.

The Scotsman was a large, imposing figure, and was unquestionably a tough, hard-headed businessman. Over the years the business grew and became one of the most recognisable and popular shopping locations for St. Louisans.

However, as the 1896 presidential race neared its climax, election fever seemed to consume him. He was an ardent supporter of the gold standard but he decided to canvass his employees and found – to his horror – that many of them were 'free silver men'. Crawford's immediate reaction was to call 12 department heads into his office and tell them to clear their desks as they were no longer in his employ.

The Scotsman did not mince his words. According to the *San Francisco Call* newspaper, he told the men that he 'did not want any anarchists to breathe the air of his establishment'. Crawford told them, 'Spread the news throughout the city. Let it be known as far and near as you choose that you are discharged because you are in favour of the free coinage of silver'.

The plight of the sacked men fuelled public ire throughout America, and there was outrage at Crawford's actions, even among many fellow 'gold bugs'. Apart from anything else it was flagrantly in breach of employment laws and legislation governing free elections. Local Democrats and trade unions vowed to take the men's case to court.

But the court of public opinion hurt Crawford more than any court action. The *St. Louis Post-Dispatch* newspaper carried scores of letters denouncing the Scot. One letter, signed 'Yours with Indignation, St. Louis', described Crawford's behavior as an 'act of tyranny'.

The letter went on: 'Doesn't he make his money off the earnings of silver as well as gold men and women? He should go to a foreign country, live in Russia for instance. He has no business living in a country that ought at least to be free. What is American manhood coming to anyhow? Excuse my rather incoherent remarks but having spent a great deal of hard-earned money in that store, I feel very indignant. I actually would rather go cold and let my children do so than to buy one cents worth there now.'

Crawford had blundered badly. He had misjudged the mood of the people whose custom had kept him in business all these years and he faced a serious backlash. He was charged with intimidating and coercing his employees in their right of franchise, although the case was dismissed on a technicality. Judges, however, forced him to re-hire his employees.

Crawford need not have worried. McKinley won the election and the gold standard remained in place. Seven years later, however, the Scotsman went bankrupt and his great store in the centre of St. Louis closed down. Perhaps the public threat to boycott the shop caused his downfall.

Granville Pattison

A review in *The Lancet* medical journal of a 2005 biography of Granville Pattison says everything about the man. It states, 'There are, and doubtless always have been, men who are like Staffordshire bull-terriers. Wherever they go they pick a fight. Granville Sharp Pattison, anatomist, surgeon and inveterate quarreler, was just such a man whose fights and largely self-inflicted troubles were unusually flamboyant'.

Pattison was already a rogue by the time he arrived in America in his mid-20s. He had been charged with body-snatching, accused of medical malpractice and found himself at the centre of a bitter divorce case after an affair with the wife of a colleague.

The young anatomy lecturer did not so much leave his native Glasgow; he was run out of the city. He had been born in 1791 in a luxurious mansion in the Kelvingrove area of the city and was welcomed as a member of the Faculty of Physicians and Surgeons in Glasgow in 1813. He became an assistant lecturer at the Andersonian Institute, now

Strathclyde University, but his entanglement with the wife of Andrew Ure brought him public disgrace and he fled to the U.S.

His troublemaking did not end when he arrived in America in 1818 – far from it. Controversy and wrangling followed him everywhere he went. At a variety of educational establishments on America's east coast, Pattison made a string of enemies, warred with them, belittled them in public and was a thorn in the flesh of the establishment. He even shot a rival with a pistol in a dawn duel.

By all accounts he was a charming, brilliant and enthusiastic lecturer who was much loved by his pupils. Among his teaching peers, he enjoyed a high reputation. Sadly for the Glaswegian though, a cloud seemed to follow him around, and the negative side of his personality always came to the fore.

He arrived at the University of Pennsylvania in Philadelphia but was denied a professorship, a fact he laid at the door of the institution's cantankerous medical professor Nathaniel Chapman. On one occasion, the ill-feeling between the two men was so intense that Chapman spotted Pattison walking in the street, crossed the road and beat him with his cane.

Pattison left Philadelphia in 1820 when he was appointed to the chair of anatomy, physiology and surgery at the University of Maryland in Baltimore. It was the senior job he had been seeking and he held it for five years before resigning on the grounds of ill-health.

However, even from a distance, his hatred of Nathaniel Chapman intensified, and he never wasted an opportunity to put down the reputation of the American. When Chapman's brother-in-law, General Thomas Cadwalader, publicly opposed Pattison, an early-morning duel between the two men was arranged.

It took place in April 1823 in Delaware. Pattison had the better of the exchange, shooting Cadwalader in the right elbow, a wound that left him unable to use his arm properly for the rest of his life. Pattison was uninjured, although a ball from Cadwalader's pistol 'passed through the skirt of his coat near the waist'.

Pattison left America to take up a post at the University of London but he lasted only three years, having to leave when colleagues and students questioned his competency. He was back in the U.S. in 1831 when he was appointed to the post of professor of anatomy at Jefferson Medical College in Philadelphia.

He held the post for 10 years until landing a similar role at the University of New York. However, his constant quarrelling and bickering with colleagues made him look constantly foolish, regardless of the quality of his teaching.

The Lancet described him as a 'competent anatomist and a brilliant lecturer'. He displayed, it said, 'a belligerence, obstinacy, and quickness to take offence that made him an impossible colleague'.

Pattison, alleged grave-robber, adulterer, duellist, troublemaker, antagonist, and a man of general ill-repute, passed away in November 1851. He left behind a wife, Mary, and a legacy of having wreaked havoc at medical establishments on two continents.

Bibliography

A great deal of the research for this book has been made possible thanks to that incredible resource known as the internet that is available to us nowadays. In particular, the ancestry.com, findagrave.com, Scotlandspeople.gov.uk, and electricscotland.com websites have been invaluable for allowing me access to details of times, dates and places, the search for which would have been a lot more painstaking only a few years ago.

I have trawled through information in libraries, chiefly but not exclusively the Mitchell Library in Glasgow. Old and current newspapers, mostly from the United States, have provided a wealth of information that has added colour to the stories I have told. These journals, many of which have long ceased publication, stretched from Rhode Island on the east coast to California on the west, and it was fascinating to study their accounts and reportage.

A number of works have been invaluable reference points in several chapters, most notably *Tam Blake & Co.* by the Scottish author Jim Hewitson, published by Canongate Press in 1993. I also pored over *A Dance Called America* by Dr. James Hunter, published by Mainstream Publishing in 1995, and *Frontier Scots*, written by Jenni Calder in 2010 and published by Luath Press.

The U.S. National Archives has been a great source of information, as has *Encyclopaedia Britannica*, and many other dictionaries and biographical reference books.

The following is a chapter-by-chapter bibliography of the works I referenced:

Chapter 1 – Adam Stephen

The American Experiment: A History of the United States, by Steven M. Gillon and Cathy D. Mason. Cengage Advantage Books. 2008.

The Battle of Germantown, by John B. B. Trussell, Jr.. Pennsylvania Historical and Museum Commission. 1974.

Benjamin Rush: Revolutionary Gadfly, by David Freeman Hawke. Ardent Media. 1971.

The C&O Canal Companion: A Journey Through Potomac History, by Mike High. JHU Press. 1997.

George! A Guide to All Things Washington, by Frank E. Grizzard, Jr.. Mariner Media. 2005.

George Washington's Enforcers: Policing the Continental Army, by Harry M. Ward. Southern Illinois University Press. 2006.

Gone For a Soldier, by Jeffrey Hepple. Elisco Publishing. 2008.

Major General Adam Stephen and the Cause of American Liberty, by Harry M. Ward. University Press of Virginia. 1989.

Nathanael Greene: A Biography of the American Revolution, by Gerald M. Carbone. Palgrave Macmillan. 2008.

The North Carolina Continentals, by Hugh F. Rankin. University of North Carolina Press. 1971.

The Ohio Expedition of 1754, by Adam Stephen. Historical Society of Pennsylvania. 1894.

The Peterson Magazine, Volume 106. 1894.

Rebels & Redcoats: The American Revolution Through the Eyes of Those Who Fought and Lived It, by George F. Scheer and Hugh F. Rankin. Da Capo Press. 1957.

Seldens of Virginia and Allied Families Volume 2, by Mary Selden Kennedy. State Historical Society of Wisconsin. 1911.

Chapter 2 – Charles Forbes

Dead Last: The Public Memory of Warren G Harding's Scandalous Legacy, by Philip G. Payne. Ohio University Press. 2008.

High Treason: The Plot Against the People, by Albert E. Kahn. Christie Books. 2014.

The Inside Story of the Harding Tragedy, by Harry Daugherty. Churchill Company. 1932.

The Roaring Twenties, by Thomas Streissguth. Infobase Publishing. 2001.

Scandal and Reform in Federal Veterans' Welfare Agencies, by Jesse T. Tarbert. Case Western Reserve University. 2011.

Star-Spangled Men: America's Ten Worst Presidents, by Nathan Miller. Simon & Schuster. 1998.

Uphill All the Way: The Fortunes of Progressivism, 1919-1929, by Kevin C Murphy. PhD submission, University of Columbia. 2013.

Chapter 3 – Thomas Cream

Bitter Nemesis: The Intimate History of Strychnine, by John Buckingham. CRC Press. 2007.

The Chicago of Fiction, by James A. Kaser. Rowman & Littlefield. 2011.

Dead Men Do Tell Tales, by Troy Taylor. Whitechapel Productions, Illinois, USA. 2008.

Famous Trials: Thrill-Killers, by Alex McBride. Penguin. 2012.

The Madman of McGill, by Jackie Rosenhek. 2005.

Monsters of Medicine: The Lives of Five Serial Killer Physicians: Is There a Common Thread?, by William W. Colliflower. FriesenPress. 2013.

A Prescription for Murder: The Victorian Serial Killings of Dr Thomas Neill Cream, by Angus McLaren. University of Chicago Press. 1993.

Ripper Notes: Suspects and Witnesses, by Dan Norder, Wolf Vanderlinden, and Stewart P. Evans. Inklings Press. 2005.

'Trust me, I'm your doctor', by Julie L McDowell. *Modern Drug Discovery Magazine*, November 2001.

Who's Who? Serial Killers. The Top 100, by David Elio Malocco. CreateSpace Publishing. 2014.

Miller-Keane Encyclopedia & Dictionary of Medicine, Nursing and Allied Health, Saunders 2003.

The Shame of the Cities, Lincoln Steffens, Amereon. 1904.

Chapter 4 – William Stewart

Account of the Mountain Meadows Massacre as described by John D. Lee. Mormonism Research Ministry. 2009.

'America's True History of Religious Tolerance', by Kenneth C. Davis. *Smithsonian Magazine*, October 2010.

Blood of the Prophets: Brigham Young and the Massacre at Mountain Meadows, by Will Bagley. University of Oklahoma Press. 2002.

Children of the Massacre. Barclay & Co. 1877.

Encyclopedia of Frontier Biography, by Dan L. Thrapp. University of Nebraska Press. 1988.

Massacre at Mountain Meadows, by Ronald W. Walker, Richard E. Turley, Jr, and Glen M. Leonard. Oxford University Press. 2008.

The Mormon Problem: An Appeal to the American People, by Rev. C. P. Lyford. Phillips & Hunt. 1886.

The Mountain Meadows Massacre, by Juanita Brooks. University of Oklahoma Press. 1950.

Chapter 5 – Robert Millar

The American Cricketer, Volumes 38-39. 1915/16.

The American Soccer History Archives.

English Speaking World, Volume 3, May 1920. E. H. Bennett.

www.phillysoccerpage.net

www.stmirren.info

Julius Caesar, William Shakespeare 1599

Chapter 6 – David Jack

Carmel-By-The-Sea: The Early Years, by Alissandra Dramov. AuthorHouse. 2013.

David Jacks – Land Baron. Mayo Hayes O'Donnell Research Library, Monterey. 1989.

Dismantling the Pueblo: Hispanic Municipal Land Rights in California Since 1850, by Peter L. Reich. Temple University. 2001.

Encyclopedia of Immigration and Migration in the American West, by Gordon Morris Bakken and Alexandra Kindell. Sage Publications. 2008.

The History of Dr Hart's Mansion & the Early Days of Pacific Grove, by Bob Kohn. Theoria. 2008.

Land King: The Story of David Jack, by Kenneth C. Jack. Monterey County Historical Society. 1999.

The Real Story of David Jack, The Land King, by Alton Pryor. Stagecoach Publishing. 2011.

Storied Land: Community and Memory in Monterey, by John Walton. University of California Press. 2003.

Across The Plains: With Other Memories and Essays, Robert Louis Stevenson, Charles Scribner's Sons. 1897.

Chapter 7 – James Callender

In Defense of Thomas Jefferson: The Sally Hemings Sex Scandal, by William G. Hyland, Jr.. Macmillan. 2009.

John Adams, by David McCullough. Simon & Schuster. 2001.

The Partisan Press: A History of Media Bias in the United States, by Si Sheppard. McFarland & Company. 2008.

The Presidents and the Supreme Court, by James F. Simon. Simon & Schuster. 2012.

Public Affairs: Politics in the Age of Sex Scandals, by Paul Apostolidis and Juliet A. Williams. Duke University Press. 2004.

Scandalmonger, by William Safire. Harcourt. 2000.

Sedition in the Old Dominion: James T. Callender and The Prospect Before Us, by James Morton Smith. Southern Historical Association. 1954.

Transoceanic Radical: William Duane, by Nigel Little. Routledge. 2010.

With the Hammer of Truth: James Thomson Callender and America's Early American Heroes, by Michael Durey. University of Virginia Press. 1990.

Chapter 8 – William Dunbar

Antebellum Natchez, by D. Clayton James. LSU Press. 1993.

The Black Experience in Natchez 1720-1880, by Ronald L. F. Davis. 1993.

Complete Baronetage: English, Irish and Scottish, 1665-1707. W. Pollard & Co. 1904.

Critical White Studies: Looking Behind the Mirror, by Richard Delgado and Jean Stefancic. Temple University Press. 1997.

A Documentary History of Slavery in North America, by Willie Lee Rose. University of Georgia Press. 1999.

Encyclopedia of Arkansas History and Culture.

The Final Victims: Foreign Slave Trade to North America, 1783-1810, by James A. McMillin. University of Southern Carolina Press. 2012.

Lives of Mississippi Authors, 1817-1967, by James B. Lloyd. University Press of Mississippi. 1981.

Sir William Dunbar: The Pioneer Scientist of Mississippi, by Franklin L. Riley. Mississippi Historical Society. 1899.

Slavery and Frontier Mississippi, 1720-1835, by David J. Libby. University Press of Mississippi. 2008.

Slavery in Alabama, by James Benson Sellers. University of Alabama Press. 1950.

Voyagers to the West: A Passage in the Peopling of America on the Eve of the Revolution, by Bernard Bailyn. Knopf Doubleday Publishing. 1986.

William Dunbar: Scientific Pioneer of the Old Southwest, by Arthur H. DeRosier, Jr.. University Press of Kentucky. 2007.

Chapter 9 – Mary Garden

Civil War America, 1850-1875, by Richard F. Selcer. Infobase. 2006.

'Distant Voices, Mary Garden', by Dean Southern. *Classical Singer Magazine*, 1 November 2011.

Famous Firsts of Scottish-Americans, by June Skinner Sawyers. Pelican Publishing. 1997.

The Grove Book of Opera Singers, by Laura Macy. Oxford University Press. 2008.

Massenet, Mary Garden and the Chicago Opera, 1910-1932, by Bruce Duffie.

The Merchant of Power: Sam Insull, Thomas Edison, and The Creation of the Modern Metropolis, by John F. Wasik. Macmillan. 2008.

Musical America Magazine, Volumes 33-34, January 1921. John Christian Freund.

The Prima Donna and Opera, 1815-1930, by Susan Rutherford. Cambridge University Press. 2007.

The Sybil Sanderson Story: Requiem for a Diva, by Jack Winsor Hansen. Amadeus Press. 2005.

Mary Garden's Story, Mary Garden & Louis Leopold Biancolli. Simon & Schuster. 1951.

A Drunk Man Looks at a Thistle, Hugh MacDiarmid. 1926.

Chapter 10 – James Abercrombie

Charles Lee: Self Before Country, by Dominick Mazzagetti. Rutgers University Press. 2013.

Empire of Fortune: Crowns, Colonies and Tribes in the Seven Years War in North America, by Francis Jennings. W. W. Norton & Company. 1988.

The Epic Battles for Ticonderoga, by William R. Nester. SUNY Press. 2008.

Francis Parkman's Works, Volume 10. Little, Brown. 1897.

Proceedings of the New York Historical Society, January-May 1847.

Recollections of an Old Soldier: The Life of Captain David Perry (1741-1826), 1822.

Washington County, New York: its history to the close of the nineteenth century, by William Leete Stone. The New York History Company. 1901.

Chapter 11 – John Dowie

American Medicine, Volume 2, July-December 1901.

The Big Con: John Alexander Dowie and the Spread of Zionist Christianity in Southern Africa, by Barry Morton. University of Leiden, African Studies Centre. 2013.

Divine Healing: The Holiness-Pentecostal Transition Years, 1890-1906, by James Robinson. Wipf and Stock Publishers. 2013.

The Independent Magazine, January-June 1906.

John Alexander Dowie, by Gordon Lindsay. Nazarene Israel Faith. 1980.

John Alexander Dowie and the Christian Catholic Apostolic Church in Zion, by Rolvix Harlan. R.M, Antes. 1906.

John Alexander Dowie and Zion City, Illinois, by Stephanie Wolfe. Washington University in St. Louis.

Leaves of Healing, various editions, by John Alexander Dowie. Various dates.

Life: A Monthly Magazine of Christian Metaphysics, January 1903.

Western Druggist Magazine, Volume 23. 1901.

Worlds of Their Own, by Robert J. Schadewald. Xlibris. 2008.

Zion City, Illinois: Twentieth-Century Utopia, by Philip L. Cook. Syracuse University Press. 1996.

Ulysses, James Joyce. Shakespeare and Company. 1922.

Chapter 12 – Jock Semple

'The Real Story of Kathrine Switzer's 1967 Boston Marathon'. www.kathrincswitzer.com. 2007.

'Angry Overseer of the Marathon', by Myron Cope. *Sports Illustrated,* 22 April 1968.

'The Boston Marathon's Guardian', by Roger Robinson. *Runner's World,* 14 April 2015.

Boston Marathon History By the Mile, by Paul C Clerici. The History Press. 2014.

'Jock, Beef Stew, and the Boston Marathon', by Bennett H Beach. *Harvard Crimson,* 18 April 1969.

Chapter 13 – Alexander Cuming

Alexander Cuming – King or Pawn? An Englishman on the Colonial Chessboard of the Eighteenth Century American Southeast, by Ian Chambers. University of California, Riverside. 2014.

Cherokee Heritage Documentation Center.

The Cherokee Struggle to Maintain Identity in the 17th and 18th Centuries, by William R. Reynolds, Jr.. McFarland & Company. 2015.

Cherokee Voices: Early Accounts of Cherokee Life in the East, by Vicki Rozema. John F. Blair, Publisher. 2002.

The Dividing Paths: Cherokees and South Carolinians through the Revolutionary Era, by Tom Hatley. Oxford University Press. 1995.

London Magazine, Volume 27. 1757.

One Drop of Blood: The American Misadventure of Race, by Scott L. Malcomson. Macmillan. 2001.

One Heroic Hour at King's Mountain, by Pat Alderman. Overmountain Press. 1990.

Revolutionary Negotiations: Indians, Empires and Diplomats in the Founding of America, by Leonard J. Sadosky. University of Virginia Press. 2010.

Scottish Tartans Authority.

Touring the Western North Carolina Backroads, by Carolyn Sakowski. John F. Blair, Publisher. 2011.

Where No Flag Flies: Donald Davidson and the Southern Resistance, by Mark Royden Winchell. University of Missouri Press. 2000.

Scots in the North American West, Ferenc Morton Szasz. University of Oklahoma Press. 2000.

Dictionary of National Biography 1885-1900, Smith, Elder & Co.

Chapter 14 – James Duff

Battle or Massacre? The Incident on the Nueces, by Stanley S. McGowen. Texas State Historical Association. 2000.

Camp Verde: Texas Frontier Defense, by Joseph Luther. The History Press. 2012.

The Dogs of War Unleashed: The Devil Concealed in Men Unchained, by Joe Baluch. West Texas Historical Association. 1997.

'Historical Friction', by Helen Thorpe. *TexasMonthly Magazine*, October 1997.

The Seventh Star of the Confederacy: Texas During the Civil War, by Kenneth W. Howell. University of North Texas Press. 2011.

Texas State Historical Association.

A Hundred Years of Comfort in Texas, Guido E Ransleben. Naylor Company. 1954.

Chapter 15 – John Murray

America's First Villain, by Ted Brackemyre. U.S. History Scene. 2015.

The Clans of the Scottish Highlands, by James Logan. David Bryce and Son. 1899.

A Cock and Bull for Kitty: Lord Dunmore and the Affair that Ruined the British Cause in Virginia, by George Morrow. Telford Publications. 2011.

Colonial Williamsburg Foundation.

The Revolution's Black Soldiers, by Robert A. Selig. AmericanRevolution.org. 1997.

Shades of Liberty: A Black Man's Destiny, by Harry Schenawolf. Time Traveler Publishing. 2014.

War: Patrick Henry's Finest Hour, Lord Dunmore's Worst, by George Morrow. Telford Publications. 2011.

Dictionary of National Biography, Volume 39, New York Macmillan. 1885.

Chapter 16 – John Mein

The Adams Papers. Massachusetts Historical Society. 1954.

Bibliographical Notes on Boston Newspapers, 1704-1780, by Albert Matthews. John Wilson and Son. 1907.

Dr. Benjamin Church, Jr. Online blog by Edward J. Witek.

The Edinburgh History of the Book in Scotland, Volume 2, by Stephen W. Brown and Warren McDougall. Edinburgh University Press. 2011.

Essays in the Economic History of the Atlantic World, by John J. McCusker. Routledge. 1997.

The Founding of a Nation: A History of the American Revolution, by Merrill Jensen. Hackett Publishing.

Legal Papers of John Adams, Volume 1. Harvard University Press. 1965.2004.

Mapping Revolutionary Boston. The Bostonian Society and Wellesley College.

Old Landmarks and Historic Personages of Boston, by Samuel Adams Drake. James R. Osgood & Co. 1900.

Publications of the Colonial Society of Massachusetts, Volume 11, 1906-1907.

The Scots Magazine, Volume 38. July 1776.

Thomas Hutchinson and the Origins of the American Revolution, by Andrew Stephen Walmsley. New York University Press. 1998.

Transactions and Collections of the American Antiquarian Society, Volume 6, 1874.

Chapter 17

Billy the Kid: A Short and Violent Life, by Robert Marshall Utley. I. B. Taurus. 1991.

'Button Gwinnett and Lachlan McIntosh Duel', by Wayne Lynch. *Journal of the American Revolution*. 24 September 2014.

Encyclopedia of the Great Plains, by David J. Wishart. University of Nebraska-Lincoln. 2004.

www.legendsofamerica.com

Royal College of Physicians and Surgeons of Glasgow.

The West of Billy the Kid, by Frederick Nolan. University of Oklahoma Press. 1999.

The American Fur Trade of the Far West, Hiram Chittenden. FP Harper. 1902.